CW00330330

The Road to Soweto

The Road to Soweto

Resistance and the Uprising of 16 June 1976

JULIAN BROWN

Department of Political Studies
University of the Witwatersrand

James Currey
is an imprint of Boydell & Brewer Ltd
PO Box 9
Woodbridge, Suffolk IP12 3DF (GB)
www.jamescurrey.com

and of

Boydell & Brewer Inc.
668 Mt Hope Avenue
Rochester, NY 14620-2731 (US)
www.boydellandbrewer.com

Published in paperback in Southern Africa in 2016
(South Africa, Namibia, Lesotho, Swaziland & Botswana)
by Jacana Media (Pty) Ltd
Orange Street, Sunnyside
Auckland Park 2092
Johannesburg
South Africa

British Library Cataloguing in Publication Data
A catalogue record for this book is available on request from the British Library

ISBN 978-1-8470-1141-1 (James Currey cloth edition)
ISBN 978-1-4314-2400-9 (Jacana paperback edition)

The publisher has no responsibility for the continued existence or accuracy of
URLs for external or third-party internet websites referred to in this book, and
does not guarantee that any content on such websites is, or will remain, accurate
or appropriate.

This book is printed on acid-free paper

Typeset in 10/12 Melior
by Avocet Typeset, Somerton, Somerset TA11 6RT
Printed and bound by CPI Group (UK) Ltd, Croydon, CR0 4YY

Contents

For my family

Acknowledgements

This book was written in Johannesburg, between January and December 2015.

It draws extensively on research I conducted and arguments I developed during my doctoral studies at the University of Oxford, between 2004 and 2009. It also draws upon further research conducted during a period as post-doctoral research fellow at the National Research Foundation Chair in Local Histories and Present Realities at the University of the Witwatersrand, between 2010 and 2012.

We see the past through the lens of the present. These recent years have been ones of dissent and disruption within South Africa. As I began this research, new social movements – including the Treatment Action Campaign and Abahlali baseMjondolo – were articulating a critique of the post-apartheid settlement, and beginning to insist on a more substantive form of democratic politics rooted in shared experiences of exclusion and protest. At the end of this writing process, university students across the country are embarking upon protests against economic inequality, social exclusion and the continuing influence of colonial thought on the contemporary academy.

Consequently, as I have looked back at the 1960s and 1970s – the period under study in this book – my attention has been drawn to the elements of those times that most resonate today. Fifty years ago, students were at the heart of South African politics, and new organisations were articulating a fierce critique of the apartheid social order. Their politics were frequently expressed through protests that were spontaneous and often disorganised, occasionally short-sighted and rarely sustainable. In a few short years, they remade politics in South Africa. Previously unimaginable ideas emerged in the course of these protests, and formed the basis of new political organisations. New classes and categories of activists became visible – not just students, but also workers. New identities became available, and new alliances – between students of different races and backgrounds, as well as between students and workers and others – became possible.

These elements of the 1960s and 1970s were always there, but they have rarely been as visible as they are today. In this moment, making sense of the past may be a way of understanding the present. In this book, I have tried to respect the integrity of past events and processes without losing sight of the moments in which I have been working – of the moments of disruption and discontent, of the reinvention of popular politics and of the emergence of new actors within South Africa. It is in the shadow of our shared history – a different history to that which is ordinarily told – that the post-apartheid present is developing. This book is a product of a dialogue between past and present, between the politics of the apartheid era and the politics of today.

As may be obvious, the book has had a long gestation and, in the dozen years that I have been working on it, intermittently, I have accrued a correspondingly long list of debts. First among these, is to William Beinart. His supervision of the original thesis combined scepticism and support, encouragement and challenge: without necessarily agreeing with any of my interpretations, he has consistently pushed me to strengthen my positions and defend my ideas. His influence has shaped me, and has made this book better than it would be otherwise.

Towards the end of my doctorate I moved to Johannesburg and completed the final work on the thesis with the support of Phil Bonner and Noor Nieftagodien. I am deeply grateful for their warmth and encouragement, as well as for the institutional support that allowed me to both continue to think about this work while exploring its resonances in contemporary politics. I spent three years as a post-doctoral fellow under their supervision, and re-learned what it meant to be part of a shared project. With their support – and with the support and friendship of colleagues in the Department of Political Studies, where I have since begun to teach – I have come to make a new home at the University of the Witwatersrand. The intellectual fellowship and friendships I have found as part of the University's History Workshop have been the bedrock of my life there.

Over the years, I have been the beneficiary of several scholarships. I must gratefully acknowledge the support of the National Research Foundation of South Africa – first as a doctoral student and then as a post-doctoral fellow. As a student, I have received support from the University of Oxford's African Studies Centre and Faculty of Modern History, from the Skye Foundation and from the Oppenheimer Trust. Without their support, I would not have been able to do this work.

I have also been the beneficiary of the work of archivists and librarians – without whose support any academic is bound to struggle. I would like to acknowledge the staff at the Rhodes House library in Oxford, at the University of the Witwatersrand's Historical Papers archive, at the archives of the University of Cape Town, and the Alan Paton Centre at the University of KwaZulu-Natal.

Friends have entertained, encouraged and challenged me throughout the writing of this project. In Oxford, I had the support of a group of South

Africanists, including Tim Gibbs, Simonne Horwitz, Kelly Rosenthal, Genevieve Klein, Franziska Rueedi and Marcelle Dawson. Outside this group, the friendship of Daniel Russell and Dalia Majumder-Russell, Miriam Prys, Naysan Rafati, Graham Harvey and Elena Schak brought me through many years of interwoven frustration and excitement. In South Africa, Vashna Jagarnath and Richard Pithouse, Prinisha Badassy, Mandisa Mbali, Annie Devenish, Kerry Chance, Arianna Lissoni, Tshepo Moloi, Shireen Hassim, Joel Quirk, Stacey Sommerdyk, Anne Heffernan and many others have given me both friendship and support. In particular, I must also thank both Zahn Gowar and Gillian Renshaw, both for their friendship and for going out of their way to make my life administratively easier over the past half-dozen years.

My husband, Stuart Wilson, has listened to me talk about this book since we met. He is my first and my closest reader. As I have written this book, he has never ceased to probe my arguments and challenge my conclusions. He has encouraged and supported me. He has my heart.

This book is dedicated to my family – to my parents, Keith and Carol, my sister, Gabrielle, and my uncle, Tony. As long as I can remember, I have had their support and their love. Without them, I would have written nothing – and without them I would be nothing.

A Note on Language

The choice of language is always a political one. In the period under study in this book, racial terminology was at the heart of the South African social order, and of resistance to it.

Under apartheid, South Africans were divided into four principal racial categories: White, African, Indian and Coloured. In the official language of the time, Africans were also known as 'Bantu'. Colloquially and sometimes formally, all African, Indian and Coloured persons were grouped together as 'Non-Whites'. These terms are all problematic.

In the late 1960s, a political movement emerged within the African, Indian and Coloured populations of South Africa. This movement rejected apartheid categories and – in place of the negative concept of 'Non-White' – asserted a shared identity under the name of blackness. They spoke about their Black Consciousness, and called themselves Black. This language evolved over time, however, and was not consistently used in the 1970s.

In this book, I have largely adopted the terminology of Black Consciousness. Nonetheless, there are instances in which I have had to use the language of apartheid racial categorisation – most obviously, when quoting directly from statements made at the time or when closely paraphrasing these statements. I have also avoided the regular capitalisation of 'Black', in part because there is little consistency in this usage during the period. When capitalised, Black Consciousness refers to the specific ideological movement. When not capitalised, it generally refers to a broad trajectory of thought.

Abbreviations

ANC	African National Congress
ARM	African Resistance Movement
BAWU	Black Allied Workers' Union
BCP	Black Community Programme
BPC	Black Peoples' Convention
BWP	Black Workers' Project
NUSAS	National Union of South African Students
PAC	Pan Africanist Congress
SASO	South African Students' Organisation
SRC	Student Representative Council
SSRC	Soweto Students' Representative Council
TRC	Truth and Reconciliation Commission
UCM	University Christian Movement
UCT	University of the Cape Town
UDW	University of Durban-Westville
UNP	University of Natal, Pietermaritzburg
UWC	University of the Western Cape
Wits	University of the Witwatersrand

'throws new light on the background to the Soweto Uprising, providing insight into white and black student politics, worker protest and broader dissent.'

– William Beinart, University of Oxford

'an extremely important contribution to the historiography on protest in South Africa. It links black and white student protests (too often studied in isolation from one another) to workers' movements by looking at the changing forms of protest during the 1960s and 1970s, and the apartheid government's changing responses.'

– Anne Heffernan, University of the Witwatersrand

'By showing how the Soweto Uprising served as a precursor for later historical and political events, the author convincingly shows the continuity from one from one protest and decade to the next.'

– Dawne Curry, University of Nebraska-Lincoln

Introduction

THE ROAD TO SOWETO

On 16 June 1976, students from secondary schools across Soweto marched through the township towards the Orlando Stadium. They planned a peaceful procession and gathering to demonstrate their opposition to the government's plan to change the medium of instruction in their schools from English to Afrikaans. Many of the students believed that this would be a carnivalesque occasion, filled with laughter and the reversal of social norms, with one student remembering that he had thought that, on the day, 'female students will wear our trousers or their fathers' trousers and we will wear our sisters' dresses.'[1]

This was not to be.

In the early hours of the morning, the South African Police began to gather at street corners scattered along the students' route. From about 08h00 they began to challenge isolated groups of students. These early incidents gave rise to rumours of police violence, which ran through Soweto, and then erupted into fact at 11h00 outside the Orlando West High School.

Here, a group of between thirty and fifty policemen confronted a large crowd of students. The students had been halted in their march, and they were standing in place. They were singing, whistling at the police and brandishing placards. In a moment, though, this changed. In the words of Sophie Tema, a journalist at the scene: 'a White policeman hurled what seemed to be a teargas shell – which released a cloud of smoke and gas – into the crowd ... [I saw] a White policeman pull out his revolver, point it, and fire it. As soon as the shot was fired other policemen also began firing.' The shots sped into the crowd, where they killed two youths. Tema saw 'a young boy ... fall with a bullet wound'. She reported: 'He had a bloody froth on his lips and he seemed to be seriously hurt so I took him to the ... clinic in a press car but he was dead when we arrived.'[2]

The child's name was Hector Pieterson, and his image was flashed across the world, becoming an emblem of the apartheid state's brutality and cruelty. But his was not the only death that day.

[1] Paul Ndaba, quoted in S.M. Ndlovu, *The Soweto Uprisings: Counter-Memories of June 1976* (Johannesburg, Ravan: 1998), p. 26.
[2] *The World*, 17 June 1976.

1

In the hours after Pieterson's death, violence spread across Soweto. As the police attempted to restrict the students' movements, and suppress their protest, large numbers of the youth began to resist the state's efforts. Instead of accepting the authority of the state – or even choosing to bend before its overwhelming force – students began to fight back: they picked up stones and threw them at the police, they used sticks to resist assaults, they set fire to a post office and the local administration office and, as the day progressed, they made makeshift Molotov cocktails from petrol, glass and rags. They ran from the police, taking advantage of their knowledge of backyards and alleyways; they evaded arrest, and turned the streets of Soweto into a battlefield.

This was a rebellion – localised, to be sure, and massively outgunned, but a rebellion nonetheless. Over the next week, students and police clashed in Soweto. Families became involved. The violence spread, rapidly, to other sites and other townships across South Africa. Within the month, much of South Africa was involved in an open struggle with the state. In Soweto itself, students and their supporters set up an alternate structure of local governance, working in the gaps left by the withdrawal of the state's bureaucracy from the township. These efforts provided the foundations for the development of an organised opposition within South Africa, which would link up with the exiled liberation movements and begin to organise a concerted challenge to apartheid rule. In the 1980s, this coordinated opposition would render the country ungovernable.

The argument of this book

The explosion of protest in Soweto thus reshaped South Africa's politics and began the processes that led to the end of the apartheid order and the creation of the new post-apartheid state. This much is widely accepted, and yet, very little is known about the context of this explosion.

At the time, scholars and commentators struggled to locate the Uprising in a political history. The official explanation for the protest, offered by the state-sponsored Cillié Commission of Inquiry, was that it was caused by an unfortunate confluence of unusual and exceptional events: 'the application of the policy on the medium of instruction in Black secondary schools, the organised resistance in Soweto to this application, the handling of this resistance, and the failure of the education officials and the police ... to take precautionary measures.'[3] In contrast to this bland conclusion, other scholars – both within and

---

[3] *Report of the Commission of Inquiry into the Riots at Soweto and Elsewhere from the 16th of June 1976 to the 28th February 1977* (Cillié Commission), 2 vols. (Pretoria, RSA: 1980), p. 643.

outside of the country – sought to connect the protest to other forms of resistance. Some suggested that labour disturbances offered a model for the students in Soweto; others argued for the influence of Black Consciousness thought on the students; yet others suggested that the ANC and other exiled liberation movements, through their clandestine underground organisations, had shaped the development of the resistance.[4]

In the four decades since the Soweto Uprising, a consensus account of the politics of the mid-1970s, and the role of Soweto in them, has emerged. In this account, the Uprising arises out of a period of political quiescence. It is the moment of the emergence of a new generation of activists – mostly under the age of twenty years – who would go on to drive politics in the future. And it was the product of local resistance to national state policies and practices, shaped by the experiences of students in Soweto, of youth gangs in the neighbourhood and their contingent encounters with the police, and taken up nationally.[5] This consensus story sees the Soweto Uprising as a moment of transition, from apartheid hegemony to popular resistance. But was the decade before 1976 ever as quiescent as this story supposes?

In this book I take up that question. I answer it by examining the emergence of new forms of politics, of ideology and of public protest in the decade before the explosion of the Uprising.

When looked at through this lens, the years immediately before the Uprising seem to be characterised by seething activity: by repeated interruptions of the public order, and by the emergence of new ideas of dissent and new forms of protest. In these years, students, factory workers and other South Africans experimented with forms of politics and resistance – recreating models of protest, and creating new forms of political behaviour. The events of this decade provided South Africa's dissidents with a repertoire of resistance, a set of tools

---

[4] In order, Baruch Hirson, *Year of Fire, Year of Ash: The Soweto Revolt – Roots of a Revolution?* (London, Zed: 1979); John Kane-Berman, *Soweto: Black Revolt, White Reaction* (Johannesburg, Ravan: 1978); Alan Brooks and Jeremy Brickhill, *Whirlwind Before the Storm: The Origins and Development of the Uprising in Soweto and the Rest of South Africa from June to December 1976* (London, IDAF: 1980). See also Nozipho Diseko's later article, setting out a case for the involvement of the ANC underground in the protest: 'The Origins and Development of the South African Students' Movement (SASM): 1968–1976', *Journal of Southern African Studies*, 18(1) 1992, pp. 40–62.

[5] This story can be found in, for example: P. Hopkins and H. Grange, *The Rocky Rioter Teargas Show: The Inside Story of the 1976 Uprising* (Cape Town, Zebra: 2001) and A.K. Hlongwane (ed), *Footprints of the "Class of 76": Commemoration, Memory, Mapping and Heritage* (Johannesburg, Hector Pieterson Museum: 2008). Among other texts, these survey accounts draw upon the long local history of P. Bonner and L. Segal, *Soweto: A History* (Cape Town, Maskew Miller Longman: 1998) and the study of gang culture in the period by Clive Glaser, *Bo-Tsotsi: The Youth Gangs of Soweto* (Oxford, James Currey: 2000) to situate the standard account of the Uprising in a richer social history of the area.

that could be used to challenge apartheid's control over the country.

The efforts of these activists in this period were directed at the reinvention of protest, in the wake of the suppression of most public opposition to the apartheid state in the early 1960s. They embarked upon often-unplanned protests with little preparation, and equally few expectations. In the process of engaging in politics, new political possibilities emerged – arising organically from the processes of struggle and engagement, of repression and re-orientation. These new possibilities reshaped the political field in this decade, both in public and in private. New forms of public action developed and were taken up by different groups in different places. New identities and ideologies became available and were adopted by young men and women.

In this book, I trace the events of this decade from their origins in student protests through to strikes and mass public rallies. I argue that these protests were the product of experiments: they were often unplanned, emerging spontaneously out of contingent events and circumstances. Even when planned, they exceeded the expectations of their organisers. They disrupted and disturbed the political order, and opened the eyes of participants – and perhaps observers – to the expanding possibilities for opposition. After each experiment, a new set of ideas became available – and each protest created the conditions for the next. Students became radicalised; their protests echoed those of workers and other groups in society; new social groups began to embark upon protest, and began to adopt the methods and forms first tried out by students.

This is a story about the emergence of a new opposition – not in a single explosion of protest, but rather through an unplanned series of experiments taking place over the course of a long decade.

South African political history, 1966–1976

But this is not the story that is usually told about the time before the Uprising. Instead, the years between the banning of the aboveground African opposition movements and the explosion of protest at Soweto have commonly been portrayed as the period in which the apartheid state's power reached its zenith, and opposition its nadir. In this context, the decade before the Uprising is seen as an interregnum, a period in parenthesis, a time of airless quiescence caught between the dramatic events of the early 1960s and those that followed in the late 1970s.

The starting point of any story about this period is the massacre of peaceful protesters at Sharpeville, outside Johannesburg, on 26 March 1960. This massacre inaugurated a wave of state repression aimed at the aboveground African political opposition; within weeks, these organisations were banned, and membership of them declared illegal.[6] The movements were forced either into exile or underground, where they sought to organise a clandestine resistance to the apartheid state. This resistance was armed, and carried out acts of sabotage against public structures and – occasionally – acts of violence against members of the white public.[7] The state continued its intensive campaign against these activists and, by the later months of 1963, had largely succeeded in dismantling the most effective of the underground structures. The suppression of an insurrection associated with the Pan Africanist Congress in Paarl in 1963, and the arrest and trial of the leaders of the African National Congress's underground in 1964, marked the end of a brief period of struggle, and of three years in which the state was threatened.[8]

In this moment, the apartheid state seemed triumphant. The liberation movements were exiled, and their underground structures scattered. The remaining aboveground opposition was weak and disunited. The emergency powers established in the period of insurrection remained and became part of the state's ordinary toolkit. The apartheid state's control over the public sphere seemed total: newspapers were gagged, opposition politics neutered and order imposed.

The standard stories of quiescence go further, and suggest that this order was largely undisturbed for the remainder of the decade. Dissent simmered in private spaces, but was excluded from the public arena. The underground movements were paralysed, waiting for instructions from their exiled leaders – who were, themselves, caught up in the struggle to establish structures that could sustain the movements internationally. In the early years of the next decade, as the movements were increasingly established in their external locations, the struggle in South Africa resurfaced in the form of intellectual and cultural resistance by young black students. The adoption of ideas of Black Consciousness shaped experiences, and provided a means through which private dissent could be made public. Black Consciousness also sowed the seeds of resistance that flowered during the Soweto Uprising, which itself remade South African politics in a violent convulsion. These ideas, though, failed to coordinate a political

---

[6] For the Massacre and its immediate aftermath see Philip Frankel, *An Ordinary Atrocity: Sharpeville and its Massacre* (Johannesburg, Wits University Press: 2001) and Tom Lodge, *Sharpeville: An Apartheid Massacre and its Consequences* (Oxford, Oxford University Press: 2011).

[7] An extremely detailed early work on this period of revolt is Edward Feit, *Urban Revolt in South Africa, 1960–1964* (Chicago, Northwestern University Press: 1971). See also: B.B. Maaba, 'The PAC's war against the state, 1960–1963,' and S. Mathabata, 'The PAC and Poqo in Pretoria, 1958–1964,' both in South African Democracy Education Trust (SADET), *The Road to Democracy in South Africa, Volume 1, 1960–1970* (Johannesburg, Zebra: 2004).

[8] The best account remains Tom Lodge, *Black Politics in South Africa since 1945* (London, Longman: 1983).

opposition, and their proponents soon joined one of the exiled liberation movements. After the Uprising, these actors brought their ideas into the ANC – whose structures made them effective.[9]

In this story, the dozen years between the Rivonia Trial of 1964 and the Uprising of 1976 are compressed to a period of quiescence, a time of private dissent and public caution. Liberation politics are located in the diaspora of banned and exiled South Africans, and a generation of activists is read out of history, their political beliefs relegated to the domestic sphere.

This narrative can be challenged on several grounds. For example, Raymond Suttner has argued that it overlooks the actual operations of the ANC's underground inside the country during these years. He suggests that the underground was actively recreating itself, recruiting new members, distributing propaganda, and establishing the structures that would allow the ANC to return to prominence in the wake of the Soweto Uprising. These processes took place in the spaces overlooked by standard histories, and by institution-centred accounts of political activity: the ANC's underground was present in people's homes, its politics preserved and passed on through treasured symbols and memories. The inability of narratives of quiescence to account for activity in domestic spaces – and the implicit assumption that acts in those spaces do not constitute politics – has led them to provide a desiccated account of political activity after Rivonia and before Soweto.[10]

In this book, I echo some of Suttner's critique. Like him, I see this decade as a period of political activity; like him, I am suspicious of accounts of politics that locate struggle only within public fora, and within official or unofficial public institutions. However, my account differs from his in at least two substantial ways. First, I place little emphasis on the significance of the reorganisation and development of the ANC's underground movement inside South Africa during this decade. Second, I argue that the public sphere was in fact the site of dissent, resistance and political contest. In doing so, I extend the definition of political activities and organisations to include not merely organisations that openly (or covertly) worked for the overthrow of the government and state, but also organisations that expressed partial

[9] This story is found, with varying differing emphases in scholarly surveys, such as Tom Karis and Gail Gerhart's magisterial *From Protest to Challenge: A Documentary History of African Politics in South Africa, 1882–1990: Volume 5: Nadir and Resurgence* (Bloomington and Indianapolis University of Indiana Press: 1997); in biographies of post-apartheid political leaders, such as Nelson Mandela, *Long Walk to Freedom* (London, Macdonald Purnell: 1994) and Elinor Sisulu, *Walter and Albertina Sisulu: In Our Lifetime* (Cape Town, David Philip: 2002); and in many popular accounts.

[10] Raymond Suttner, *The ANC Underground in South Africa to 1976: A Social and Historical Study* (Johannesburg, Jacana: 2008). See pp. 59–83.

and incomplete forms of dissent – particularly student organisations. These organisations have been largely neglected in the standard accounts of the time, and this neglect is replicated in Suttner's critique of these histories.

These organisations are, however, coming to the fore in recent work by graduate students. This work has directed attention at under-explored elements of political activity in this period. Ian Macqueen has argued, in his doctoral thesis, that the intellectual project of white students and activists was of greater importance to the development of a new South African political identity than has previously been recognised. He suggests that the localised organisations set up by these activists helped shape the development of a body of radical dissenting ideologies and political practices that posed a threat to the ideological stability of the apartheid state, and that fed into the development of later resistance.[11] Similarly, Helen Lunn emphasises the politics of culture and counter-culture amongst students in this period.[12] Anne Heffernan has written a rich and detailed study of the development of student politics in Limpopo, adding vital insights into the ways in which local contexts shaped political practice.[13] In my doctoral work, I sought to show how notions of violence shaped the emergence of public forms of protest between the election of the apartheid government and the eruption of protest in Soweto.[14] Our shared focus on aboveground activities has influenced new surveys of the period. Saul Dubow's recent history of apartheid, for example, builds upon this – still largely unpublished – work to flesh out the conventional account of this period and add detail to the history of a neglected decade.[15]

Beyond these examples, a lengthy article by Martin Legassick and Christopher Saunders, published as part of the South African Democracy Education Trust project, has outlined the range of aboveground political activity in this period, and – in compiling the records of this activity – suggested its scope.[16] Other scholars have focused on the activities associated with Black Consciousness activists, and have

---

[11] Ian Macqueen, 'Re-Imagining South Africa: Black Consciousness, Radical Christianity and the New Left, 1967–1977' (PhD Thesis, University of Sussex: 2011).

[12] Helen Lunn, '"Hippies, Radicals and the Sounds of Silence': Cultural Dialectics at Two South African Universities, 1966–1976' (PhD Thesis, University of KwaZulu-Natal: 2009).

[13] Anne Heffernan, 'A History of Youth Politics in Limpopo, 1967–2003' (DPhil Thesis, University of Oxford: 2014).

[14] Julian Brown, 'Public Protest and Violence in South Africa, 1948–1976' (DPhil Thesis, University of Oxford: 2009). Although this book emerges out of this work, it has developed in a very different direction.

[15] Saul Dubow, *Apartheid, 1948–1994* (Oxford, Oxford University Press: 2014)

[16] Martin Legassick and Christopher Saunders, 'Above-Ground Activity in the 1960s', South African Democracy Education Trust (SADET*), The Road to Democracy in South Africa, Volume 1, 1960–1970* (Johannesburg, Zebra: 2004), pp. 661–89.

suggested that the standard account of their activism needs reconsideration.[17] In a more popular vein, Glen Moss's memoir of activism in the decade recovers many of the personal stories of a neglected generation of activists.[18] Other memoirs and biographies, too, have highlighted the stories of activists of this generation and the impact of their experiences in this period on the political education and evolution. These include accounts of and by members of the Black Consciousness generation, Beverley Naidoo's biography of Neil Aggett, and Billy Keniston's recent account of Rick Turner's life.[19]

Although these authors focus on different – and sometimes sharply divergent – aspects of public politics in this period, they all set out to consider public dissent and resistance in this period, and to take the claims of contemporary activists seriously. In doing so, both scholarly and popular works build upon and significantly reframe earlier studies. In particular, a rich body of scholarship on Black Consciousness has often contained useful information on the organisational development of black student organisations, and their local political struggles, while nonetheless seeing these as incidental to the development of an ideological and philosophical project.[20] Work on the re-emergence of a labour movement in the middle years of the 1970s, too, often suggests at the activities in the years before.[21] By mining these earlier sources for information and hints as to the activities of the period, the authors of this new body of writing have sought to recover these activities for historical study – and to challenge the emphases of an earlier generation of scholars – suggesting new subjects of study.

These new works have a number of shortcomings, however. First is their routine acceptance of a set of structuring dichotomies: between

[17] See for example: Saleem Badat, *Black Man You Are On Your Own* (Johannesburg, Steve Biko Foundation: 2009) and Daniel Magaziner, *The Law and the Prophets: Black Consciousness in South Africa, 1968–1977* (Athens, Ohio University Press: 2010).

[18] Glenn Moss, *The New Radicals: A Generational Memoir of the 1970s* (Johannesburg, Jacana: 2014).

[19] See: Mamphela Ramphele, *Mamphela Ramphele: A Life* (Cape Town, David Philip: 1995); L. Schuster, *A Burning Hunger: One Family's Struggle Against Apartheid* (London, Jonathan Cape: 2004); Lindy Wilson, *Steve Biko* (Johannesburg, Jacana: 2011); Xolela Mangcu, *Biko: A Biography* (Cape Town, Tafelberg: 2012). Beverley Naidoo, *Death of an Idealist: In Search of Neil Aggett* (Johannesburg, Jonathan Ball: 2012); Billy Keniston, *Choosing to be Free: The Life Story of Rick Turner* (Johannesburg, Jacana: 2014).

[20] Key works on Black Consciousness ideas include: Gail Gerhart, *Black Power in South Africa: The Evolution of an Ideology* (Berkeley, University of California Press: 1978); Sam C. Nolutshungu, *Changing South Africa: Political Considerations* (Cape Town, David Philip: 1982); Robert Fatton, *Black Consciousness in South Africa: The Dialectics of Ideological Resistance in White Supremacy* (Albany, SUNY Press: 1986).

[21] See, in particular: Steven Friedman, *Building Tomorrow Today: African Workers in Trade Unions, 1970–1984* (Johannesburg, Ravan: 1987).

public and private spaces and politics, between organisations and individuals, structures and agency, and between white and black activists and their political practices. Second, they continue to be shaped by an implicit theorisation of political activity. Although they no longer presume that politics can be identified with formal organisations and the institutionalisation of dissenting ideas, these works do still tend to associate politics with open contests for access to the power of the state. As such, acts that did not succeed in significantly disturbing the apartheid government's control over the state are regarded – to a varying extent – as failed politics: as frustrated efforts to change the state, and as abortive forerunners of later, more successful, challenges to the apartheid order.

These theoretical presumptions tie these texts to the ideological structures of their predecessors. Dichotomies function to fragment the political activities of the period: protest and ideological development are separated from each other, the actions of white and black students are studied separately, as are the politics of workers and students. The presumption that political efficacy can be measured through an assessment of the immediate effects of a particular act also serves to remove alternate understandings of politics from study. When considered together, they lead scholars to re-emphasise the presumption of general quiescence – even while seeking to recover the actions of a particular fragment within that history.

In telling the story of a decade of seething activity, this book aims to do something different. I hope to destabilise the standard dichotomies of South African struggle histories of the period, and in doing so recover the complex interactions that shaped the development of politics in this period. This then reveals a political landscape that requires a different theory of politics – one that highlights both the spontaneity and temporary nature of political acts, and one that emphasises the productive potential of political disruption.

Destabilising dichotomies

The first of these efforts – the destabilisation of dichotomies – can perhaps be best introduced in the context of a broader reconsideration of the politics of the late 1960s and early 1970s globally.

In this context, the single most prominent political event of this period took place in Paris in May 1968. In this month, French students embarked on a series of protests, occupations and public marches; they disrupted the ordinary operations of the social order, building barricades in the street and challenging the authority of the state and police. They also exceeded the boundaries of their spatial and class location, occupying factory spaces alongside workers and arguing for a broad reshaping of capitalist class relations and culture.[22] These protests contributed to the emergence of the 'New Left' and a range of social movements and new political forms.[23]

However, the events have not been remembered this way. In her account of the political disruptions of May 1968, Kristin Ross argues that the linked struggles of students and workers in these protests have been separated from each other in popular histories and political accounts of the events. This is despite the fact that students and workers were protesting simultaneously, through May and into June, and despite the fact that students and workers were communicating with each other, and adopting each other's strategies.

Ross suggests that the student protest has been enshrined as the primary episode of the period, while the workers' strike has been largely erased from histories. In doing so, the political implications of the student protest have been minimised – instead of being seen as part of a challenge against the capitalist order, linked to broader social and economic struggles, they have been portrayed as the product of generational discontent. This allowed the protests to be domesticated within the French social order – and allowed some of the most prominent activists of the time to enter into the formal arena of official state politics as commentators, public intellectuals and elected representatives. Ross argues that the effect of this has been to skew the public memory of the events of May 1968, creating a dichotomy between the generational struggles of the students and the class struggles of the workers which, consequently, permitted the social order – momentarily threatened by these disruptions – to renew itself by incorporating the energies of the moment.[24]

This argument has a particular significance for South African history of this period. The country's social order has long been defined by a series of sharp dichotomies – the most notable of which has been, of course, the dichotomy between white and black. These dichotomies have shaped the ways in which histories of the apartheid struggle have been written. In this period, this means that most histories separate the politics of black students from those of white students, and the politics of students from those of workers.

[22] Among a wide range of accounts of the events, see: Angelo Quattrochi and Tom Nairn, *The Beginning of the End: France, May 1968* (London, Verso: 1998); Ian Birchall, 'France 1968,' in Colin Barker (ed.), *Revolutionary Rehearsals* (Chicago, Haymarket: 2002); Daniel Singer, *Prelude to Revolution: France in May 1968* (2nd edition, Chicago, Haymarket: 2013).
[23] See, for example, the arguments in: Julian Bourg, *From Revolution to Ethics: May 1968 and Contemporary French Thought* (Montreal and Kingston, McGill-Queens University Press: 2007), as well as the introductory comments in Razmig Keucheyan, *The Left Hemisphere: Mapping Critical Theory Today* trans. Gregory Elliot (London, Verso: 2013).
[24] Kristin Ross, *May '68 and Its Afterlives* (Chicago, University of Chicago Press: 2002).

In doing this, studies have often adopted the self-image of many participants at the time: black students emphasised their difference from white students, while workers argued that their politics were driven by immediate economic crises, rather than by the intellectual agendas of students. Thus, while excellent work has shown how the intellectual world of black students developed in this period, much of this work has tended to accept a strict segregation between the experiences of these black students and their white counterparts.[25] Likewise, studies of the resurgence of a black labour movement in this period have separated these activities from those of both black and white students – except insofar as some white intellectuals chose, in the later part of the 1970s, to become part of the new trade union movement.[26]

But as Ross suggests in the French context, adopting these divides as the basis of political analysis and historical narrative domesticates potentially disruptive forms of politics. Adopting these divides splits the politics of the period into multiple strands, and hides the extent to which they may have been woven together. By studying these strands independently of each other, they are artificially completed, and rendered into self-contained wholes. The effect is to foreclose analysis, and to allow the potential of each strand of politics to amplify the effects of all others to be lost.

In this book, I seek to emphasise connections rather than differences. These connections sometimes involved personal relations – between student leaders, for example, or between students and workers. More often, though, the connections were less immediately material, and found expression in shared approaches to protest, similarities in political organisation and action, and inter-related reactions to divergent social and spatial contexts. The forms of organisation and protest adopted by students and by workers, in their contexts, are thus at the heart of this account.

From this perspective, the relations between black and white students do not diverge dramatically. The break between their two organisations – the South African Students' Organisation (SASO) and the National Union of South African Students (NUSAS) – did not bring engagement to an end. Instead, this break altered the terms of the relationship. SASO rejected attempts by NUSAS to dictate the terms of student protest while adopting and adapting many of the same organisational structures. Both organisations learned from the experiences of the other; both – as student unions – developed comparable strategies for making use of the peculiar dynamic of university spaces. When considered in this fashion, the activities of students can be seen to

---

[25] See, for example: Gerhart, *Black Power in South Africa*, and Magaziner, *The Law and the Prophets*.

[26] e.g. Friedman, *Building Tomorrow Today*, and the early sections of Jeremy Baskin, *Striking Back: A History of COSATU* (London, Routledge: 1991).

constitute a radical challenge to the norms of organisation and expression in the formal political sphere – a challenge that is defanged by the scholarly erasure of the activities of white students, and the incorporation of Black Consciousness histories into those of the ANC in the years after the Uprising.

Similarly, the divide between students and workers needs to be challenged. By dividing these efforts, the activities of workers can be seen as being primarily part of a longer trajectory of union organisation and labour politics – and only tangentially as part of the specific historical conjuncture of the decade before Soweto. This approach de-emphasises the importance of spectacular protests by workers, and emphasises the importance of behind-the-scenes organisation and institutionalisation. As such, the spectacle of protest is seen as an early stage of political action, prior to the real work of organisation – and, as such, the events of the first half of the 1970s slip into the background of the history of the re-emergence of African trade unions. However, if labour protests are understood in the context of the other activities taking place around them, then the similarities between the forms of protest and spectacle adopted by students and workers becomes important – and the claims made by workers cannot simply be streamlined into calls for formal trade union activism.

Politics as disruption

Destabilising the dichotomies that have structured political histories of the period in this way, and emphasising the connections between classes, movements and struggles within the particular conjuncture of this decade, also works to dethrone a standard approach to conceptualising politics. This standard conceptualisation assumes the primacy of a particular version of the public sphere – a 'political sphere' within which legitimate political struggles may take place. This sphere is located in the terrain of parties, liberation movements, and civil society organisations; action that occurs in it is defined by its relation to these bodies. It thus emphasises the importance of organisation and institution building, of the powers of the state, and of the development of organised and coordinated movements that seek to counter the unjust exercise of those powers.

This vision of politics relegates unplanned and uncoordinated protest to a secondary position: at best, these events provide the context within which organisation can occur, but without transcending the conditions of their emergence in this way they are merely ephemeral, lacking lasting significance. This vision has, of course, been challenged from different directions in recent decades – including by many political theorists who emerged from the explosion of protest in the late 1960s. Several scholars associated with the 'New Left' have suggested that protests provide the conditions under which new social movements organise themselves as emergent – rather than planned – structures. Others have attempted to reframe Marxist approaches to politics through a reconceptualisation of class relations as relations of social and cultural power.[27]

Another approach – one that I adopt in this book – focuses on the ways in which exceptional political actions disturb the operations of the social order, and expose its contingency. There are a number of different sources for this approach. Henri Lefebvre's immediate response to the events of May 1968, *The Explosion*, provides an important precursor – building on and transcending the dreams of the Situationist International. Alain Badiou's highly influential account of the aporetic nature of political events has returned to these themes in the light of revolutionary theory. In addition, Slavoj Žižek's account of the centrality of the subject and subjectivity to politics has cast a wide shadow over contemporary political theory. However, although I have been influenced by each of these thinkers, I find the key to my approach in a different body of work.[28]

I find it in the work of Jacques Rancière, as adapted to respond to the particular circumstances of South Africa's political history.[29] In the wake of May 1968, Rancière rejected an early allegiance to Althusserian Marxism and began work on a series of historical investigations into a radical pedagogic experiment in the early eighteenth century, and into the political activities of worker-poets in the nineteenth.[30] In these examples, he found evidence of individuals and groups acting politically without access to the privileged theoretical knowledge that Althusser and his followers suggested was necessary. Instead, each of these acts were motivated by the insistence of the actors that they had not been accounted for in the ordinary distribution of society, but were nonetheless capable of acting as equals with those who had been counted.

[27] Among other works, I am thinking of: Michael Hardt and Antonio Negri, *Empire* (Cambridge, Massachusetts, Harvard University Press: 2000), and their *Multitude: War and Democracy in the Age of Empire* (Harmondsworth, Penguin: 2005), as well as Ernesto Laclau and Chantal Mouffe, *Hegemony and Socialist Strategy: Towards a Radical Democratic Politics* (2nd edition, London, Verso: 2001).

[28] Henri Lefebvre, *The Explosion: Marxism and the French Revolutions*, trans Alfred Ehrenfeld (New York, Monthly Review Press: 1969) and Kristin Ross and Henri Lefebvre, 'Lefebvre on the Situationists: An Interview,' *October*, 79 (Winter 1997); Alain Badiou, *Metapolitics*, trans. J. Barker (London, Verso: 2005); Slavoj Žižek's, *The Ticklish Subject: The Absent Centre of Political Ontology* (London, Verso: 2000).

[29] In this section, I provide a brief summary of this approach. For a lengthy discussion see: Julian Brown, *South Africa's Insurgent Citizens: On Dissent and the Possibilities of Politics* (London, Zed Books: 2015).

[30] Jacques Rancière, *The Ignorant Schoolmaster: Five Lessons in Intellectual Emancipation*, trans. Kristin Ross (Stanford, Stanford University Press: 1991); Jacques Rancière, *Proletarian Nights: The Workers' Dream in Nineteenth Century France*, trans. John Drury (London, Verso: 2012).

13

Moving from these examples, Rancière argued that politics do not begin when groups organise themselves to openly contest the structures of power, but rather that politics begin when any established order is disrupted by acts premised on the existing but as-yet-unacknowledged equality of the actors. These actions disturb the seamless operations of the social order and deny its naturalness. Instead, they expose its contingency by making its hidden exclusions visible.[31]

This requires some elaboration. Rancière divides the idea of 'politics' into two elements: first, the visible and invisible institutions of power and authority that shape the social order and, second, acts that disrupt that order. Rancière calls the first 'the police' – and refers to the ways in which it enacts a 'distribution of the sensible'.[32] This is meant to suggest how actors, roles, and knowledge are imagined and parcelled out within a social order so that everything and everyone has its place. Only acts that disrupt that order and are based on the presumption of an unrecognised equality can be called, in Rancière's code, 'politics': 'political activity is always a mode of expression that undoes the perceptible divisions of the police order by implementing a basically heterogenous assumption ... [which is] the equality of any speaking being with any other speaking being.'[33]

Speech is important. Rancière locates the metaphorical origins of the divisions that structure the police order in Aristotle's distinction between those who can speak – and are thus citizens – and those who cannot – and are thus barbarians. In the Greek polis, those who could speak were adult men. Those who could not speak were foreigners – but also, in somewhat different ways, women and slaves. In all these cases, their speech was not recognised as such, or as being capable of rational construal – but rather as sounds without meaning, brute and instinctual in the case of foreigners, domestic and banal in the case of women. Democratic politics are thus defined from the start by practices of exclusion, by the incomplete count of potential citizens and potential actors. The ability to speak is important, because it is the only way to make oneself understood – and thus the only way to verify one's equality: 'only an equal understands an equal'.[34] When those who have not been counted speak, they require their interlocutors to recognise an already-existing equality.

The performative aspects of this model have lead some scholars to suggest that Rancière approach sets up a kind of 'theatrocracy' –

---

[31] Jacques Rancière, *Disagreement: Politics and Philosophy*, trans. Julie Rose (Minneapolis, University of Minnesota Press: 1999).

[32] In describing these institutions as 'the police', Rancière is of course drawing upon the expansive connotations the term in French, as perhaps most famously used by Michel Foucault in *Discipline and Punish: The Birth of the Prison*, trans. Alan Sheridan (London, Allen Lane: 1977).

[33] Rancière, *Disagreement*, p. 30.

[34] Rancière, *The Ignorant Schoolmaster*, p. 71.

that is, a political order defined by aesthetic acts of self-definition.[35] There is some truth to this, in that the analysis of aesthetic categories has influenced Rancière's thought and in that some degree of performance is implicit in the idea of speech. However, the idea of a theatre implies a stage, a proscenium arch and an audience beyond it. This separation between actors and audience is antithetical to Rancière's notion of equality. In its place, he continues to insist that speech relations must be relations between equals. As it is only in the process of conversation and dialogue that equality can be demonstrated and verified, everyone who can speak is simultaneously actor and audience.

This also suggests that there is no theatrical space set apart from everyday life. In the context of political struggles, this must mean that there is no privileged site of politics and no political sphere – that is, no site in which actions are understood to be political, and no site in which actions are not political. Indeed, Rancière is explicit on this point: 'the same thing – an election, a strike, a demonstration – can give rise to politics or not give rise to politics. A strike is not political when it calls for reforms rather than a better deal or when it attacks the relationships of authority rather than the inadequacy of wages. It is political when it reconfigures the relationships that determine the workplace in relation to the community.'[36] This reconfiguration of relationships can take place in multiple sites, and unfold through multiple different kinds and forms of action. All that is essential is that the existing distribution of authority and order is disrupted and the relationships of power that underpin it are rendered visible, and shown to be merely contingent.

The revelation of the contingency of the social order – and of the institutions that shaped it – allows for new political ideas to emerge. This suggests that a function of the disruption caused by political action is to initiate new possibilities, and to remake the boundaries of the political. In other words, once we consider 'politics' as a product of the disruption of existing orders, then we must alter implicit chronologies of theory and practice, organisation and action, in which theory shapes practice, and organisation precedes action. Instead, it is the unpredictable excess of action that allows for the development of theory, and the forms of solidarity and connection that emerge in acts that permit organisation. As Ross puts it, in her discussion of the Paris Commune: 'the thought of a movement is generated only with and after it: unleashed by the creative

---

[35] The term comes from Peter Hallward, 'Staging Equality: Rancière's Theatrocracy and the Limits of Anarchic Equality', in Gabriel Rockhill and Philip Watts (eds), *Jacques Rancière: History, Politics, Aesthetics* (Durham, Duke University Press: 2009).

[36] Rancière, *Disagreement*, p. 32.

energies and excess of the movement itself. Actions produce dreams and ideas, and not the reverse.'[37]

In the context of this study, Rancière's ideas provide a way of conceptualising the political nature of the protests of the period. Instead of considering these events in light of their potential to contribute to the development of a coordinated opposition to the apartheid state – or even, perhaps, in light of their contributions to the post-Soweto resurgence of organised struggle – these events can be considered in the light of their potential to disrupt the apartheid social order. In disrupting the social order, these acts of dissent and experiments in resistance could both expose the contingency at the heart of that order, and frustrate the attempts of apartheid's ideologues to establish hegemony. By exposing the contingency of specific decisions and policies – whether to withdraw the offer of employment to an African academic, or to implement a wage policy based on a supposedly neutral 'poverty line' – these decision and policies were shown to be the product of particular political processes, made for the benefit of particular political interests. They could no longer be seen as natural or inevitable – or even as the consequence of a popular ideological consensus. Once perceived as contingent, therefore, they were shown to be challengeable, and alternate choices were proven to have been possible.

The structure of this book

This book thus sets out to show how the eruption of disruptive actions, as a consequence of unpredictable experiments in resistance, reshaped the boundaries of political possibility in the decade before the Soweto Uprising. It tells the story of the emergence of new groups of activists, new forms of protest, and new political dreams and ideas in these years. It does so by tracing lines of activity from initial starting points into entanglement: that is, showing how apparently separate strands of politics intertwine, shadow each other, and become bound up in each other. The interweaving of these politics took place organically, over time – and were neither planned nor coordinated, despite the occasional fantasies of the apartheid state throughout this period.

The first chapter focuses on the politics of the National Union of South African Students (NUSAS) in the middle years of the 1960s. A multi-racial student union, dominated by white English-speaking liberals, NUSAS had a history of opposing the apartheid state's attempts to enforce segregation within universities. It was also one of the few such organisations to survive the wave of repression that followed the Sharpeville Massacre. As such, it became an unlikely torchbearer

---

[37] Kristin Ross, *Communal Luxury: The Political Imaginary of the Paris Commune* (London, Verso: 2015), pp. 6–7.

for opposition politics – an identity that it and its members struggled with in these years. In 1966 and 1968, NUSAS organised large protests on affiliated university campuses. These protests inspired NUSAS's leaders to adopt increasingly radical positions in opposition to the state. As events erupted, and exceeded expectations, new possibilities were brought to light.

The efforts of NUSAS to oppose the state and the apartheid order had consequences. Within the movement itself, racial divisions became apparent: white students claimed to organise and lead public protests on behalf of the black majority while neglecting the complaints of black students within NUSAS. Chapter 2 examines how black students found that their shared experiences gave them a basis on which to organise, and to assert both their solidarity with each other and their difference from the relatively privileged white leaders of NUSAS. They formed a new student union, the South African Students' Organisation (SASO) and set out to distinguish this new organisation from NUSAS. In part, this meant rejecting the confrontational approach to political opposition that the older union was adopting in the last years of the 1960s. In its place, SASO sought to develop a new politics of community organisation and personal political education, based on cultural and social identity.

However, as the third chapter shows, it was not possible for the two movements to develop independently. NUSAS's confrontational measures were rejected by SASO's leadership, but were nonetheless popular amongst black students. The pressures exerted on SASO by its members forced the organisation to adopt a more confrontational public stance, and to abandon or neglect many of its alternative ideas. During the first years of the 1970s, both student movements adopted similar methods of protest – in dialogue with each other, and with university administrations. Although the divergent responses of their respective universities meant that their protests sometimes differed, they both developed in response to a continuing engagement with practices of policing and repression. The experiments in resistance undertaken by NUSAS and SASO provided examples and inspirations – both direct and indirect – to other groups and communities, as well as to each other.

The activities of students provided an important component of the context within which the labour strikes that paralysed the port city of Durban in the first months of 1973 took place. They helped shape the ways in which these strikes were reported, understood and responded to. Chapter 4 examines the development of these strikes, and the ways in which they reshaped the boundaries of political possibility for other workers across the country. These labour strikes spilled out onto the streets of the city, redrawing the social geography of protest, while the interaction between workers and the police developed. The relative success of the Durban Strikes – the minimising of violent confrontations, the concessions won from owners, and the relatively smooth resumption of economic activity – all carved out a space for labour politics to continue to develop over the coming years.

The emergence of this space, however, coincided with a shrinking of the spaces available for students to act politically. The government instituted a Commission of Inquiry into the behaviour of student movements, and imposed severe restrictions both on the individual leaders of the movements and on their public activities. The fifth chapter considers how student movements reimagined their political options in light of these restrictions. Both NUSAS and SASO sought to engage with the workers, whether through providing them with research and organisational support or through attempting to launch new trade unions. At the same time, the first waves of black students were leaving university, either after graduation, or after expulsion for political activity. They began to launch new movements, including the Black Peoples' Convention (BPC), to remake politics for the context of township life. These different initiatives took the experimental politics developed on university campuses and translated them into new arenas. The context of the country was changing around them, though, and activists faced increasingly brutal forms of repression – including murder – at the hands of the state.

In 1974, SASO and BPC advertised a national series of mass rallies to celebrate the success of the Mozambican liberation movement, Frelimo, in ousting the Portuguese colonial government. Only two of these rallies took place, one in Durban and the other at the University of the North. However, the threat of these rallies – and the possibility of the re-emergence of a mass opposition, adopting the methods of protest and organisation associated with student protests in the years immediately before – provoked a violent response from the police. The rallies also provided the state with the excuse to suppress the newly-visible Black Consciousness movement, leading to a high-profile trial of the leaders of SASO and BPC. From the end of 1974 until the second half of 1976, black activists – almost all of whom had emerged in the student movement, and several of whom had attempted to liaise with militant workers – sat in court, watching the world change. Chapter 6 focuses on these rallies and their aftermath, showing how the constriction of political space frustrated the ability of these movements to act before the Uprising.

Despite the state's attempts to restrict the space for public protest, the experiments in resistance undertaken by students and workers paved the way for the insurrection in Soweto. The seventh chapter thus examines the unfolding of the Uprising in the context of the decade that preceded it. The examples of public protests by SASO and other organisations were known to school-going students in the country's most prominent township; a number of student activists were living in Soweto at the time, either working as teachers or living in the area after being excluded from university in the wake of recent state crackdown. These examples helped shaped the politics of young students, and provided a template for their planned actions on 16 June 1976. They also provided a framework within which later forms of organisation could be conceptualised, and supported.

The final pages of this book return to the theoretical ideas outlined in this Introduction, and show how they emerge from the story of the development of dissent and resistance in the decade before the Soweto Uprising. These ideas shed light both on the politics of the period, and those of the decades that followed. They also shed light on the ways in which histories of protest and politics can be written. In these pages, I will argue that histories need to destabilise the dichotomies that structured – and continue to structure – the country's social order if they are to uncover sources of solidarity and histories of political struggle in unexpected corners of the past.

1 White Student Activism in the 1960s
'THE CHOICE BETWEEN SILENCE AND PROTEST'

In September 1963, South Africa's Minister of Justice, Mr Balthazar John Vorster, used the occasion of a speech made before a public audience in Potschefstoom to attack the National Union of South African Students. NUSAS, he told his audience, was 'a damnable and detestable organisation … a cancer in the life of the nation'. He hinted, darkly, that it would have to be 'cut out'. He urged all students to resign 'in the interest and for the sake of our country'.[1]

Vorster was not alone in his assault on NUSAS. At the same event, the Minister of Posts and Telecommunications suggested that parents should themselves take action and refuse to send their children to any university where NUSAS might be active. Eight months later, in a parliamentary debate on education funding, several MPs vented their own indignation. A representative for Pretoria was particularly vehement. He told his fellow parliamentarians that NUSAS was the breeding ground of 'Communists … and all the other staunch leftists'. NUSAS, he said, 'as we know it today, should be destroyed root and branch'.[2]

The Minister for Education, Johannes de Klerk, took up his colleague's words in a lengthy speech. He reminisced about his experiences with NUSAS in the past, and suggested that there had once been an attempt to set it on a different path. But now, he said, NUSAS had embarked upon 'a changed course of action which I must say is frightening':

> These people no longer stand by the original objects but encroach on the political sphere. They arrogate to themselves the right as immature people, to a large extent, to criticize any actions of the Government. We receive the greatest criticism from them, but I take no notice of it. When I receive criticism from that association, it goes into the wastepaper basket without any acknowledgement.[3]

[1] These remarks were widely quoted, and taken up in international student writing. See, for example: Richard Suzman, 'Will South African Students Stay Defiant?' *Harvard Crimson* (16 October 1963), <http://www.thecrimson.com/article/1963/10/16/will-south-african-students-stay-defiant>, accessed 8 December 2015.

[2] RSA, *Debates of the House of Assembly* (Hansard – Parliament of South Africa), 1964, col. 5978.

[3] Hansard, 1964, col. 5980.

This chapter will consider the efforts of the government to suppress NUSAS, and examine the perverse effects that these efforts had on white students in South Africa. I will argue that, although the government was able, at times, to push students out of the 'political sphere', more often than not it failed to do so in the middle years of the 1960s. Instead, its efforts at repression sometimes galvanised student activism, leading to the organisation of some of the most publicly visible demonstrations and protest actions of these years. As these events developed, NUSAS began to fulfil the fantasies expressed by these different ministers and parliamentarians in 1963 and 1964. Rather than remain limited to providing pastoral care to students on university campus, NUSAS and its members began to experiment with ways of opposing the government in public.

These experiments were not always successful in achieving their immediate goals, but often served instead to remake the boundaries of political possibility – opening up new perspectives on the apartheid system, highlighting its injustices, and demonstrating that it was possible for students to organise and resist individual attempts by the state to impose its will on universities. These possibilities helped to re-open spaces of political action in the wake of the repression of public opposition to the apartheid state at the start of the 1960s – and, as such, began the process of reinventing public forms of protest and dissent at the height of the apartheid era.

Between silence and protest

In the years before the Minister's vitriolic statements, the apartheid state had faced down the challenge posed by the ANC, the PAC and other black opposition movements, and had driven them into exile or underground. By the mid-1960s, only a very small number of white liberal organisations remained publicly active. The most notable of these were the Black Sash, a group of women opposed to aspects of the apartheid system, and NUSAS, a group of young white students.

Of these, it was NUSAS that would now attract the state's ire.

At the core of the ministers' complaints was the idea that NUSAS was now encroaching upon 'the political sphere', that it had abandoned its proper task – of mediating between students and university administrators – in favour of overtly political actions. This was grounded in two intertwined assumptions: first, that the government and its parliamentary opposition were the sole legitimate occupiers of the political sphere and, second, that students were particularly illegitimate interlopers onto this terrain. They had their own world, their own realm of legitimate interest – the university. If they were responsible, they would remain within that realm.

These were both widely held assumptions: there is nothing peculiar about the apartheid state's belief either in the sanctity of a parliamentary political sphere or in the impropriety of students acting outside of a university setting. Indeed, similar assumptions would – later in this decade – guide the responses of the French, North American, Japanese and other governments to the student protests that rocked these countries during and after 1968.

Nonetheless, there were significant local particularities that shaped the South African situation and the government's response to student activism. One element of this was NUSAS's institutional history. In its early years, NUSAS had sought to represent all students at white and open universities in South Africa – but failed to build a consensus between English and Afrikaans speaking students. Indeed, the students at South Africa's white Afrikaans-medium institutions disaffiliated from NUSAS in the 1930s – in part in protest against an application by the students at the University of Fort Hare (the oldest and most prestigious African institution in the country) to affiliate themselves to the union. Despite this drama, African students were not in fact admitted to NUSAS until 1945 – and then, half a dozen years later, these students found that the Union could not, or would not, accommodate their political interests. Nonetheless, the nascent Afrikaner Nationalist movement – which would become the National Party, and form the heart of the apartheid order – indelibly defined NUSAS as sympathetic to the project of African nationalism.[4]

Until the mid-1950s, NUSAS limited itself strictly to addressing student issues and to using consensual, negotiated forms of action to do so: it restricted its actions to taking part in discussions and official inquiries, circulating petitions and writing letters of protest to government officials. In the 1950s, however, more public and more confrontational forms of protest such as those organised by other white liberal opposition organisations, including the Black Sash and the Torch Commando, became more popular and thus more visible.[5] NUSAS joined them in protest.

Still, none of these organisations were regarded by the state as posing any immediate threat to the political status quo. They were

[4]   See: M. Legassick, *The National Union of South African Students: Ethnic Cleavage and Ethnic Integration in the Universities* (Occasional Paper no. 4, African Studies Center, University of California, Los Angeles: 1967).

[5]   For the Black Sash, see: Mirabel Rodgers, *The Black Sash: The Story of the South African Women's Defence of the Constitution League* (Johannesburg, Rotonews, 1956); Cherry Michelman, *The Black Sash of South Africa: A Case Study in Liberalism* (Oxford, Oxford University Press: 1975); Kathryn Spink, *Black Sash: The Beginning of a Bridge in South Africa* (London, Methuen: 1991). For the Torch Commando, see: Michael Fridjon, 'The Torch Commando & the Politics of White Opposition: South Africa 1951–1953', Paper Presented at the University of the Witwatersrand African Studies Institute (March 1976); Neil Roos, *Ordinary Springboks: White Servicemen and Social Justice in South Africa, 1939–1961* (Aldershot, Ashgate: 2005).

constituted by groups of citizens outside of the mainstream of political life in apartheid South Africa: the Black Sash by white women,
the Torch Commando by war veterans, and NUSAS by young, largely
white, students. Of these, only the Torch Commando was seen as
posing a threat to the state – and it responded by passing a law to
prevent veterans from joining the group. NUSAS and the Black Sash
were different: both represented people in liminal positions within the
white society of the period. Neither women nor young students were
taken seriously by the representatives of the government – and both
were thus marginally protected from repression when, in the wake of
the 1960 Sharpeville Massacre, the state led a violent crackdown on
the country's extra-parliamentary opposition.[6]

The government imposed a national State of Emergency, rushed
a mass of legislation through parliament; and took advantage of a
changed political and legal terrain to informally detain or (sometimes)
formally arrest the leaders of the African National Congress, the Pan
Africanist Congress, and other aboveground opposition organisations.
Membership in these organisations was made illegal, and anyone who
might have once been a member was likely to be harassed, threatened,
or even assaulted by the police. In the weeks following, about 18,000
people were rounded up and arrested under a wide variety of formal
charges – some of which were explicitly political, and others of which
appeared to be purely opportunistic.[7] This trawl through South Africa's urban areas netted many of the sympathisers of the opposition
movements, placing them in cells and removing them from the public
sphere. Here, at least, the state could know that they would not be
participating in any threatening – or even just mildly embarrassing –
public protests.

In this period the broad trajectory of South Africa's political history
intersected with the history of NUSAS. While the constraints imposed
on public action by the Emergency regulations and the state's assault on
the ANC and the PAC also impacted upon liberal and white opposition
organisations, they did so to a far lesser extent. These organisations
– including NUSAS – continued to operate and, by doing so, found
themselves among the few remaining agents of public opposition to
the state.

NUSAS embarked on a tentative series of protests against the
government's repressive actions: for example, in 1962 its members took

---

[6] The Massacre itself has given rise to a number of accounts, the best of which are:
    Philip Frankel, *An Ordinary Atrocity: Sharpeville and its Massacre* (Johannesburg,
    Wits University Press: 2001) and Tom Lodge, *Sharpeville: An Apartheid Massacre
    and its Consequences* (Oxford, Oxford University Press: 2011). In addition, Ambrose
    Reeve's *Shooting at Sharpeville: the Agony of South Africa* (London, Gollancz: 1960)
    is an important document written in its immediate aftermath.
[7] Muriel Horrell, *A Survey of Race Relations, 1959–1960* (Johannesburg, SAIRR, 1961),
    p. 84.

part in a series of protests against the new General Law Amendment Act. This Act was designed to entrench the government's Emergency powers to detain, arrest, and imprison potential and actual opponents. NUSAS was not alone in these protests, nor was it the primary organiser of them. Nonetheless, white students were publicly prominent: the student bodies at the Universities of Cape Town, the Witwatersrand, Natal and Rhodes drew up petitions asking the government to withdraw the proposed Act. Representatives of these student bodies met with the Minister in Cape Town to hand over the petitions.

More importantly, approximately 2,000 students took part in a march in Johannesburg, while a further 800 congregated in Durban and in Pietermaritzburg. A similar protest march in Cape Town was prohibited, and replaced by a less confrontational combination of a mass meeting on the university campus and a 'poster demonstration'. These protests were controversial: in Johannesburg, for example, an angry crowd followed the student protesters on their march, throwing raw eggs, tomatoes and rotten fruit at them.[8] In the weeks after this march, the Wits student newspaper wondered whether this would be the last mass protest that the government would allow. Its editorial noted:

> The days when students could protest, secure in the faceless anonymity of a crowd are gone; he who protests now must stand single and alone, fanned by a cold wind of censure from a ruthless and intolerant government ... the choice between silence and protest has been made infinitely more difficult.[9]

There was a great deal of truth to these observations. Protests drew the ire of the government and its ministers, provoking Vorster's rhetorical assault in September 1963. No doubt the so-called 'tall poppy syndrome' played its role in attracting attention to NUSAS: after the other, more radical, organisations had been (apparently) disbanded or de-clawed, NUSAS found itself – by default – one of the principal faces of opposition to the government. And the government began to treat it as such.

A brood of vipers

The ministers' attacks intensified in 1964, after the press published a leaked copy of a confidential paper compiled by the president of NUSAS, Jonty Driver. It included contributions from two former members of the executive, Martin Legassick and Magnus Gunther. The document was

[8] Muriel Horrell, *A Survey of Race Relations in South Africa*, 1962 (Johannesburg, SAIRR: 1963), pp. 40–43.
[9] As quoted in Suzman, 'Will South African Students Stay Defiant?', p. 2.

in part a response to criticisms that had been levelled by other student movements on the rapidly-decolonising African continent, and was intended to launch a discussion on the nature and future of NUSAS in the new South African order; it was to be read out and discussed at a private seminar for about seventy members of NUSAS. It was also – importantly – a patchwork document, including a range of beliefs and ideas held to differing degrees by each of the three.[10]

This was not, however, how it was reported.

The most radical proposals were extracted from the document and printed, denuded of context. It was implied (and at times stated) that these proposals had been adopted by NUSAS, and were official policy. These proposals included suggestions that NUSAS should move towards having an African-majority membership, that it should pre-emptively promote existing African members to leadership positions, and – most controversially – that NUSAS should consider dissolving itself as a legal organisation and become 'a genuine wing of the liberation movement' operating from exile 'through "front groups" while the real work goes on underground'.[11] Given these opportunities for selective quoting, it is perhaps unsurprising that the government would seize upon this document. It was used both to justify their recent attacks on NUSAS, and as grounds to launch another.

Thus, on 14 May 1964, as these quotes were appearing in the media, the government used the excuse of a parliamentary debate on education funding to once again smear NUSAS. As already quoted, parliamentarians called upon NUSAS to be eradicated 'root and branch' and the Minister of Education poured scorn on it. They attacked the union's associations with 'communists' and 'liberalists'; they suggested that the earlier membership of prominent 'staunch leftists' in NUSAS demonstrated an ongoing interaction between the forces of revolution and the student union; and they suggested that NUSAS should simply abandon all of its political pretensions.

This new wave of attacks had a greater impact on NUSAS than Vorster's assault the previous year. According to Driver, in 1963, the Minister's suggestion that all students resign from the union had only prompted 335 students (out of a total of 18,500 members) to leave.[12] In the immediate wake of the scandal following the leaking of the

[10] See the discussion of the authorship of this document in: Martin Legassick and Christopher Saunders, 'Above-Ground Activity in the 1960s', in South African Development in Education Trust (SADET) (ed.), *The Road to Democracy in South Africa, Volume 1, 1960–1970* (Cape Town, Zebra: 2005), p. 680.
[11] 'NUSAS: Paper by Jonty Driver, President, delivered at NUSAS National Seminar, April 1964,' in T. Karis and G. Gerhart (eds), *From Protest to Challenge, Volume 5: Nadir and Resurgence, 1964–1979* (Bloomington and Indianapolis, University of Indiana Press: 1997).
[12] These figures were reported in Muriel Horrell, *A Survey of Race Relations in South Africa, 1963* (Johannesburg, SAIRR: 1964), p. 244.

discussion document, and the renewal of the government's attacks, about 1,000 students left NUSAS. Four hundred of them came from a single university – the University of Natal, and the scale of these resignations drove the student representative council (SRC) there to contemplate disaffiliating the entire institution from NUSAS. In a sign of the complexity of local student politics, however, this disaffilia-tion process was a shambles: the SRC agreed first to disaffiliate from the union, then to suspend its disaffiliation until the union's annual general meeting in July, and then decided, after all, to remain inside NUSAS.[13] Despite the collapse of this initiative, the tumultuousness of the process reflected the discontent of the students at this and other institutions, as well as showing NUSAS's newly weakened position.

Meanwhile, as students across the country disputed with each other over the legitimacy – or otherwise – of Driver's positions, the actions of another movement provided the state with further justifications for its attacks against NUSAS. The African Resistance Movement (ARM) announced its existence in June 1964, and launched a series of sabo-tage attacks in Cape Town and around Johannesburg. At first, these attacks targeted power pylons, electricity substations and railway sidings – all targets picked to avoid the loss of human life. In July, however, as the leaders of the small group were being arrested, one of its members planted a suitcase bomb on a 'whites-only' platform at the Johannesburg central train station. He called the police to warn them, but failed to do so in time. The bomb exploded, killing one woman and seriously injuring twenty other people.[14]

It was a fruitless attack. By this time, ARM had already been crushed. Its leaders were imprisoned or had fled the country. Damningly, in the eyes of the state at least, many of these leaders had recently been active members of NUSAS. Among those arrested were Adrian Leftwich, a former president of NUSAS, and Hugh Lewin, a former vice-president; among those in exile was another former president, Neville Rubin. These men – alongside other members of ARM – had started their political activism in NUSAS. Their actions lent a degree of plausibility to the government's otherwise-fantastic attacks on NUSAS: in their eyes, students, or at least men and women who had very recently been students, had aligned themselves with the armed underground, had embarked upon violent resistance to the state, and had brought death and injury to ordinary white South Africans.

It is unsurprising, given this context, that few members of the official

[13] See Muriel Horrell, *A Survey of Race Relations in South Africa 1964* (Johannesburg, SAIRR: 1965), pp. 297–300.
[14] For the history of the ARM, see M. Gunther, 'The National Committee of Libera-tion (NCL)/African Resistance Movement (ARM),' in SADET (ed.), *The Road to Democracy, Vol. 1*, and A. du Toit, 'The National Committee for Liberation (ARM) 1960–1964: Sabotage and the Question of the Ideological Subject,' MA Thesis (Cape Town, University of Cape Town: 1990).

opposition could bring themselves to defend the rights of students to act politically – to, in the words of the Minister of Education, 'encroach upon the political sphere'. Their defences were mealy-mouthed, half-hearted, and hedged. For example, in the midst of a defence of the union, the Education spokesman for the official opposition, Mr Marais Steyn, found it necessary to tell parliament that if there was any substance to these charges, then 'we on this side of the House will not find it possible to defend NUSAS'.

The effect of these defences was to surrender the discursive ground to the government: NUSAS was assumed to be playing with fire. Assaults against NUSAS became common, and unremarkable. In the wake of the ARM attacks and the station bombing, Driver was arrested and held – without charge – for 28 days. So too was another recent president of NUSAS – held for 21 days, and then released uncharged. Anonymous pamphlets were circulated on university campuses, associating NUSAS with 'revolution, sabotage, and the invasion of South Africa'.[15] In November, the Minister of Justice once again addressed a public meeting and attacked NUSAS, this time describing its leaders as '*addergebroedsel*' – or, in English, 'a brood of vipers'.[16]

Charge or release!

Only a year after the Wits student newspaper had warned its readers that the government's actions were making the choice 'between silence and protest' so much more difficult than it had been, these attacks seemed likely to tip the scales permanently in the direction of silence over protest. After all, these attacks were unquestionably intended to drive NUSAS out of the political sphere, and to convince it – and its members – to turn to addressing disputes within universities, between students, and between students and lecturers, and to abandon 'the political sphere'.

There were even signs in the wake of the 1964 scandal that this abandonment might happen. At the next annual meeting of NUSAS, held midway through July that year, the majority of the student delegates voted in favour of a motion condemning Driver for drawing up the discussion document and 'expressing personal opinions which would inevitably be associated with NUSAS policy'.[17] The actions of this meeting suggest both the performance of public repentance in the motion to censure Driver, and also a performance of public conservatism – as NUSAS repeatedly disavowed totalitarianism of all kinds. More than this, though, a note of caution was being sounded: the new

[15] As quoted in Horrell, *Survey 1964*, p. 297.
[16] As quoted in Horrell, *Survey 1964*, p. 300.
[17] As described by Horrell, *Survey 1964*, pp. 298–9.

president of NUSAS defended the union against the government's attacks, distanced it from the radicalism of the ARM and – more importantly – from the apparent radicalism of his predecessors. He emphasised the normalcy of its day-to-day operations. He even invited Vorster to attend and address a NUSAS meeting – although, of course, this invitation was tinged with a kind of subdued irony. (Unsurprisingly, Vorster declined the invitation.)

This retreat into caution did not last. The government's attacks did not let up, and soon began to have the perverse response of galvanising NUSAS into new actions. In particular, the attacks themselves provided NUSAS with opportunities for organising student opposition during a period in which the state appeared to have successfully suppressed public dissent outside of parliament.

The best example of this process was the protest launched by the banning orders levied against Ian Robertson, the NUSAS president in 1966. Robertson had been collecting information on police intimidation of students and, at the start of May, embarked on a tour of affiliated campuses, where he discussed his research.[18] In addition, he had arranged for Robert Kennedy – the brother of an assassinated American president, ex-attorney general of the USA, and a future presidential candidate himself – to visit the University of Cape Town to speak at its annual Day of Affirmation of Academic Freedom.[19]

On his return from this campus tour, and less than a month before Kennedy was due to arrive in South Africa, the state served five banning orders on Robertson, preventing him from travelling within South Africa, entering the offices of NUSAS, participating in its events, and – most strikingly – forbidding him from entering any university campus for any purpose other than his own studies.[20]

The Minister of Justice refused to reveal the reasons behind his actions – but as the order was imposed shortly before Kennedy was due to arrive, most commentators associated the two. In the course of a parliamentary debate on the banning, several months later, Vorster

[18] This is described in University Christian Movement of the USA, 'Student Movements in South Africa: A study of three student movements illustrating student problems and the Government's response', (1970) in E.S. Reddy (ed.), *The Struggle for Liberation in South Africa and International Solidarity: A Selection of Papers Published by the United Nations Centre against Apartheid* (Sterling Publishers, New Delhi: 1992)

[19] For more details of Kennedy's visit see Robert Erbmann's excellent undergraduate thesis: '"Conservative Revolutionaries": Anti-Apartheid Activism at the University of Cape Town, 1963–1973', University of Oxford (2005), available online at: <http://www.sahistory.org.za/pages/library-resources/articles_papers/1963_1973_conservative_revolutionaries.htm>, accessed 8 December 2015. See also the pamphlet put together at the time: n.a., 'Robert Kennedy in South Africa: a souvenir booklet of Senator Kennedy's 1966 Tour of South Africa', *Rand Daily Mail* (1966).

[20] See Muriel Horrell, *A Survey of Race Relations in South Africa 1966* (Johannesburg, SAIRR:1967), pp. 39–41.

made a number of allegations – that Robertson had been a member of the since-banned 'Defence and Aid' committee, that he had travelled out of the country for political purposes, and that he was not, in any case, a real student but rather a paid activist. Each of these allegations was disputed in Parliament; and the specifics of each of Vorster's charges shown to be either incorrect (for example: Robertson did not visit the countries he was said to have visited) or disingenuous (all NUSAS presidents were ex officio members of the Defence and Aid committee and Robertson had not attended a single meeting before its banning). Finally, Vorster was reduced to rhetorical frothing: he announced that he was in possession of 'three fat files' on Robertson's activities and – presumably drawing upon the undisclosed contents of these files – had sought to prevent 'a second Leftwich affair' by pre-emptively banning him.[21]

The government's unconvincing attempts to assert that it had, indeed, possessed good cause to ban Robertson were provoked by the fact that this action – unlike most other banning orders – had itself galvanised NUSAS and others into public protests, in May and in June 1966.

Large public marches were organised to protest against Robertson's banning, attracting 3,000 students in Johannesburg and 2,000 in Cape Town. In Johannesburg, a week-long vigil was held. Smaller marches took place in Grahamstown and Durban. Open meetings were also organised – one of which attracted about 1,500 members of the public. More theatrical interventions included the lighting of a symbolic 'flame of freedom' at the University of Natal's Durban campus and, the printing and distribution, across the country, of 20,000 car windscreen stickers, bearing the legend 'Charge or Release'.[22] Popular support was overwhelming: Curtis and Keegan, writing some six years after the protests over Robertson's banning, described this moment as 'the high water mark in mass student support' of NUSAS.

One measure of the extent of this student support was a petition, prepared by NUSAS and handed over to the Minister of Justice. The petition was couched in legalistic terms, and called for the government to clarify its reasons for banning Robertson. It was ratified by 12,000 people, mostly students and university faculty. This represented a number equivalent to 60 per cent of the 20,000 white students who were enrolled at the four principal English-medium universities.[23]

It is notable, however, that this support was levied in protest against the banning of a white student leader and not in protest against an

---

[21] Hansard, 1966, cols. 2720–3, and summarised in Horrell, *Survey 1966*, pp. 42–3.
[22] Horrell, *Survey 1966*, p. 40.
[23] N. Curtis and C. Keegan, 'The Aspiration to a Just Society,' in H.W. van der Merwe and D. Welsh (eds), *Student Perspectives on South Africa* (Cape Town, David Philip: 1972), p. 113.

official policy or ideology of the apartheid state. At the centre of many of the protests against the government's actions – including those of the parliamentary opposition – was the idea that the Minister of Justice was abusing his powers. The limited reach of this defence of the right of students to act publicly must be emphasised – and can, once again, be summed up by a telling quote from the Leader of the Opposition: 'I am not pleading that Mr Robertson is innocent. I do not know. But I am beginning to come to the conclusion that the Minister does not know, either, that Mr Robertson is guilty.'[24] It was only by framing the dispute in this manner – as a dispute over the withholding of evidence of wrongdoing, rather than over the right to dissent – that a coalition of moderate and liberal opponents of the government could hold. Even those who believed that NUSAS was involved in some sort of subversion could protest against the Minister's refusal to provide any proof.

More importantly, however, the limits of this defence – and the limits of the coalition – point to how far student activism had fallen, in two short years, from the ambitions expressed in 1964. There was no talk of challenging the assumptions underlying the Minister's allegations: that even if Robertson had met with dissident groups outside the country that would not be good reason to ban him. Nor was the opposition to the banning order conflated with the opposition to apartheid ideology and practice. The protesters did not consistently draw the obvious connections between this act and all other acts of political repression over the previous half-dozen years in South Africa.

In other words, the protest against Robertson's banning order was not the product of the relatively radical commitments of Driver and Legassick and others; instead, it was the product of the more cautious and politically conservative trends that had emerged within the student movement after the successes of the government's attacks on NUSAS. This protest was not a development. It was an experiment in reinventing dissenting politics within a new context.

Given this, it would be easy to conclude, as Robert Erbmann does in his study of student politics at the University of Cape Town, that the successes of this protest 'did little to alter the essentially defensive position of the student movement on campus'.[25] After all, students were largely satisfied with the appearance of lawfulness in the state's actions; they were soon distracted by disputes with university administrators. It seemed as though the possibilities for building upon this action, and the broad public support for it, were likely to be squandered.

The effects of this protest should not be minimised, however. As cautious and limited as it was, it did serve an important purpose: after NUSAS's retreat from the public sphere two years before, it now re-

[24] As quoted in Horrell, *Survey 1966*, p. 43.
[25] Erbmann, 'Conservative Revolutionaries', p. 8.

introduced the possibility of public action. If the response of students to the government's earlier assaults had been to be disheartened and to retreat from public challenges, then the successes of this protest in mobilising opinion in favour of the right of students to protest was newly invigorating. Steps could now be taken towards imagining a new regime of action.

Decorous demonstrators

The protests over Robertson's banning order were not the only attempts by white students affiliated with NUSAS to use public forms of action in the service of political ends. At Rhodes University, in Grahamstown, for example, a small group of students staged a day-long 'sit-in' on the steps of the university's library. Their protest was aimed at a very local problem: the decision of the Bantu Affairs Department to forbid Africans from attending university rugby matches. This outdoors 'sit-in' was – as Eddie Webster recalls – 'influenced at the time by the civil rights movement in the Southern States of the USA and their non-violent desegregation struggles in particular. Not surprisingly,' Webster adds, the students 'sang "We Shall Overcome"'.[26]

This small event was perhaps more typical of the development of student protest in this period than the mass marches of the 'Charge or Release' campaign. Nonetheless, both indicate the direction within which NUSAS and its student members were moving in these years: towards new forms of confrontational protest, inspired in part by events scattered across the globe.

The culmination of this phase of NUSAS's move towards confrontation occurred late in 1968, in response – once again – to an attempt by the state to interfere in the internal workings of a university. This interference, however, unlike the attempts of the state to impose University Apartheid in the late 1950s, was aimed at one man in one university.

On 1 May 1968, Archie Mafeje – a black South African scholar, who was at the time completing his doctorate at Cambridge – was appointed to the position of Senior Lecturer in Social Anthropology at the University of Cape Town (UCT). However, his appointment letter was never sent. Soon after the decision had been made, the university's Vice-Chancellor received a letter from the Minister of National Education recommending that UCT reconsider its decision. The Vice-Chancellor, Sir Richard Luyt, met with the Minister of Education and attempted to interrogate the government's position.

Luyt's records of this meeting suggest that the Minister threatened

---

[26] Edward Webster, 'Rebels with a Cause of Their Own: A Personal Reflection on my Student Years at Rhodes University, 1961–1965', *Transformation* (2005), 59, pp. 98–108.

the university, and told him that 'the Government will not hesitate in taking such steps as it may deem fit' to prevent Mafeje's appointment – including rushing legislation through Parliament to this purpose. Luyt recalled the climax of the meeting:

> The Minister emphasised that he greatly respected the principle of autonomy for the universities and would not wish to interfere in any way if this could be avoided, but the Government also had its principles and the racial separation of higher education was a principle of great importance which accorded with the accepted traditional outlook of South Africa. It was determined that this principle be applied.[27]

On 5 June – just over a month after their decision to appoint Mafeje had provoked the Minister's threats – the University Council held its next meeting. Here, despite the strong objections of Mafeje's supporters, it was decided by a vote of 12 to 8 to rescind Mafeje's appointment and also to 'express dismay' at the Minister's interference.[28] At the end of the month, Luyt invited two members of UCT's Student Representative Council to a meeting, where he 'gave them an outline of the Mafeje affair'. He asked them to keep the information confidential until after the Council could issue an official statement – which it did in July, after its next monthly meeting.[29] This was the start of the winter vacation, and so effectively postponed student reaction. Still, the affair was widely reported, and a slow-burning scandal was ignited.[30]

At the annual NUSAS conference, also held in July, a resolution condemning the university's decision to 'capitulat[e] to the Minister's threats' was adopted; this resolution urged the UCT SRC to 'organise effective and significant protest' against the university's decision.[31] On 7 August, the first of a series of public meetings was held on the UCT campus; a further meeting was announced for 14 August. In between these two meetings, students met with the Vice-Chancellor. He attempted to persuade them to avoid mass protests, emphasising the formal role of the SRC, and warning them that 'there could be no escape from the responsibility of leadership in the plea that democratic principles require yielding to the views of the majority if the latter were clearly wrong in terms of disorder and lawlessness'.[32] After these meetings, the Vice-Chancellor left the country for a long-planned trip to Australia; he flew on 11 August and would only return two weeks later.

[27] University of Cape Town Manuscripts and Archives (UCTMA) BC1072/B1.2 Sir Richard Luyt, *Memo*, p. 5.
[28] See: Lungisile Ntsebeza, 'The Mafeje and the UCT Saga: Unfinished Business?' *Social Dynamics* (2014) 40(2), pp. 274–88.
[29] UCTMA BC1072/B1.2, *Notes*.
[30] See, for example: 'UCT Offer to African is Rescinded', *Cape Times*, 4 July 1968.
[31] Quoted in F. Hendricks, 'The Mafeje Affair: The University of Cape Town and Apartheid,' *African Studies*, 67/3 (2008).
[32] UCTMA BC1072/B1.2, *Notes*.

Meanwhile, the public meeting planned for 14 August took place. A large crowd arrived, estimated at about 1,200 students. The ability of this meeting to mobilise student support – if not its ability to shift the University's Council – prompted student organisers (drawn from the student council, the NUSAS local committee, and the Student Radical Association) to propose a further, more ambitious, protest.[33] The gathered students were asked not only to adopt a resolution calling upon the university to 'consider the reappointment of Mr. Mafeje' but also to agree to a demand to 'call upon the mass meeting to accompany the student delegation to the administration building as a sign of solidarity and sit-in until the student demands are met'.

The organisers proposed that the students occupy the administration building and stage a sit-in – the largest to have been organised in South Africa. While the form of protest adopted was influenced by events in France and the United States in this period, the immediate cause was certainly uniquely local. Of the approximately 1,200 students attending the meeting, 300 then continued into the administration building, planning to occupy it 'overnight if necessary'.[34] This was imagined to be a notably sedate protest: record-players and guitars were brought into the building; the students gathered to sing folk songs and held study sessions in the building's corridors.[35]

The university was reluctant to eject the students, preferring to wait until the Vice-Chancellor returned, and so the students settled in – announcing that they would remain until the university's council met. This would only happen nine days later: meanwhile, the students would remain in occupation.

As the sit-in continued, the number of students participating increased to between 400 and 500 at any one time.[36] These students developed a society in the corridors. They held 'teach-ins' – discussing topics such as 'The Church and Student Power' and 'Students and Social Change'. An internal police force was constituted – a 'peace corps' – of student volunteers who patrolled the corridors and perimeters of the building, both to maintain order amongst the students and to ensure than no external force, such as other students opposed to the protest, entered. Threats were occasionally made – a smoke-bomb was exploded inside the building, the back entrance was assaulted one evening, and a further bomb scare telephoned in over the weekend – but the students responded with notable discipline, forming 'sleeping-cells' under the direction of cell-leaders and instructing the

[33] The overlap between these three bodies was substantial. The Student Radical Association was a revival of the older Radical Student Society, which had provided the NCL/ARM with many of its Cape Town recruits.

[34] *Cape Times*, 14 August 1968.

[35] *Cape Times*, 15 August 1968.

[36] *Cape Times*, 16 August 1968.

'peace corps' to patrol at night.[37] The orderliness of their responses to these provocations no doubt helped to confer a degree of public respectability on their protest.

This respectability was attested to in the local newspapers. One weekend columnist described: 'UCT's decorous demonstrators' and reassured his readers that, despite their expectations: 'the Republic's first 1968 style sit-in is the very picture of Boy Scout and Girl Guide decorum ... There was not a drop of liquor in sight. Not a whiff of hashish.'[38] The seriousness and sobriety of the students suggested harmlessness, and the letters in the pages of the Cape Times were mainly supportive, although more often than not offering this support in a spirit of parental indulgence.

Elsewhere, the sit-in provided a focus for further student protests. The University of the Witwatersrand became prominent nationally after students were refused permission to march. In response, students formed a picket along the edge of the Wits campus, facing Jan Smuts Avenue, a major city road. They held placards condemning the refusal of the police to permit the march. This picket then caused controversy when it was assaulted by students from the neighbouring Rand Afrikaans University, who threw tomatoes, eggs, paint and whitewash at the Wits students.[39]

Meanwhile, in Cape Town a number of UCT students opposed the sit-in and announced that they would hold their own counter-protests – but these did not materialise. Students from the University of Stellenbosch, located about 50 km (30 miles) from Cape Town, also threatened protests throughout the period.

These threats materialised on the sit-in's last afternoon, when a group of approximately 1,000 students unexpectedly arrived at UCT from Stellenbosch and laid siege to the administration building. They demanded that the sit-in end immediately, and then threatened to invade the building and forcibly disperse the protesting students if it did not. By the late evening, the mood was increasingly violent: journalists heard the invading students shouting, 'Come out, Ikeys, or we'll fetch you out.'[40]

The protesters would not leave, and prepared themselves to be stormed. Female students congregated in an interior room for safety; the balconied Senate Room was locked and sealed off. (The decision to lock the Senate Room proved wise: one counter-demonstrator was reported to have climbed to its balcony to tear down a banner suspended

[37] *Cape Times*, 19 and 20 August 1968.
[38] *Cape Times*, 17 August 1968.
[39] Muriel Horrell, *A Survey of Race Relations in South Africa 1968* (Johannesburg, SAIRR: 1969), p. 264.
[40] 'Maties invade sit-in', *Cape Times*, 23 August 1968. 'Ikeys' were University of Cape Town students; University of Stellenbosch students were known as 'Maties'.

from it.) The 'peace corps' members took up positions behind the main entrances to the building, apparently holding firehoses in readiness; others made arrangements to barricade the windows, in case stones were thrown through them; yet others patrolled the building's corridors. According to reports of the incident, published in the local news: 'Some sang folk songs and there was no evidence of panic.'

Half an hour passed. The Stellenbosch students surged forward, shouting down faculty members appealing for calm. They battered at the administration building's main door, attempting to force entry. Some milder voices attempted to remind their fellows not to 'foul the good name of Stellenbosch' by causing too much physical damage to the building. When this failed – and when the door remained shut – a shout was reported to pass around the mob: 'Windows are cheaper than doors – try the windows!' The group abandoned its assault on the main entrance and streamed round the building; 'one group discovered the rear entrance, damaged two nights ago by another demonstrator, and yelled for support'.

The rear doors shook under the violent assault; the glass windows shattered.

At this point, the police finally acted to disperse the crowd. The counter-protesters left reluctantly, returning to Stellenbosch, and the police informed the protesting students at UCT that they would no longer guarantee their safety against any possible future assault if they remained.[41]

Ironically, the protesting students had already decided to end their sit-in. The Vice-Chancellor's return to Cape Town on 23 August was thought by the organisers to constitute a sufficiently symbolic moment at which to end their long protest – before fatigue could set in and end it for them.[42]

Ultimately, the protest was unsuccessful in forcing the university to reconsider the appointment of Mafeje: the University Council met on the following Monday and decided not to rescind their earlier rescission of Mafeje's appointment. The students promised further protests but, for the moment, their energy seemed to have been expended in sustaining the lengthy sit-in.

The students had failed to achieve their goal, but had demonstrated the potential reach of this ambiguously confrontational form of protest: they had sustained a sit-in for nine days, NUSAS local committees had been able to organise protests in sympathy with the UCT students, and they had alerted the national newspaper-reading public to their actions. This protest also demonstrated the effectiveness of the institutional structures of NUSAS. The executive had been able to pass a resolution empowering UCT's SRC to act on its behalf; that SRC had

---

[41] *Cape Times*, 22 August 1968.
[42] *Cape Times*, 22 August 1968.

then collaborated with the local campus committee of NUSAS and other groups to organise the protest meetings. The sit-in itself had then been able to inspire protests in sympathy at campuses across the country.

On UCT's campus itself, the protest helped reshape student politics. Elections for a new SRC were held shortly afterwards, and the campus's radical left wing did exceptionally well. Raphael Kaplinsky – one of the main instigators of the sit-in, and a central member of the Student Radical Association – was elected to the SRC, alongside several of his colleagues.[43] This signalled a shift at UCT towards a greater acceptance of some radical politics; and although there would continue to be disagreements over the politics of NUSAS and its allies, this did signal the effective creation of a new political consensus – one that rejected the caution of the mid-1960s in favour of a nascent commitment to opposition and, possibly, confrontation.

At first, the state's response to the sit-in and its associated protests was muted. Although the police were occasionally present at the sit-in, they did not intervene to disperse the protesters; on the other hand, neither were they eager to assist or defend them. The day after the sit-in ended, B.J. Vorster – having risen to Prime Minister in the years since his earlier attacks on NUSAS – told an audience that the police had in fact been instructed to forcibly end the protest, although this instruction had coincided with the students' own decision to end their sit-in.[44] The timing of this statement makes it difficult to credit. Nonetheless, Vorster's speech signalled the continued willingness of the state to continue to threaten protesting students and their official leaders.

But this intimidation was less successful than it had been before. For some NUSAS organisers the attention of the state was a badge of honour. In September 1969, for example, Duncan Innes, the president of NUSAS – also president of the UCT student council at the time of the sit-in – told an audience that: 'these police signify our triumph. They can break up our pickets but they cannot break our message. They can ban our protest marches but they cannot ban our protest.'[45]

Upsetting calculations

In none of the protests after 1964 did the students of NUSAS and its affiliated campuses succeed in their explicit goals: Ian Robertson's banning order was not lifted before the visit of Robert Kennedy, the government's refusal to allow Africans to attend rugby matches at

[43] See Erbmann, 'Conservative Revolutionaries', pp. 9–10.
[44] *Cape Times*, 26 August 1968.
[45] Quoted in Legassick, *NUSAS*, p. 683.

Rhodes University was unshaken, and Archie Mafeje remained – at the end of the sit-in – without employment at the UCT. In at least the two most prominent of these protests, however, NUSAS did succeed in less explicit ways: it raised the profile of student protests and student politics in the public eye, including its own profile as an effective political organisation. It convinced many of the student participants that political action was possible – that dissent could shape opinion, even if in these cases it had not forced a new outcome. At best, these were ambiguous successes, but they were also undeniably exciting for the participants, and opened up new possibilities.

Before fully embracing the implicit teleology of this account of repression, resistance, and progression, though, it is worth concluding this chapter by considering the role of contingency in the development of NUSAS into a protesting organisation in these years. Although an obvious movement can be discerned from the protests of the late 1950s and early 1960s to those emerging from Cape Town and elsewhere at the end of the 1960s, that movement cannot be said to have been consciously planned – or even to have proceeded uninterrupted.

Instead, the process of reinventing protest was fragmented and partial – a reflection, that is, of the political moment within which it took place. It occurred in stops and starts. Innovations in one part of the country and in one kind of protest did not lead directly or inevitably to further developments in another part of the country and in another kind of protest. Some protests fizzled out, unable to sustain their initial passion; others were suppressed by the state; still others burned bright, achieved their immediate goals, and faded away; and only a few of these entered into a broader public imagination and – in doing so – came to provide later protests with a set of models and examples on which they could draw.

The story that emerges from these events therefore resists attempts to streamline its narrative, and construct of a kind of hero's progress. It is, in many ways, the story of partial failures and incomplete actions – and yet, despite this, and despite the difficulty inherent in the idea of tidying up the messy reality for the purposes of a good story, it does still add up to something more than the sum of its fractured parts. The kinds of protest that could take place changed, even if the change was neither uniform nor directed. The story that results is of a gradual, partial and decentralised movement of students towards an increasingly radicalised, increasingly public and increasingly confrontational form of dissent. It is a story of experimentation, not of planning.

This is clear when one considers the interruptions of chance events that shaped this movement: the shooting at Sharpeville sparked the period of repression that left NUSAS as one of the few remaining representatives of aboveground opposition in South Africa; the scandal that emerged around Driver's seminar address forced NUSAS to retreat and rethink its approach to public politics; the state's banning of Robertson provided NUSAS with an opportunity to experiment with publicly supported protests; and the interference of the state in the internal appointments processes of the UCT – coinciding, as it did, with an international wave of student protest – provoked the students there to embark upon their sit-in and, in so doing, reshape not only public opinion but – more importantly – their own shared sense of what was now politically possible. None of these events were expected, and none could have been coherently planned for.

This may help explain why NUSAS did not face the same kind of repression as other opponents of the government: the state could no more predict that NUSAS would develop into an effective protesting organisation than anyone else could. Nor could the state predict that its efforts to suppress its opponents in NUSAS would not succeed and would, instead, move the organisation into a position where public opposition was increasingly thinkable. This development was the result of chance events impacting on students and state alike; the force of these impacts altered the direction of NUSAS – even if that direction was already implicit at the start of the decade.

Overall, the events of the years between 1964 and 1968 could be described in the terms used by Henri Lefebvre to understand the impact of the student protests in France: they were events that, by their nature, 'belie forecasts; to the extent that [these] events are historic, they upset calculations'. Lefebvre, in a brief opening salvo of aphoristic thought, suggested that events like these 'pull thinkers out of their comfortable seats and plunge them headlong into a wave of contradictions … Good and bad conscience, ideological labels and scraps of obsolete practices are swept away like refuse'. In the wake of this rush, new possibilities open up and new ways of seeing emerge: 'Under the impact of events, people and ideas are revealed for what they are.'[46]

In the aftermath of the suppression of the aboveground opposition to the apartheid state, and the arrest, detention, trial and imprisonment of the leaders and active members of the armed underground movements, it was difficult to see the apartheid state as anything other than unassailable. The few radical activists who remained within the country turned their attention to building underground networks, and defending them against the state's attempts to ferret them out; those liberal activists who were able to work aboveground largely seem to have resigned themselves either to providing a symbolic resistance or to working cautiously within the system. Certainly, this was NUSAS's approach in the aftermath of the government's attacks in 1963 and 1964.

However, the disruptions to the organisation's own status quo brought about by the protests against the banning of Ian Robertson

[46] Henri Lefebvre, *The Explosion*, trans. Alfred Ehrenfeld (New York, Monthly Review Press: 1969), pp. 7–8.

in 1966 and against UCT's treatment of Archie Mafeje in 1968 upset NUSAS's own calculations, and drove it towards a more public form of politics. These events also upset the government's calculations: its efforts to drive NUSAS from the political sphere, and to confine it to campus activities, did not have the intended effect. Instead, what had seemed a process of limiting NUSAS's audience had expanded it.

With this expansion in audience came an expansion in imagination: although the Cape Town sit-in involved fewer people than the national demonstrations in 1966, they represented a new confidence in the possibilities of protest. The forms of activism adopted were new – at least, in the context of student politics. The ability to sustain the sit-in over time demonstrated a new belief in the validity of protest. The positive reception granted to the protest – in the media, and among a significant section of the liberal white population – emboldened student activists. In a very short time, possibilities that had seemed to have been closed off began to open up again.

But one of the characteristics of events is that they simply keep on coming, and another, that their impact is unpredictable. In these years, NUSAS had benefited from the occurrence of events, but at the end of 1968 something else happened – a new student movement announced itself, and threw the potential development of NUSAS as a national political force into disarray.

2 The Formation of the South African Students' Organisation

'CARVING OUT THEIR OWN DESTINY'

At the conclusion of a three-day meeting held in December 1968 at St Francis' College, the Catholic high school in Mariannhill, half-way between Durban and Pietermaritzburg, a group of black students – representing 'Non-white Universities, University Colleges, Seminaries, Training Colleges and other centres of higher learning' – announced their decision to launch a new student movement.

The students stated that although they agreed that it was 'ideal that any country should have one National Student Organisation, and that such an Organisation should cater for the interests of all the students of the country', they also agreed that NUSAS was not that organisation.

They accused the existing union of no wrongdoing, but simply identified 'circumstances beyond [its] control' that limited its effectiveness – namely, that 'students at some Non-white Centres are unable to participate in the National Student Union of this country.' Therefore, they added,

> since we believe that contact among the Non-white Students so affected is of paramount importance, we regard ourselves as duty bound to examine all possibilities of establishing the necessary contact. As a result of our discussions we have provided for the establishment of a Co-Ordinating Body called the SOUTH AFRICAN STUDENTS ORGANISATION (SASO) which amongst other things shall serve to promote practical co-operation; represent Non-white students at a National level; and bring about contact in general among SOUTH AFRICAN STUDENTS.[1]

For all its apparent modesty, this declaration was revolutionary.

It marked the first attempt of black students to assert their own political and social agency after the suppression of the aboveground organisations of the 1940s and 1950s. SASO would become a national union for black students, an alternative to NUSAS – with, significantly, a far clearer source of legitimacy. It would represent the political aspirations of black students as defined by black students, as articulated by black students and as fought for by black students, and not, as had

---

[1] University of the Witwatersrand Historical Papers (WHP) A2675/III/743, *Press Statement*: Mariannhill, 3 December 1968.

previously been the case, by those few white students who wished to represent them. In doing so, SASO would articulate a new philosophy – Black Consciousness – that sought to place the experiences of men and women of colour at the centre of political, cultural and social developments. These ideas would soon reshape South Africa's political worlds.

But they would not do so in the measured tones of this first statement. Despite the caution of their early announcements, many of the founders of SASO were driven by dissatisfaction with the internal workings of NUSAS – and not merely with the state-imposed limitations on the ability of black university campuses to affiliate centrally to NUSAS. These young black students – many of whom had been active participants in NUSAS in the 1960s, and some of whom had even been singled out for future leadership positions in the organisation – saw the white members of NUSAS as intransigently opposed to attempts to articulate black political experiences and, at the same time, saw the supposedly-radical white leaders of the organisation hamstrung by their political caution and ideological blind spots. Intentionally or not, both the majority of the members and the leaders of NUSAS had alienated these black students and, in consequence, NUSAS would not only lose their membership, but also the moral authority that came from representing them.

These two things – the ideas of Black Consciousness, and the restructuring of student politics – shaped the development of protest in the decade that followed SASO's founding. In this chapter, I focus on the second of these, but the political actions of SASO are only truly understandable in the context of its ideological originality. SASO's emergence created a new space for black students to organise as activists, allowing for the development of a new wave of political projects on the edges of the apartheid era's political sphere. This did not occur in isolation. As students, SASO's leaders were able to organise in dialogue with – and sometimes challenge to – NUSAS, and to build a set of networks while the government's attention was turned to addressing the white student protest.

This dialogue was a complicated one. In the initial years of its operation, SASO continued to act in concert with NUSAS. It acknowledged NUSAS as a legitimate national union of students, and sought to establish a fraternal relationship of equals with it. However, this did not last. In 1970, NUSAS embarked upon a public protest that attracted the attention of the state, and led to the mass arrest of white students in Cape Town. NUSAS's leaders saw this as a badge of honour, and attempted to instruct other student bodies – including SASO – to follow their example and launch confrontational protests. The tone and content of this instruction infuriated SASO: the communication made it clear NUSAS saw itself as the senior partner in its relationship with SASO. This left no room for real equality between the movements – and SASO broke publicly with NUSAS.

In this moment, SASO's leaders challenged the right of white students to speak or act on behalf of black students. They articulated a radical claim: that the shared experiences of black students provided the basis for their own political action. The inability of white students to share these experiences rendered them incapable of participating in this action – and made it impossible for them to lead, coordinate, or instruct black students.

The ideas of Black Consciousness – as this form of theorising from experience came to be known – provided new models of political identity. Instead of committing oneself to an explicit and ordered political programme of change, linked to specific policies and institutions, Black Consciousness provided black students with a new sense of self, and a new way of being in the world. Its emergence as a philosophy of experience permitted a looser set of identities and identifications to form, and provided a broad and flexible system of thought, culture and social orientation that could ground a wide range of political practices.

Both these ideas and the models of organisation developed by SASO would play significant roles in the rediscovery and development of popular politics and public protest in the 1970s. It is important to recognise, though, that they did not develop in a vacuum – and that the apparent dichotomy between white and black student politics was a product of a continuing, if conflictual, exchange of ideas between students. In this chapter, I show how this dialogue developed over the first two years of SASO's existence. The split between SASO and NUSAS developed around contrasting approaches to confrontational forms of protest, but incorporated a range of other issues – including, most importantly, a challenge to the unconscious assumption of authority on the part of white students. SASO refused to accept this, and insisted upon the equal ability of black students to speak – and, more than this, their greater ability to speak about their own experiences. This reshaped the foundations on which opposition activism took place, and opened up new possibilities for a different kind of politics.

The road to SASO

To understand the birth of SASO, though, we need first to understand how black student politics changed dramatically after the banning of the ANC and PAC (Pan Africanist Congress) in 1960. The Youth Leagues of these organisations were also banned in the course of this wave of repression, and a number of student organisations attempted to replace them on the black campuses. None, however, developed a mass following – and all were forced to disband within a short time. These included the ANC-aligned African Students Association (ASA) and the PAC-aligned African Students Union of South Africa (ASUSA). The 'balkanisation' of the black campuses from each other – caused by the absence of any national coordinating body – was further reflected by divisions within the campuses themselves. In addition, Student Representative Councils (SRCs) were banned on many campuses, further limiting the ability of black students to meet and coordinate activities between faculties and age groups. Finally, those SRCs that did exist were forbidden to affiliate with NUSAS – for fear that its liberal ideas would spread to the campuses of the Universities of Fort Hare or Zululand, or that of the newly-created University of the North.[2]

For many students at these institutions, NUSAS thus became the only plausible vehicle for political actions. Although black institutions were forbidden to affiliate, individual students could often do so on their own account and – by the mid-1960s – the black membership of NUSAS had increased fourfold. Black students were also notably active in this period, constituting between one-third and one-quarter of the delegates at its national conferences.[3]

But NUSAS was not an ideal home for black student politics. Despite the increasing numbers of black students in NUSAS, many students began to feel disenchanted with the union. Several ran for high office, but only one (Thami Mhlambiso, who served as vice-president in 1961–62) was actually elected. Black students perceived themselves as a token presence in the union, and saw that all important decisions were being taken without consulting them – even when these decisions were ostensibly being taken on their own behalf.

Steve Biko – a black student at the University of Natal's Non-European section who would go on to found SASO and act as its first president – later described the situation as one in which 'whites of liberal opinions' found that they could 'make representations for blacks in a way that had not happened before in the past'. The difference between the relations established in the later 1950s and that of the mid-1960s, he suggested, was that liberal white students were now acting 'unaccom-

[2] The conditions of this period are surveyed effectively in Saleem Badat, *Black Student Politics, Higher Education & Apartheid: From SASO to SANSCO, 1968–1990* (Pretoria, HSRC: 1999), as well as in Donovan Williams, 2001. *A History of the University College of Fort Hare, South Africa – 1950s: The Waiting Years.* Lampeter, The Edwin Mellen Press: 2001; T.V.R. Beard, 'Background to Student Activities at the University College of Fort Hare: Conflict, Consensus and Political Mobilisation on a University Campus', in H.W. van der Merwe and D. Welsh (eds), *Student Perspectives on South Africa* (Cape Town, David Philip: 1972).
[3] Thomas G. Karis and Gail M. Gerhart, *From Protest to Challenge: A Documentary History of African Politics in South Africa, 1882–1990: Volume 5: Nadir and Resurgence, 1964–1979* (Bloomington and Indianapolis, University of Indiana Press: 1997), pp. 69–70.

panied by black opinion'.[4] Blacks were a national majority, but not a majority within NUSAS – and without the institutional support of black-majority organisations such as the Youth Leagues, the black minority in NUSAS found itself in a clientalist relationship with the union's white student majority. Thus, even as black student participation in NUSAS increased in response to outside phenomena, the hope of a fraternal relationship among all students – held out in the late 1950s – was no longer tenable.

Many members of the NUSAS executive in the 1960s had been aware of these growing tensions, but few had ready solutions. Jonty Driver had come closest to serious reform in 1964, when he suggested that the union's policy of affiliating university campuses be replaced by individual membership; it seemed likely that these members would be more committed politically – and would more likely than not be black.[5] The proposal was leaked and rejected. Any members of NUSAS sympathetic to the position of black students within the union then turned their energies on developing internal black leadership training programmes.

Before founding SASO, Steve Biko was one of the early participants in these leadership programmes. His student life had already been interrupted by the state: in 1963, after his older brother was jailed for allegedly participating in the PACs's underground activities, Biko was expelled from Lovedale College in the Eastern Cape. The following year he was admitted to St Francis' College at Mariannhill, in Natal. In 1966 he started a medical degree at the University of Natal's Non-European section in Durban, attended his first NUSAS leadership training seminar and the annual NUSAS conference. According to Karis and Gerhart, he was singled out by the NUSAS executive during that year as being a potential future president.[6] His increasing participation in these programmes and in the ordinary work of the NUSAS leadership, however, also confronted him with the intransigence of many of its members: in particular, Biko would later remember the July 1967 national conference as being a pivotal moment in his relationship with NUSAS – and a pivotal moment in the processes leading up to the foundation of SASO.

At this conference, held at Rhodes University in Grahamstown, a crisis developed over the question of overnight accommodation at the conference: unexpectedly, the university refused to accommodate black students. The NUSAS executive struggled to make contingency plans, and came up with a controversial proposal: dividing the

[4] WHP A2675/Interviews, Interview with Steve Biko, conducted by Gail M. Gerhart (24 October 1972).
[5] 'NUSAS Paper by Jonty Driver, President, delivered at NUSAS National Seminar, April 1964', in Karis and Gerhart, *From Protest to Challenge*, Vol. 5.
[6] Karis and Gerhart, *From Protest to Challenge, Volume 5*, pp. 93–5.

students up according to apartheid categories. Indian and Coloured delegates to the conference would be housed in the city itself, while African delegates were asked to sleep on the floor and on the pews of a church in the neighbouring African township. As the university's catering department refused to serve non-white students, meals on campus would only be served to the white student delegates. Indian, Coloured and African students would have to find alternative sources of food.

Unsurprisingly, Biko and the other students from Natal's Non-European Section raised an immediate protest, calling for an adjournment until a non-segregated venue could be found. The NUSAS executive, however, hesitated to risk alienating its white student base and suggested, instead, that the conference continue. It proposed that the university be formally censured in a motion passed from the floor. From Biko's perspective, this was hardly satisfactory: it would result in the students spending the following nights in segregated, makeshift accommodation and would entrench, for the length of the meeting, a visible and tangible inequality between black and white students. Biko and his fellows thus remained awake all night attempting to raise support for their alternate proposal – that the meeting adjourn.

In the morning, though, the delegates voted 42 to 9 against adjournment. For Biko, this shook his confidence in liberal non-racialism. He began to 'feel that our understanding of our own situation in this country was not quite coincidental with that of the whites'. Even those white students who claimed to be the most sympathetic to the struggles of black students – the leaders of NUSAS – had proved themselves unwilling to risk the political consequences of taking a stand against the convenience of their white members.[7]

After the conference, many of the black delegates met again in Port Elizabeth. Here, Biko sat down with Barney Pityana and began to discuss the idea of founding an alternative national organisation for black students.[8] Although he was a few years older than Biko, Pityana shared several of his experiences – both, for example, had been expelled from Lovedale College. Pityana had been involved in a student group initiated by the ASA in the early 1960s – and could thus, unlike Biko, be placed in a genealogy of ANC-derived politics. During 1967, at the time of these meetings, Pityana was still studying at Fort Hare. As a forerunner of some of the problems that black students would face in the course of organising politically, he would soon be expelled from

[7] S. Biko, *The Testimony of Steve Biko*, ed. M. Arnold (London: Maurice Temple Smith, 1979), p. 8. See also: S. Buthelezi, 'The Emergence of Black Consciousness: An Historical Appraisal,' in Barney Pityana, Mamphela Ramphele, Malusi Mpumlwana and Lindy Wilson (eds), *Bounds of Possibility: The Legacy of Steve Biko and Black Consciousness* (Cape Town, David Philip: 1991).

[8] L. Wilson, 'Bantu Stephen Biko: A Life,' in Pityana et al. *Bounds of Possibility*.

that university – charged with organising an unauthorised student protest.

Nothing was decided in Port Elizabeth, but the seeds of the break-away had been sown. They would bear fruit a year later when the next NUSAS national conference was held at the University of the Witwatersrand, in Johannesburg. Here, once again, Biko and his allies found themselves and their ideas sidelined in the course of the debates over NUSAS policy, and often in favour of discussions of the potential crisis sparked at the UCT over the university's withdrawn offer of employment to Archie Mafeje, as discussed in Chapter 1.

This time, though, the black students moved directly from the NUSAS conference to the second annual conference of the newly formed University Christian Movement (UCM). This had been founded a year earlier by a number of clergymen at the country's English-medium universities, with 'the intent to revive interracial and ecumenical links among university students'.[9] It represented an attempt to revive a network of religious – explicitly Christian – organisations that had been caught up in the wave of repression that had drenched the country in the early 1960s. Many of these organisations had been active on black university campuses and had seemed, for a brief moment, to offer these students a possible alternative to the white-led politics of NUSAS. That alternative – a space for organising under the umbrella of Christianity, rather than under that of liberalism – did not last, and African students had left these groups. Now, at the end of the decade, the UCM seemed to hold out the same hope.

Many black students were open to the UCM's potential: over half the delegates to its inaugural conference, in 1967, were black. At its second conference, in 1968, this percentage rose to almost two-thirds of the delegates. Unlike NUSAS, the UCM offered black students a place in which they could dominate the discussions, they could set the agendas, and they could – most importantly – hear and be heard by each other.

They put this space to good use. At the conference, Biko, Pityana and their allies began to canvas support amongst the student delegates. They were able to assemble a group of university students representing the University of Fort Hare, the University of the North, and the Non-European section of the University of Natal; they were then joined by a number of others representing theological seminaries and teacher-training colleges. It was soon clear that none of these students were any more willing to tailor their ambitions to fit the strictures of a religious institution than they were willing to subsume themselves in NUSAS's existing structures. Instead, they were set upon launching their own new organisation.[10]

[9] Karis and Gerhart, *From Protest to Challenge, Volume 5*, p. 72.
[10] WHP A2675/III/744, *Notes on the Formation of SASO*.

The student delegates agreed to meet again in December, at Mariannhill. In the months between, they returned to their universities and canvassed support for a new organisation. Then, in December, the delegates agreed to form SASO, and released the statement that opened this chapter. They drafted a constitution for the organisation and agreed that its first General Students' Council would be held six months later, during July 1969. There, they agreed, the organisation would be formally constituted.[11]

The idea of Black Consciousness

SASO was not intended to be a simple student organisation, designed to articulate the academic concerns of black students. Instead, from its inception, the organisation was committed to a broader ambition: to challenge the foundations of apartheid's racial structures and ideologies. SASO sought, in other words, to remake black identity.[12]

The core element of this was a challenge to apartheid's racial categories, and the positing of an alternative source of identity and pride within a broad 'black' community. The state did not only differentiate between 'white' and 'non-white' groups, but also – within the broad category of 'non-white' – between African, Indian and Coloured men and women. Each category was subject to different restrictions, each held a different legal status and, although all were disenfranchised in comparison to the white population, a complex web of minor privileges and significant deprivations threatened to force the groups into competition with each other. SASO set out to challenge this implicit differentiation: instead of using the language of apartheid, it insisted that Africans, Indians and Coloureds shared a common blackness, a common experience of disenfranchisement, and a common hope. Rather than define themselves by their differences from each other, they should define themselves by their commonalities, and rather than use the terms of others, they should make their own language.

In rejecting the terminology of the state, activists sought to remake the language of race. In place of the idea of a community defined in the negative – i.e. as non-whites – they put forward the idea of a community defined positively, as being black. This meant asserting that groups separated by the state (in racial terms, African, Indian and Coloured groups) in fact shared experiences of oppression and exclusion – and that these shared experiences could ground a politics of solidarity. Beyond this, it also meant asserting that – having

[11] WHP A2675/III/744, SASO Pamphlet, SASO Communiqué; Biko, *The Testimony of Steve Biko*, pp. 10–11.
[12] See the writings collected in Steve Biko, *I Write What I Like: Selected Writings* (London, Bowerdean: 1978).

been excluded from white society – these groups had developed ideas, identities and cultures that were unique and – although often unrecognised – deserving of respect on their own terms. Where the state conflated race and culture, Black Consciousness activists emphasised the links between race and exclusion, and between culture and the creative re-appropriation of experience.

This gave rise to a series of explorations. Intellectually, Black Consciousness thought encouraged students and others to read widely in the international literature on black experiences on the continent and in the diaspora. Engagement with the works of the Harlem Renaissance, of Frantz Fanon, of Nkrumah and Nyerere, and other African leaders, remained controversial in the apartheid era – and often these texts were circulated secretively, in samizdat form. Culturally, in seeking to enable practices of self-definition, some Black Consciousness activists emphasised the importance of reclaiming everyday practices, investigating pre-colonial histories, and asserting communal identities. This could take material forms, such as the adoption of clothing and dress styles from elsewhere on the continent, or the adoption of different regimes of grooming, hair-care and self-presentation. Religiously, the influence of radical elements within the country's Christian tradition brought notions of Black Theology to the fore. Influenced by Latin American Liberation Theology, churchmen within the movement sought to develop an interpretation of Christian teachings that emphasised both a reparative ethos and a radical notion of equality at the heart of Christianity. This acted as an explicit challenge to the racism that marked many mainstream Christian churches in South Africa, including the Dutch Reformed Church, which provided separate sites and practices of worship to congregations of different races. In this context, Black Theology provided a conventional moral core to the concepts of Black Consciousness in its early years.

These intellectual, cultural and religious developments gave rise to a new conception of black humanity, one that was linked to racial identity in South Africa but not dependent on apartheid presumptions. If it was the shared experiences of oppression that allowed black South Africans to unite, it was these alternative sources of identity that gave the humanism of Black Consciousness thought its particular character. Rather than attempt to straightjacket identity, humanist strands of Black Consciousness thought sought to ground it in a re-valuation of everyday practices. Ordinary life was seen to possess depths of meaning, and brought into dialogue with historical and comparative examples of black diasporic culture. In so doing, Black Consciousness emphasised the value of what Manganyi calls 'being black in the world'.[13]

---

[13] N. Chabani Manganyi, *Being-Black-In-The-World* (Johannesburg, Spro-Cas and Ravan: 1973).

The political implications of these developments, however, were not always self-evident, and were the subject of passionate debates within SASO and other organisations throughout these years. Some suggested that activists should refrain from entering into national politics, and rather focus on building consciousness within black communities; others thought that some of the instruments of the apartheid system – including the Bantustans or homelands project of establishing dependent ethnic colonies within South African territory – could be used to create opportunities for developing an independent black politics.[14] These approaches could be contrasted with others that saw SASO and other Black Consciousness organisations as being on a collision course with the state, either immediately – as a way of establishing the difference between the expansive notions of black community developed by SASO and the constrained ones espoused by the state – or in the future, when the implications of Black Consciousness became clear. The various approaches – caution, co-option, resistance, challenge – were debated during the early years of SASO, with different approaches dominant at different times.

The politics of Black Consciousness are thus perhaps best understood in liquid metaphors: intersecting streams of experience and ideology combining together in unstable fashion. Some ideas spun off into side-streams and ox-bowed lakes; others fed into the main rush of ideas and excitement, driving the movement forward. Conflicts took the forms of eddies and whirlpools, disrupting the smooth flow of the stream but not stopping. In this context, a great deal of intellectual and political fluidity was possible, and consistency was less important than embracing new ideas.

However, all contributors to the ideas of Black Consciousness agreed on at least one thing: whatever politics were adopted, it was no longer possible to accept the efforts of white students or activists to represent black claims. Blacks must speak for themselves, and act for themselves – to do anything else was to accept a junior or inferior position within an existing system. It was also to accept that the implicit hierarchy of knowledge and authority that assumed that white experiences were universal, while black experiences were exceptional.

This put SASO on course for an inevitable collision with NUSAS.

The structure of SASO and its relationship with NUSAS

At first, the ideological differences between SASO and NUSAS were not reflected in their institutional structures – nor, indeed, in their

---

[14] See for an example of a prominent argument that was rejected: Themba Sono, *Reflections on the Origins of Black Consciousness in South Africa* (Pretoria, HSRC: 1993).

49

relations in the aftermath of SASO's launch. As SASO developed in confidence, though, these relations began to alter.

The first constitution of SASO – supplemented by communiqués and internal memoranda – set out a provisional structure for the organisation. Multiple forms of membership were to be permitted: an SRC could choose to affiliate its entire institution on behalf of its student body, a majority vote of the student body could bypass recalcitrant – or non-existent – SRCs and affiliate the institution, or individuals could affiliate themselves. Ten or more of these individual members could form a local SASO branch and represent their institutions at SASO general councils. The national executive – elected annually at the general council – would include a president, two vice-presidents, regional representatives, a sports organiser, a fieldwork director, a chairman of publications, and directors of cultural activities and education. This national executive was primarily intended to coordinate the activities of the various affiliated campuses; it would present a national front for SASO, provide guidance on national events and generally act to organise the development of the organisation. Local committees – called, at this point, 'SASO local committees' on the model of the NUSAS local committees – would be responsible for initiating campus-based activities. These committees would be locally funded, often set up and supported by SRCs on different university campuses.[15]

There are a number of similarities between this institutional structure and those of earlier organisations. On the one hand, it is reminiscent of the structures of the African opposition movements in their period of aboveground activity: a national executive, provincial and regional committees, and local branches. On the other hand, it also seems to be have been modelled on the existing structure of NUSAS. Both student organisations relied on local committees and campus branches to mediate between students at affiliated universities and the national executive; in both cases, overall policy was to be set in annual meetings – both to be held during the winter vacation, in July. The respective executives were to be elected at these meetings, and were be responsible for ensuring the continuing application of formal policies. In addition to these coincidences – and not the least of them – both set out to act as national bodies, representing students across South Africa.

This coincidence of aims had the potential to lead to conflict: NUSAS still claimed to represent all students nationally, including affiliated students at black universities.

At first SASO sought to side-step this clash, suggesting that 'in terms of structure SASO operates like a National Union although she does

[15] WHP A2675/III/743, *SASO Constitution* (1969) & 'Report on the 1st National Formation School' (December 1969).

not claim to be one'.[16] SASO went further at its inaugural national council, acknowledging NUSAS as the *only* national student union and suggesting that it was only the racial policies of the state – forbidding many black universities from affiliating with NUSAS – that had created the situation in which a separate black student union had had to be formed.[17] This apparently congenial relationship could also be seen in the communications between the leaders of SASO and those of both NUSAS and the UCM; indeed, in this initial period, SASO depended heavily on both movements for their political and financial support. The UCM was active in sourcing international funding for SASO, and a number of letters exchanged between Biko and Colin Collins at the UCM testify not only the importance of this financial support, but also to the relative informality of the personal relationship between these men. Similarly, correspondence between Biko and Neville Curtis – the president of NUSAS in 1969 and 1970 – suggests that their common history within the student movement was used to maintain a certain camaraderie between the two men, with Curtis asking for Biko's opinions on tactical matters within NUSAS. Beyond this, Curtis also approached Biko for advice on his proposals to change the institutional structures of NUSAS.[18]

SASO's emergence came at a moment when NUSAS itself was in organisational – and, to an extent, ideological – transition, and the creation and acts of the new union had an immediate impact on the older institution. Early in 1969, Duncan Innes fell ill and had been replaced as NUSAS president by Neville Curtis – who immediately announced that the July conference would discuss the organisation's reorganisation and redirection. At this conference, delegates debated the failure of the 1968 sit-in to achieve its stated goals. They agreed that other forms of confrontational protest should be investigated, while also agreeing that NUSAS should be restructured to more clearly define the fields within which it acted.

At the end of 1970 – eighteen months after the decision to reorganise NUSAS – Curtis announced, in the newly launched *NUSAS Newsletter*, that his organisation had 'shifted [its] emphasis from [being] a service organisation to [being] a campaigning organisation – from an organisation which talks and provides benefits to an organisation which initiates, leads, and involves people'. Although he did not suggest what it was that NUSAS might initiate and lead, it was clear by implication that he envisaged this to mean public forms of protest. NUSAS had now shifted, Curtis suggested, from 'involvement in society for nega-

---

[16] WHP A2675/III/744, 'SASO Budget'.

[17] WHP A2675/III/743, 'SASO Communique'. See also the account in: Sono, *Reflections.*

[18] WHP A2675/III/743, Correspondence (1969). WHP A2675/III/744, Correspondence (1970).

tive reasons (that our rights were being infringed by the curtailment of academic freedom) to involvement for a positive reason (that it is our duty to work for the achievement of greater rights for all)'. This shift was accompanied by an institutional reorganisation: the core organisation of NUSAS was separated out from new sections dedicated to responding to educational, welfare and cultural issues. This left the core of the NUSAS executive with the ability to focus its attention on its new political priorities.[19]

NUSAS thus claimed a duty to a much broader public, one that included its constituent student members but was not limited to them. Instead, these students were no longer expected to think and act as students but as members of a South African public opposed to the apartheid state. They were to campaign for social change, and not just to protect the embattled autonomy of their universities. This shift was substantial and significant. Although Legassick and Saunders suggest that NUSAS was without direction in this period, the years between 1969 and early 1971 saw both the national executive of NUSAS and several of its local branches embark on public protests – the most notable of which occurred in the week of 11–18 May 1970.[20] This would help galvanise SASO into action – and would be, in part, responsible for its official break with NUSAS in July 1970.

NUSAS and 'the first mass arrest of students'

In December 1969, Winnie Mandela – the activist, and wife of the imprisoned Nelson Mandela – was brought to court, along with twenty-one other defendants; their trial dragged on for two months, until February 1970, when the Attorney-General suddenly withdrew all charges. The defendants were formally acquitted and released. However, they were not permitted to leave the courtroom. They were immediately detained without charge, rounded up by the police in the court room and the corridors outside. The context of this repeated arrest was significant: several of the defendants had already accused the police of brutality and assaults while in detention. These accussations were given plausibility by a concurrent investigation into the death in detention of a religious figure.[21]

In March 1970, the Black Sash began a series of public vigils to protest against the cynical detention of Mandela and her co-

---

[19] N. Curtis, *NUSAS Newsletter*, December 1970, p. 1.

[20] Martin Legassick and Christopher Saunders. 2004. 'Above-Ground Activity in the 1960s', South African Democracy Education Trust (SADET), *The Road to Democracy in South Africa, Volume 1, 1960–1970*. Johannesburg, Zebra p. 686.

[21] Some of the material in this section and the next has been previously published as J. Brown, 'SASO's Reluctant Embrace of Public Forms of Protest, 1968–1972', *South African Historical Journal*, 62 (4): 2010, pp. 716–34.

defendants. These were to be held every Monday until the detainees were either charged or released. The Black Sash continued the vigils from March through to May, when NUSAS began to involve itself. The NUSAS president, Neville Curtis, called upon students to observe a 'national day of protest' on Monday 11 May 1970 – a date obviously chosen to coincide with the Black Sash's weekly public vigil. This day of protest was to be marked by a national 'student strike' – lectures would be boycotted, pickets would be manned, placards would be displayed, pamphlets would be distributed and an all-day public vigil would be held.[22]

These protests succeeded in mobilising student groups on NUSAS-affiliated campuses, most notably the University of the Witwatersrand. Students decided to extend the day of protest into the following week as it was 'the duty of students – in sincere search of the truth as they are – to bring to the full attention of the public injustices of this kind and magnitude'.[23] In addition, a public march was proposed at a mass meeting.

On Tuesday, 12 May, the president of the Wits SRC, Kenneth Costa, sent a letter to the Johannesburg Town Clerk requesting permission to hold a public march on the following Monday. The Town Clerk granted permission, so long as it was uninterrupted and disciplined, and that 'any posters to be carried or displayed by marchers are to be in good taste'.

On the Sunday immediately preceding the planned march, however, the Acting Chief Magistrate for the district of Johannesburg unexpectedly overruled the Clerk's decision and forbade the march. He claimed to have 'reason to apprehend that the public peace will be seriously endangered by the assembly of a public gathering in a certain public place'. His notice did not describe this threat, leaving the SRC with little ground on which to argue against it. It was also served late in the day, curtailing the possibility of any potential legal challenge.

On the morning of Monday 18 May, the SRC called a public meeting in the campus's Great Hall and proposed a motion condemning the prohibition of the march, and empowering 'a delegation to visit the Minister to protest against various aspects'. The council did not propose that the students ignore the ban and risk confronting the state; instead, it sought to register a formal protest and to continue to oppose the state within the bounds of the law. This did not appeal to many of the students present. According to the account given by John Dugard – then a lecturer in the university's law department, and active in the South African Institute of Race Relations (SAIRR) – several students

[22] *NUSAS Newsletter*, 8 May 1970.
[23] Here, and below, the details come from a series of affidavits filed by participants in the march, and archived by their attorney. See: WHP AK3166/11 (Raymond Tucker, Attorney).

stood to oppose the motion and 'spoke vaguely about other action, without specifying what in particular they meant'.

As the debate continued to rage within the Great Hall, a number of students walked out of the meeting. They congregated on the building's steps and gathered up pre-prepared placards and posters. Several more students fell into step behind them, and a spontaneous march then left the campus along the route originally planned. As news filtered back into the Great Hall, several members of the SRC abandoned their own meeting and rushed to join the march – officially, as responsible marshals hoping to be able to keep the peace should any confrontation develop.

Their fears were not entirely unjustified. The march was planned to end outside the police headquarters in John Vorster Square and, just as the marchers began to arrive in its vicinity, the police appeared. They surrounded the students and instructed them to seat themselves on the street. All the students present complied.

Meanwhile, a number of lecturers and bystanders who had followed the march found themselves on a traffic island in the middle of Commissioner Street. They intended to act as witnesses – and, to some extent, as chaperones. Several of these were carrying cameras, intended to record the progress of the march; they photographed the encounters between the students and the police – an act to which some members of the police, both in uniform and in plainclothes, objected. The photographers were hassled, arrested and taken into the police station. Once there, they were joined by a large number of students. In total, 357 people were arrested for taking part in the march. They were processed, fingerprinted, harassed, beaten, insulted and then finally released after hours of detention.

That weekend, the *NUSAS Newsletter* announced triumphantly that 'the last week has been the most significant in the history of student protest in South Africa'. This statement was printed in capital letters at the top of its front page. The accompanying article pointed out that the march had taken place 'in defiance of prohibition' and had resulted in 'the first mass arrest of students (357) in this country'.[24] For NUSAS, this was a badge of honour.

Both the march and the mass arrest also received a great deal of national press attentions, which served to enhance NUSAS's public image, suggesting that the state saw it as a significant threat to its hegemony over white opinion. This was confirmed ten days later, on 28 May, when the Minister of Justice announced that formal charges would be laid against thirty of the 357 arrested students – while, at the same time, announcing that charges would be formally laid against Mandela and her fellow detainees. NUSAS's protests were thus

[24] *NUSAS Newsletter*, 22 May 1970.

suddenly vindicated: linking the prosecution of its members with the state's acceptance of the necessity of finally charging Mandela and her fellows certainly made it appear as though NUSAS's actions had finally forced the state's hand.

The continuing coincidence of the two trials – of the thirty students, and of Mandela and her 21 co-accused – only reinforced this perception. Both trials stumbled, however, to a halt in the later part of the year. The state dropped its primary charges – of contravening the Riotous Assemblies Act and of contravening the Criminal Law Amendment Act – against the thirty students, and settled instead for allowing them to plead guilty to a minor charge of contravening a Johannesburg city by-law. They paid an admission-of-guilt fine of R50 each, and were allowed to go free. Similarly, Mandela's trial fizzled out, eventually being dismissed due to the similarity between the state's initial, abandoned, case and the second charges.[25]

SASO's break from NUSAS

The national executive of NUSAS soon attempted to capitalise on the unexpected success of the march. The publicity surrounding the march and the novelty of the mass arrests seemed to provide the organisation with the opportunity to position itself firmly at the centre of oppositional student politics; it communicated with other student groups – including SASO, which was still formally aligned with NUSAS – and challenged them to join their protests.

In response, Biko circulated a statement to SRC presidents across the country, analysing NUSAS's recent protest and explaining why SASO did not support it. First, he condemned the assumption – held by SASO to be that of the NUSAS executive, and to have been communicated by their challenge – that black students should automatically support the protests of white students. 'We hold it as absolute arrogance', he wrote, 'for any student leader from the privileged group to give a directive reading what black student leaders should do at times like these.' He explained that the issue at stake in SASO's refusal to participate was not 'whether the 22 [i.e. Mandela and her co-defendants] are released or not' nor 'whether the Terrorism Act is repealed or not' but rather a 'far more basic' issue – the 'disinheritance and dispossession' of black agency implicit in the actions of white student leaders claiming to lead the struggles of black students. If SASO were to embark upon public forms of action, it would act on its own behalf, at a time of its own choosing, and in a manner of its own choosing – not at NUSAS's bidding.[26]

[25] Muriel Horrell, *A Survey of Race Relations in South Africa 1970* (Johannesburg, SAIRR: 1971).
[26] WHP A2675/III/744, Memo re: Recent Protest (1970).

After establishing this, Biko went on to offer a pointed critique of the protest. First, he argued that the march was aimed to prick the collective conscience of the white electorate, and thus to spur it into taking action against the government. As such, it was politically pointless: as far as SASO was concerned, 'we do not recognise the South African "electorate" as it is presently constituted. Nor do we believe that they have any conscience that anybody can appeal to.' Second, he argued that any protest or campaign that limited itself to opposing only one aspect of the apartheid state – whether that be the Terrorism Act, or the detention without trial of the 22 – was incapable of dismantling that state. This type of protest, he suggested, 'focuses all strength on one item' and thus 'invariably leads to frustration'. Even when a protest did succeed in changing the approach of the state – as, for example, in the case of the twenty-two detainees – this change still left the structures of the apartheid order intact.

Biko's comprehensive dismissal of the relevance of NUSAS's targeted protests was not unprecedented. A similar critique of the 1968 UCT sit-in had been made during SASO's first Formation School – a political training and leadership retreat – held in December 1969. Here, the sit-in had been described as a 'reactionary type of protest' that 'fails to change the situation' and thus 'leads people to believe that the value of protest is little'. It was suggested that, 'protesting at the fact that Mafeje's appointment has been cancelled is different from protesting against the erosion of academic freedom' and that the two were not necessarily compatible. 'NUSAS must always differentiate between the specific and the general' in designing its protests; unless it did so, the two would become tangled up and the failure of a protest to alter a specific issue would lessen the likelihood of a more general protest ever succeeding in mobilising mass participation.[27]

The terms of both this initial critique and Biko's slightly later variation were once again reiterated at SASO's second General Student Council (GSC) in July 1970. At this, tensions between student organisations boiled over. Several resolutions intended to establish SASO as distinct from all rivals were passed. The UCM was praised for its 'practical' projects – work-camps and literacy projects, explicitly derived from Paolo Freire's theories of education. The SASO executive was instructed by its membership to collaborate with the UCM on these 'practical and meaningful projects'. The new National Federation of South African Students – an initiative of the student council at the Afrikaans-medium University of Stellenbosch – was dismissed with 'contempt'. The Afrikaanse Studente Bond also attracted a substantial dose of vitriol: its 'cultivation of racist tendencies' meant that it was clearly 'an incorrigible group'.[28]

[27] WHP A2675/III/744, Memo re: Critique of NUSAS. (1969).
[28] In this and subsequent paragraphs, all quotes are taken from: WHP A2675/III/744, 'Resolutions adopted at the 1st SASO General Students Council, July 4–10' (1970).

The tenth motion presented to the general council proposed that SASO withdraw its recognition of NUSAS as the country's sole national student union. This particular motion was premised on the ground that black self-sufficiency was inherently preferable to dependence and clientalism; NUSAS, 'as presently constituted', could not claim to truly represent black students in the country, 'despite the openness of its membership'. Several delegates felt that this language was not strong enough, and proposed an amendment from the floor, suggesting that SASO 'condemn' and 'reject' NUSAS outright. This amendment was not accepted. However, the vast majority of the delegates – 85 per cent of them – voted for the original motion.

The passage of this motion marked a formal break between SASO and NUSAS. Nonetheless, it is striking that that this was not an absolute break. The unwillingness of the council to accept more critical language suggested that they remained open to the possibility of interaction. Indeed, the final motion passed instructed the SASO executive to study NUSAS's actions and respond to them, while at the same time maintaining contact with their counterparts in other organisations. In essence, SASO now considered itself as equivalent to NUSAS in national range and potential significance. It would collaborate as an equal partner on projects with the UCM. These organisations would be tolerated, so long as they did not claim to represent black students.

Thus empowered, the student delegates used the sixty-seventh motion to define SASO's official opinion on 'the public protests and demonstrations being aimed at the white press and public'. The motion restated the organisation's sceptical approach to these protests, and stated that they were 'deficient' because 'they did not involve a strategic and continuous attempt to change the status quo'. The motion recommended that black students avoid taking part in such protests, 'particularly at this stage in South African politics and especially where student interests are not directly involved'. Instead, 'if protests are to be held' then black students should only participate in them if they were 'directed primarily at the Black population' rather than at the white electorate. Even then, any organisation planning a new protest should first consider whether it should 'possibly adopt a new form' – one which was not yet specified.

'Practical Applications of the Ideology of Black Consciousness'

The debate at the general council had made it clear that whatever new form of protest SASO might choose to adopt in the future, it should not resemble those being organised by NUSAS. These potential protests would not be aimed at the white electorate – and thus would not necessarily need to court the white press. They would not confuse responding to specific crises with its general challenge to the apartheid state and its social system. And they would take new forms, which would 'involve a strategic and continuous attempt to effect a change'.[29]

SASO's national executive continued to struggle with these ideas after the council ended. A confidential report on the council, circulated to all members of the national executive, suggests that these ideas continued to evolve. This report emphasised that although it did not immediately propose altering SASO's official policy of non-involvement in confrontational protest – as set out in the sixty-seventh motion – it did nonetheless believe that it was important to consider its limits. The report suggested that non-involvement could be abandoned under restricted circumstances – 'the only time where we can modify our approach is with reference to local authorities and even there with the obvious goal of encouraging group action'.[30]

This exception was brought up again in a second document, circulated later that year. Titled the 'Practical Applications of the Ideology of Black Consciousness', it seems to have been intended to serve as a discussion document at SASO's next Formation School. Its contents were thus intended to spark discussion, and to delineate the overall outlines of SASO's policies. Indeed, the paper specifically noted that the four categories of discussion listed were 'but a few that one can think of'. Nonetheless, the choice of these four categories outlined the range of possible practical applications – i.e. the types of political actions that could be undertaken by SASO and its members in accordance with its general guiding ideology. The categories were: (i) Directive politics, (ii) Infiltrative politics, (iii) Orientation projects, and (iv) Self-reliance projects.[31]

The first two categories suggested ways in which students involved in SASO could engage politically with non-student communities. Directive politics, for example, involved 'vocalising and popularising the idea of black consciousness'. Students should therefore present their self-belief to as wide a public as possible – it 'must be tackled by its advocates as a religion' – so as to convert neutral observers. SASO local groups should demonstrate 'the strength of group action' through 'publicity stunts' – such as slogans ('Black man, you are on your own!') and the 'cultivation of images' (on SASO tee shirts, for example). Infiltrative politics, on the other hand, described actions that were aimed not at neutral communities, but rather at fellow travellers and rival organisations – that is, at 'a group of people who direct themselves to only part of the overall goal you share with them'. Infiltrative actions

[29] WHP A2675/III/744, Resolutions.
[30] WHP A2675/III/744, Reports to the 1st GSC (1970).
[31] WHP A2675/III/744, 'Practical Applications of the Ideology of Black Consciousness' (1970). All quotes in the following paragraphs come from this document.

were intended to engage with these other groups and to move them towards accepting SASO's agenda. Students could act from outside of these groups – applying 'constructive criticism calculated to provoke some kind of action' – or could consider acting covertly from within, by the 'deliberate planting of our own people in the midst of such a group' – thus changing their practices.

The second two categories of action listed in the discussion document aimed to organise communities. Orientation projects were designed to address the ways in which black history had been 'distorted' by re-orienting black society 'along educational, cultural, religious and economical lines'. The projects would aim to establish 'black facilities and resource centres' that would help recreate a black culture outside of apartheid caricatures. Black Theology would be taught to priests, and 'black cooperative enterprises designed for the benefit of Blacks' would be encouraged. Communities would 'marshall [their] economic resources' and use 'the pooled strength of the economy to the advantage of that group'. This would enable self-reliance, which would lead to the integration of community activities with the general aims of national Black Consciousness, thus providing a 'physical and practical demonstration of the fact that salvation and emancipation of a group ultimately lies in the hands of that group'.

Implicit in the proposals for practical action presented in this document were the beginnings of a coherent approach to the mobilisation of community-based activism. While ideological unity was emphasised, most organisation would take place in response to local needs, and the end of such programmes would be the creation of a decentralised institutional base that reached beyond university campuses. This project of localised institution building began to be put into practice after a series of discussions in 1971 regarding Community Development Proposals, modelled on the orientation projects discussed at the Formation School. These proposals presented a budget for the organisation of eight regional and two national seminars, at which further education initiatives would be discussed, as well as for the production a SASO Newsletter and other periodicals which would, eventually, lay the ground for an extensive literacy project aimed both at youth and at adult learners.

In 1972, then, a new organisation – the Black Community Programme (BCP) – was created by SASO to put these proposals into practice.[32] The BCP would work on orientation and self-reliance projects in local communities while SASO itself continued to organise students, and to develop black self-consciousness amongst its particular constituency.

But these strategies all required time: time to build networks, to develop organisations, and to raise popular consciousness. It is clear

---

[32] WHP A2675/III/747, Community Development Proposals.

that SASO's leaders understood that this work would not yield rapid results: when calling upon SASO members to dedicate themselves to the work of consciousness-raising, for example, Biko and others also emphasised that 'the task to which we wish to dedicate ourselves may demand from us a lifetime of application'.[33]

The emergence of SASO and its affiliated organisations changed South Africa's political scene. The implications of this change were not immediately clear, however. At first, SASO's conciliatory approach to NUSAS obscured the radicalism of its political claims. In addition, the caution with which the organisation intervened in public politics may have obscured its challenge to the apartheid order – and may indeed have permitted the state to imagine that its ends were innocuous. Nonetheless, within two years of its emergence, the ideas and practices of Black Consciousness were beginning to demonstrate their effects on the new politics of dissent.

After 1968, Steve Biko, Barney Pityana, and other black representatives of SASO began to engage in political debates as representatives of black students, challenging the right and the ability of NUSAS to speak on the behalf of these students. NUSAS, at first, did not fully appreciate this challenge, as their actions in the wake of the 1970 protests suggest. However, the straightforward rejection of NUSAS's attempts to direct and lead all students clearly demonstrated SASO's position – and was closely connected to the movement's official break from existing student politics. In the years following, it became impossible for white students to speak on behalf of black students and, more generally, for white activists to imagine that they could represent black communities.

By placing black activists at the heart of the new politics emerging from these initial experiments in resistance, the rhetoric of political opposition shifted. Instead of representation, it became about self-expression and identification. Instead of allowing NUSAS to make demands on behalf of an excluded community of black students, that community insisted on making its own case, in its own manner. This, in turn, forced NUSAS to consider its position, to base its political claims on the social positions of its own members and to insist on their rights to participate in politics. Meanwhile, black activists were setting out on their own paths, and establishing their own projects.

Ideologically, too, the efforts of SASO to consider the intellectual, cultural and religious aspects of Black Consciousness as part and parcel of a political programme worked to reshape political possibilities. Instead of participating in a debate over the legitimacy of student participation in 'the political sphere' – as the government had earlier characterised NUSAS's attempts to engage in public politics – Black Consciousness

---

[33] WHP A2675/III/744, 'Practical Applications of the Ideology of Black Consciousness' (1970).

thought redefined the sphere of politics, including in it a range of activities and practices that would not fit the classic institutional definition in use at the time. The practices of dress and grooming, of self-definition and identity, and of belief and faith were all part of a new political field. In this expanded field, political identity could be birthed in apparently 'private' spaces, it could grow and develop away from public confrontation with the state, and it could emerge fully formed at the end of a localised process of self-development.

The effect of this was to broaden the possibilities of politics: to insist that any form of action, public or private, had political consequences and was thus political. SASO sought to exploit these new possibilities through the development of a multi-pronged approach to action, bringing together student organisation, community education and individual work on self-consciousness. These would provide a new form of organisation and activism for a new realm of politics.

SASO's members would need time to succeed in their aims, perhaps even 'a lifetime of application'. But time was one thing that could not be guaranteed and, as the state began to respond to the wave of resistance, many of the ideals of Black Consciousness would soon be forced to fall by the wayside.

3 Confrontation, Resistance and Reaction

'THE MINISTER ... CANNOT BAN IDEAS FROM MEN'S MINDS'

In 1971, SASO circulated a document titled 'The Politics of Protest for Black Students' that set out a limited case for black students' involvement in public forms of politics, over and above the forms of community engagement described in the previous chapter. This case was founded on black students' natural 'concern for social upliftment' arising out of their own 'poor family background'. Black students, SASO suggested, were uncertain about the prospects of future employment in apartheid South Africa – and would thus consider participating in politics that would provide them with greater long-term security. In addition, 'the situation in black universities' was fraught with tensions – making political activism more likely to occur in this immediate context. Overall, students would also benefit from the 'intellectual discovery' that might arise from engaging with certain forms of political protest.

If this case for action was accepted, then the aims of that action could be considered. In part, political involvement should help link SASO to broader community networks: it should 'spread the front for activism' and rouse 'the consciousness of black people'. But it should also work to deepen social engagement within university campuses: action should enable students 'to record dissatisfaction and to express opinion', it should 'instil confidence' in them, and permit them 'to rally adequate bargaining power'. In this context, bargaining and negotiation were the preferred forms of engagement between students and university authorities – but in certain cases, boycotts, marches, 'placards, statements, meetings' could also be used in the service of change.[1]

In this document, SASO sought to lay the foundations for a lengthy period of activism on campuses and in communities. Its instructions to students presumed a continuing relationship between activists and administrators. Over time, an accord would develop between all stakeholders: it was not in the interests of students to be over-aggressive in confronting the administration. Instead, SASO sought to encourage all parts of the university – students and administrators alike – to work towards a unity of purpose. Its advice presumed that, as such a shared

[1]   WHP A2675/III/748, Memo: The Politics of Protest for Black students.

purpose developed on a given campus, the 'difference in ideals' which had led to conflict would be resolved.

This approach resembles one that Biko would later describe as being a 'third idiom' of politics – action that took place 'within the ambit of the law' while challenging the existing distribution of power within apartheid society. It was an approach that eschewed confrontation with the state, and worked, instead, to provide SASO and Black Consciousness with the space to develop slowly.[2]

However, SASO found consensual 'third-idiom' politics difficult to put into practice – even given the relatively contained context of a university campus. The visibility of NUSAS's protests had had an undeniable influence on black students, and SASO faced pressures from students to support protests to alter conditions on university campuses. Before long, black students were exceeding the suggestions laid out by SASO's leaders. As activism spread on these campuses, events overwhelmed the model set out in 'The Politics of Protest' and attempts at engaging with university administrators 'within the ambit of the law' backfired. Confrontations erupted on campuses, ending the possibility of a 'third idiom' to achieve a politics of consensual engagement.

Meanwhile, white students were facing their own dilemmas. NUSAS's leaders hoped to extend their political reach, but needed to find causes that permitted them to act. Both the visibility of the campaign to charge or release Winnie Mandela and the successful defence of the students arrested in that campaign had emboldened NUSAS but neither provided the foundations for future action. NUSAS needed to reckon with SASO's critique of its practices of representation – and to reckon with the need to avoid replicating their earlier mistakes. The largest issue, however, arose from chance developments of the most effective of NUSAS's protests: its successes in the recent past had occurred when events exceeded expectations, and small protests became highly public causes. Although the 'Charge or release' campaign had been relatively planned – at least in contrast to the protests of the 1960s – it had still emerged in the context of a Black Sash campaign, and had only achieved its public impact when the police intervened and arrested several hundred students. But these events were difficult to anticipate. So long as the model of student politics relied on the chance to catalyse events, NUSAS would struggle to build on their existing successes or develop a new politics.

In the first years of the new decade, both student movements found themselves in uncertain positions and in an implicit dialogue with each other. Where SASO sought to refrain from entering into confrontations with the state, NUSAS sought for opportunities to do so. Neither movement was able to control the contexts within which they acted,

[2]   Steve Biko, *The Testimony of Steve Biko*, ed. M. Arnold (London, Maurice Temple Smith: 1979), pp. 85–7.

and both had to juggle internal and external pressures on the development of their respective approaches. In particular, both were forced to engage with university administrators to carve out a space for political action on campus. This meant that both sought to experiment with ways of developing forms of resistance and political action. Of course, experiments do not always produce the expected results.

This chapter examines how these experiments in resistance developed. They often started from small events, or from clashes on campus, and then escalated as student activism over-spilled both the ideological and the material confines of the university. As these protests developed and spread, the state began to respond to them with increasing violence – and, in the confrontations between authority and students, a new realignment of the political possibilities of public protest began to emerge, and develop.

In this process, the carefully-planned development of a 'third idiom' of politics envisaged by SASO in 1971 was soon swept away by the flood of events. These events – and the responses of the powerful – sometimes highlighted the differences between the situations of white and black students. But they also underlined the ways in which students shared experiences of protest in the face of an increasingly brutal police force, and in the face of an increasingly repressive order. In this period, both NUSAS and SASO had to deal with changing circumstances on their separate university campuses, and to respond to the unpredictable pressures placed on public forms of protest by the government, by university administrators, by courts, and by the police. These events reshaped the possibilities of public activism for both organisations, and set the stage for their development in the coming years.

Trouble at Turfloop

For SASO, the most significant of these events occurred midway through 1972 at the University of the North, known informally as 'Turfloop'. This gave rise to a large-scale protest that would shape the organisation's future.[3]

Its origins were inauspicious: during the second half of 1971, a series of clashes between students and administrators at the university prompted SASO to write to the university's Rector. In this letter, SASO

---

[3] Some of the material in this section has been previously published as J. Brown, 'SASO's Reluctant Embrace of Public Forms of Protest, 1968–1972,' *South African Historical Journal*, 62 (4), 2010, pp. 716–34. A recent article that engages with this material is Anne Heffernan, 'Black Consciousness's Lost Leader: Abraham Tiro, the University of the North, and the Seeds of South Africa's Student Movement in the 1970s', *Journal of Southern African Studies*, 2015, Vol. 41, No. 1, pp. 173–86.

suggested that the university act to resolve tensions with the student body. The letter recommended that the university's staff be increasingly Africanised – that is, that hiring practices should be altered to ensure that the majority of the teaching staff at the university were black – and that the minority of black academics already at the university be promoted to senior administrative positions, including that of Rector. The letter also recommended that a commission be established 'to look into university education' and to propose a redeveloped curriculum for the university. Finally, it advised that the administration should recognise SASO as an organisation that represented black students on the campus, and enter in dialogue with it accordingly.[4]

The content of this letter was compatible with the plans set out in 'The Politics of Protest'. Its recommendations sought to establish an engagement with the university's administration in a firm but constructive manner; they set out specific steps that could address students' issues, and remake the campus into a better environment. The letter invited future dialogue with the administration, and welcomed it into this conversation. There is no evidence that the university ever replied to this letter.

Months later, in March 1972, a confrontation between staff and students erupted. When the university's administrators saw that two texts circulated by SASO – the 'SASO Manifesto' and its 'Declaration of Student Rights' – had been included in the body of a diary distributed by the Turfloop SRC, they insisted that these texts be removed. This act of censorship sparked discontent on the campus. Students burned their diaries in a show of dissent, and elected Onkgopotse Tiro – the previous year's SRC president, now a graduate student, and a member of SASO – to address the annual graduation ceremony on their behalf. Both actions were clear responses to the university's actions, and signalled the students' support for SASO.[5]

Tiro's address, however, went beyond what anyone might have expected. It began by quoting a statement made by the country's Prime Minister, B.J. Vorster, arguing that in South Africa 'no Black man has landed in trouble for fighting for what is legally his'. Rather than draw attention to the obvious disingenuousness of the statement, Tiro used it as an excuse to speak about the government's Bantu Education system. He condemned the system as providing an insufficiently critical education. Tiro then considered the operations of Turfloop itself: he pointed out that the parents of the graduating students were made to sit in secondary locations, and said that this was a sign of disrespect on the part the administration of university. He highlighted

---

[4] WHP A2675/III/748, Memo: SASO's Recommendations.
[5] The background to these events is covered in: M. Horrell, D. Horner, and J. Kane-Berman, *A Survey of Race Relations in South Africa, 1972* (Johannesburg, SAIRR: 1973), pp. 386–92.

the relative absence of the university's few black academics from its decision-making bodies. He told his audience – made up of administrators, faculty and students, as well as parents – that, in light of all this, 'the system is failing'. He then sought to suggest solutions to this failure and quoted Helen Suzman, then the Progressive Party's lone member of parliament, saying that whatever other powers the state might have, nonetheless, 'the Minister ... cannot ban ideas from men's minds'. Tiro finally ended, saying:

> Let the Lord be praised, for the day shall come when all shall be free to breathe the air of freedom which is theirs to breathe and when that day shall have come, no man, no matter how many tanks he has, will reverse the course of events.[6]

It is easy to imagine the silence that followed these words.

On 2 May 1972, three days after the graduation ceremony, that silence was broken. The university's disciplinary committee announced that Tiro was expelled from the university.

A petition calling for his reinstatement was quickly circulated by students, and then presented to the administration. It was rejected. Students then embarked upon a more confrontational protest, beginning a sit-in at the university's main hall. The administration responded by suspending the SRC and banning all public meetings. When this proved ineffective, it announced that all 1,146 protesting students were to be immediately expelled. To enforce this expulsion, the administration invited the local police on to the campus.

Despite this, the students refused to abandon their sit-in. In the face of their recalcitrance, the university and the police acted. The police cordoned off the hall, preventing food from being brought in. The administration cut off the building's water pipes. The police then prevented the occupying students from accessing the adjacent toilets and confined them within the central building – without access to food, water or sanitation. The blockade continued overnight and into the next day, until the students were finally forced to abandon the hall. The police allowed them to leave, and then sealed the boundaries of the campus and refused to allow anyone to return. By 6 May, a week after the graduation ceremony, the university was deserted.[7]

In this moment, it was possible for the university's administrators to imagine that they had succeeded in suppressing the protest. But if this was so, it was at best a pyrrhic victory.

---

[6] 'Graduation Speech, by O.R. Tiro at the University of the North, Turfloop, 29 April 1972', in Thomas Karis and Gail Gerhart (eds), *From Protest to Challenge: A Documentary History of African Politics in South Africa, 1882–1990. Volume 5: Nadir and Resurgence* (Bloomington and Indianapolis, University of Indiana Press: 1997), pp. 497–8.

[7] See the narrative in Horrell et al., *Survey 1972*.

Even before the mass expulsion, news of these events has begun to spread across the country. The first reactions came from students on other black university campuses across South Africa. On 5 May – while the students still occupied Turfloop's main hall – the student council at the University of Durban-Westville (UDW) held an emergency mass meeting, in part to 'support the students of the University of the North'. Their expression of support was then followed by boycotts of university-provided food services and lectures at the university on 7 and 8 May.[8] At the same time, students at the University of the Western Cape (UWC) had also summoned a mass meeting to pass a resolution supporting the stand taken by their peers at Turfloop; this resolution announced that all UWC students would 'symbolise their solidarity by staying away from classes throughout Tuesday 9th May.'[9]

In the days following, these protests spread. At UDW, a further two-day boycott of lectures followed the initial boycott. At UWC, students – buoyed by the successes of the boycott of lectures on 9 May – openly planned a boycott of university food services. On 12 May, students at the University of Natal's Non-European section began an indefinite boycott of lectures. The following week, students at the University of Zululand picketed their graduation ceremony. On 22 May, 700 students at Fort Hare began an eight-day-long boycott of lectures. In each of these examples, students at these campuses planned their protests in solidarity with the students of Turfloop. They relied on their internal organisational structures, rather than on any coordination that might have come from SASO's national executive, and they often tied issues arising out of their own campus experiences – over food services, teaching practices, and other administrative challenges – to their support for the struggles of the students of Turfloop. In essence, they produced an organic critique of the education system for black students – and suggested that this critique was generalisable across all similar institutions. A challenge to one was a challenge to all.

By contrast, the central executive of SASO was unable to respond quickly. It was only on 13 May – a full week after the Turfloop campus had been closed – that SASO released an official statement. This statement was produced by forty delegates at an emergency meeting convened at the regional Formation School being held in Alice, near the University of Fort Hare in the Eastern Cape. The delegates announced (somewhat belatedly) that they believed that 'the wait and see attitude … will be a betrayal to the Black man's struggle in this country'. They argued that the event at Turfloop should not be viewed 'as an isolated incident' – after all, 'Black students have long suffered under oppression'. Given this, the singular clash at Turfloop had the potential to 'be

---

[8] WHP A2675/III/749, Minutes of Emergency Mass Meeting.

[9] The details of protests in this and the following paragraph come from: WHP A2675/III/749, SASO Fact Paper: The Student Crisis. See also: Horrell et al., *Survey 1972*.

escalated into a major confrontation'. The delegates announced that SASO would now prepare for such a confrontation. They thus called upon 'all Black students [to] force the Institutions/Universities to close down by boycotting lectures' and gave a date on which this coordinated effort would take place – 'from June 1st'.[10]

Meanwhile, on 19 May, Barney Pityana – the General Secretary of SASO – wrote to the president of the SRC at UWC, hoping to solicit his support for SASO's national boycott. Pityana emphasised that at the Alice meeting the UWC SRC's 'show of solidarity with the exiled students of the University of the North was warmly applauded by all those present'. He suggested that the delegates to that meeting had been inspired by the example of protests at UWC and at UDW and had determined that 'it was essential that black students throughout the country demonstrate solidarity and pressurize the university authorities to "rethink"'. This process could only be coordinated by SASO; but, Pityana added, 'the final execution of it will remain with student leaders at a local level. Then it cannot be said that students didn't act when events dictated that they do.' He ended by asking UWC to support 'the principles behind the Alice Declaration' by urging 'all black students to stand together, differ in togetherness'.[11] Five days later, Pityana circulated an almost identical memo to all SRCs and SASO local committees, asking them to support the national boycott.[12]

The Alice Declaration stood as a significant break with SASO's official policy of avoiding reacting to singular events and risking confrontation with the state. But despite their unexpected militancy, the forty delegates at Alice had already been outpaced by events at black universities across the country. An unnamed student at the UDW summed up the attitude of black students in these weeks, saying that 'the air is thick with protest'. Only one institution was apparently willing to delay starting protests on its campus until 1 June: the Springfield College of Education. With the obvious exception of the University of the North, black students at every other major campus were already embroiled in public confrontations with their administrators. It was expected that the University of the North would in fact re-open on 1 June – a coincidence which may explain SASO's willingness to delay starting a nationwide protest until that date – and that its students would then be able to join the national boycott.[13]

By moving away from its stated policy of negotiations and engagement, SASO attempted to respond to the actions already being taken by its members across the country. The plan to coordinate a national boycott represented an attempt to regain control over the development

[10] WHP A2675/III/749, 'The Alice Declaration'.
[11] WHP A2675/III/749, Correspondence: Pityana to Lamoela (19 May 1972).
[12] WHP A2675/III/749, Circular: re. Alice Declaration on Turfloop Crisis.
[13] WHP A2675/III/749, SASO Fact Paper: The Student Crisis.

of student protest. While students at black universities did protest on 1 June, they had been already doing so for some weeks. SASO was playing catch-up with its members. This was certainly the impression that many of its members had developed.

After SASO's failure to successfully coordinate a national boycott, a meeting of SRC presidents from black campuses across the country was convened in Durban on 17 June. Here, the presidents grilled SASO for its perceived lack of leadership. They complained that the Alice Declaration had been 'published in the Sunday press even before the SRCs were consulted' and that this pre-emption of discussion by SASO suggested that it had been trying to 'intimidate' students into following its agenda, rather than allowing them to make their own plans themselves. They recognised that 'as a national organisation whose aim it is to cater for and protect the interests of black students, SASO found itself in a dilemma where the leadership called upon SASO to keep out as the issues were local ... However, as the activities escalated, the students were looking for direction from SASO.' This meant that SASO often acted – in the eyes of the student council presidents – either inappropriately or prematurely. Its intervention was first unwanted, and then inadequately planned: 'the Alice meeting never undertook any planning for follow up on the protest nor did it perceive or give direction to the future. This tended to make demonstrations boring and unproductive.' Overall, there had been an obvious 'lack of co-ordination'.[14]

In the joint report presented by the SASO executive at its annual general council – held on 2–9 July 1972 – these complaints were addressed. The executive officially welcomed the comments, but suggested that the criticism levelled against SASO's action in the course of the crisis was inappropriate. SASO's inability to coordinate had actually risen from the SRCs themselves: 'at local level SASO was kept out of the picture by the leadership which shunned "agitators' infiltration" charges by the authorities. This effectively kept SASO out of the picture.' The executive then proposed developing policies for coordinating and planning national protests, for consulting and organising at a grassroots level, and for laying out a 'follow-up machinery' for future protests.[15]

The sequence of events that had begun at the University of the North – and that had then galvanised local protests on already-strained black campuses across the country – thus led to SASO's executive proposing a significant shift in priorities. Instead of working towards laying a national foundation from which later – as yet undefined – politics could develop, SASO now had to consider how to shape and control already-existing protests. It was lurching towards adopting exactly the

14 WHP A2675/III/749, Minutes (17 June 1972).
15 WHP A2675/III/750, Executive Report to the 3rd Annual GSC (July 1972).

policies which it had earlier dismissed: policies in which its primary function was to react to unpredictable moments of protest and attempt to manage their volatile development.

These changes were not driven by either an ideological or a practical commitment to protest. Nor did they come from the central offices of SASO or its affiliates. Instead, they emerged despite the reluctance of SASO's leaders to embrace confrontational political tactics. They emerged as products of experimental protests – protests that were occurring without precedent, and with little sense of a predictable outcome – at local sites of student politics.

Beginning from a single event, the political situation rapidly developed in 1972. Rather than risk being lost dust raised by its members' independent actions, SASO was forced into a reluctant embrace of confrontation. This embrace would radically alter the terrain of possibility in the coming months.

'A little violence'

Meanwhile, the white students of NUSAS responded to these protests in their own way. On 22 May, NUSAS launched a national Free Education campaign across its affiliated campuses. This campaign had been planned to build on the tradition of the academic freedom campaigns of the 1950s and early 1960s, but these plans were altered by the sudden explosion of activism on black campuses.

NUSAS had planned a campaign of mass student meetings on campuses, and pamphleteering. Students at each of its affiliated campuses were encouraged to elaborate on the overall scheme and to organise their own local events. Perhaps unsurprisingly, many of these events tied the issues of academic freedom and autonomy to the other student protests already underway across the country. But where the black students' protests were largely confined to the space of their universities themselves – in part due to those universities' relative isolation from large cities – white student protest began to leave university campuses and enter into urban spaces.

In Cape Town, students held a demonstration outside the Houses of Parliament on Thursday 1 June, and then – following the relative success of the demonstration – decided to meet again on the next day. They reconvened on the steps of the St George's Cathedral and, according to the report of the Minister of Police, displayed 'posters displaying seditious slogans' while, 'as could be expected, the so-called freedom song, "We Shall Overcome," was sung time and again.'[16]

[16] These quotes, and those in the following paragraphs, can be found in the records of a parliamentary debate on the protest: RSA, *Debates of the House of Assembly* (Hansard), 5 June 1972, cols. 8705–10.

This protest began peacefully, with the police – according to the Minister's account – refraining from taking any action against the singing students. The gathering did not constitute a 'public meeting' until a student began to speak to the crowd through a loudhailer and – for the purposes of the text of the law – transformed the gathering. The police took the opportunity provided by this formal redefinition to attempt to arrest the leaders. At this point, again according to the Minister, 'girls shrieked and screamed hysterically and disorder resulted'. The police 'made use of batons' – that is to say, they charged the students and assaulted them; the violence of this confrontation spilled out into the surrounding crowd, catching up bystanders and reporters. Some students ran into the Cathedral, hoping to avoid the attack. The police followed them into the sanctuary, where they assaulted, subdued and then arrested them. This violence brought the protest to an end – but launched a new phase of political resistance.

The police violence provoked a national scandal – unlike, for example, the actions taken by the police at the University of the North a month earlier. The assaults were widely reported in the country's newspapers and a parliamentary snap debate was held on 5 June, the first working day after the protest. The defensiveness of the government was on display in this debate: several representatives condemned the protesters and supported the police; they described the protest songs, decried 'the appearance of young people nowadays' and expressed shock at, in particular, the 'dirty, long dresses and coats of the women' taking part. These various signs of illegality – or at least of disrespect for societal norms – were held to have justified the actions taken by the police. Opposition parliamentarians who ventured to suggest otherwise were heckled throughout. The Prime Minister entered into the debate to shrug off any criticism of the police actions as essentially naive, given the scale of the threat apparently posed by NUSAS and the student protesters in Cape Town. He said: 'if it is necessary to use a little violence, to use rubber batons, to nip in the bud what has been planned against South Africa, we shall not hesitate to do so'.

This was not the end, though. Similar protests and similar clashes took place across South Africa. On 7 June, for example, police dogs were used to disperse a picket at the Pietermaritzburg campus of the University of Natal. In Durban a handful of students were arrested for putting up posters over the same days. In Grahamstown, 321 students and university staff members were arrested for taking part in a public protest march from the university campus.[17]

Meanwhile, throughout this period, a week-long programme of protests took place at the University of the Witwatersrand in Johannesburg. On Monday 5 June, 800 students marched from the main

[17] Horrell et al., *Survey 1972*.

university campus into Johannesburg, ending at St Mary's Cathedral. This march was declared illegal, and the police used tear gas to disperse the participants. In an echo of events in Cape Town, students and other bystanders rushed into the Cathedral to seek relief from the police assault. The next day students continued to pamphleteer residential areas around the university. Several were arrested and charged with 'obstruction'. On Tuesday, Wednesday, Thursday and Friday pickets were held on a strip of university land facing Jan Smuts Avenue, a major city byway. Each day, the police arrested students from this picket – and twice, on Wednesday and Friday, assaulted students with rubber batons. On Friday 9 June, a large group of uniformed and plain-clothes policemen used tear gas and a violent baton charge to break up the picket. Afterwards, 71 of the demonstrating students were arrested and charged with contravening the Riotous Assemblies Act.[18]

Despite the events in Cape Town, the violence of the police caught these students by surprise. The statements recorded by their legal team after the event suggest that they had come – through the course of the week of protest – to expect some restraint on the part of the police: several students believed that the police could not or would not inter-fere in a protest so long as it was held on university property. The students had come to recognise the presence of a senior police officer and had come to associate him with an approachable authority. In fact, the president of the Wits SRC remembered complaining to him about the plainclothes men lurking nearby.[19]

It was the ambiguous presence of these plainclothes men rather than the presence of the uniformed police that inspired the greatest concern amongst the students. This was not unfounded. Photographs of the area around the picket line show the uniformed police in a deep line, attended by journalists and photographer, while a mass of plainclothes men stood in suits and ties, their hand tucked into their pockets, waiting to one side. Shortly after 14h00 on that Friday afternoon, several of these plainclothes men left their positions and began to mingle amongst the students – prompting complaints about their presence. Approximately half an hour later, the uniformed police ordered all members of the public to leave the campus; they followed this order with an announcement, delivered through a loudspeaker, that the picket and the gathering of students now constituted an illegal meeting and, as such, contravened the Riotous Assemblies Act. The protesting students were given three minutes to disperse voluntarily; they were told that, after those minutes had elapsed, the police would then act to disperse them.

---

[18] Horrell et al., *Survey 1972*, pp. 393–4. See also the statements made by the arrested students to their lawyers: WHP AK3166/3 (Raymond Tucker, Attorney) WITS Students vs Minister of Justice – and Minister of Police.

[19] WHP AK3166/3, Statement of Kenneth Costa.

Students began to leave the picket. Some abandoned their posters and placards on the ground, while others chose to walk away still carrying them. Most moved towards the main campus grounds; a minority dropped their placards and sat in their original places.

At the end of the three minutes, plainclothes men charged into the retreating students: 'The next thing I remember was all the plain-clothes yanking long rubber batons out of their pockets and dashing towards us. It had never occurred to me that they had batons in their pockets.' A photograph shows six men in plainclothes gathered around a single student. His shirt has been pulled over his head and he is being pushed to the ground; at least two of his assailants are wielding batons; three of them are beating him, either with batons or with their fists. In the background, more men holding batons can be seen while a camera films the scene.

Students reported being dragged along the ground by their hair, kicked and stamped upon, and beaten. Although not every student was assaulted, all testified – in affidavits and then in the course of their eventual trial, in August – to having seen similar assaults occurring around them.[20]

In 1970, the relatively peaceful arrest of 357 students outside the police headquarters in Johannesburg had been hailed by NUSAS as 'the most significant [event] in the history of student protest in South Africa'. Only two years later, though, mass arrests – accompanied by violent threats, assaults, and serious criminal charges – were becoming normal. The arrest of 321 students in Grahamstown did not merit a headline even in the *NUSAS Newsletter*. For observers, the violence of the state was still shocking – but Vorster's glib invocation of 'a little violence' to prevent a greater violence provided activists with a taste of the untrammelled brutality that was to come.

'Terror in the suburbs'

Violence did not only erupt in the course of protests, however – and was not the sole purview of the police. In the course of June 1972 a small group of white, right-wing vigilantes in Cape Town set out to express their opposition to the actions of white students and their supporters. These incidents give an impression of how student protests were seen by radical conservatives.

The prelude to this took place a year earlier: in June 1971, a petrol bomb was thrown at a house occupied by Geoff Budlender – a prom-inent student activist and president of the UCT SRC. According to

---

[20] The photographs can be seen in the *Cape Times*, 10 August 1972. Further details of the narrative can be drawn from the affidavits and documents kept by the students' legal team WHP AK3166/3, WITS Students.

newspaper accounts, the house was blackened by the fire but its inhabitants were unharmed. In August and October that year, the tyres of cars belonging to UCT lecturers and to students known to be active in NUSAS were slashed; several of their windscreens were also smashed. No official investigation seems to have been able to identify these assailants.[21]

A year later, these assaults began again. Early in June 1972, as student protests were spreading, an attempt was made to set fire to the Ecumenical Centre in Mowbray, where the Christian Institute had its offices. The Christian Institute had been founded in the early 1960s and had campaigned openly against the apartheid system. It was led by the Rev. C.F. Beyers Naudé, a dissident member of the Dutch Reformed Church and an especial thorn in the side of the National Party government. On 8 June and 10 June petrol bombs were then thrown at the home of the Rev. Theo Kotze, the regional director of the Christian Institute. Neither bomb exploded. Then, on 22 June – almost exactly one year after the previous attempt – another bomb was thrown at Budlender's home.

At the start of July a number of pamphlets were anonymously distributed throughout Cape Town. The pamphlets linked NUSAS and the Christian Institute to communism, atheism, homosexuality, perversion, drug addiction and Judaism.[22] A month later, yet another petrol bomb was thrown at Budlender's house – a different house this time, shared with several other students. This attack was more effective, and the building was damaged by the resulting fires. Budlender had been addressing a meeting in Rondebosch, and this meeting had also been attacked, albeit by a milder intervention: 'sneezing powder thrown through the windows during the speeches had caused the meeting to end early'.[23] Shortly after that attack, on the night of 23 August, at least three shots were fired at Rev. Kotze's home. No one came forward to claim responsibility for either attack.[24]

On 10 September another pamphlet appeared in Cape Town, signed with the name 'Scorpio'. It did not directly claim responsibility for bombing Budlender's home, but instead suggested that 'the hovel of the little leftist jew Budlender' had been not been attacked, but had rather burned when 'a cache of arms and explosives had inadvertently blown up'.[25] The *Cape Times* noted on the publication of this pamphlet that 'Scorpio' had been the pen-name of the villain in the film *Dirty*

[21] *Cape Times*, 11 September 1972.
[22] *Cape Times*, 28 and 30 September 1972.
[23] *Cape Times*, 22 August 1972.
[24] *Cape Times*, 24 August 1972.
[25] This pamphlet is quoted in: *NUSAS Newspaper*, 8 September 1972. (Confusingly, this newsletter is dated 8 September, despite referring extensively to events reported to have occurred on 10 September. It seems plausible to attribute the earlier date on the newsletter to a printing error.)

Harry – which had recently been shown in Cape Town.[26] The style of this pamphlet and the adoption of the *nom de guerre* of a Hollywood villain support the idea that this was the product of a vigilante organisation, placing itself outside of the law in its policing of social boundaries.

Scorpio's assault on these individuals and their supporters continued. Over the next months, vitriolic and vicious graffiti appeared on walls across Cape Town – on the offices of the Progressive Party, for example, proclaiming the organisation to be home to 'Jew/Nigger Lovers', and on the door of the *Cape Times* itself – labelling the newspaper with a hammer-and-sickle symbol.[27] Meanwhile, a man claiming to be Scorpio telephoned the newspaper to say that he would kill Kotze – a threat serious enough to cause the police to place officers on guard duty.[28]

Throughout this period, a series of highly critical editorials appeared in the Cape newspapers, suggesting that the government had little interest in investigating the case: 'as things stand now, no South African can feel free to express anti-Nationalist views in strong terms without risking a petrol bomb in the night'. The overall theme of these editorials was found in one phrase – 'terror in the suburbs' – used by the *Cape Times* on at least four occasions in the period; the violence of these vigilantes had exceeded all ordinary bounds, and entered into suburban space.[29]

The authority of the state was in fact challenged by the existence of the vigilante group – and although their aims might not differ, the state could not permit Scorpio to continue to operate. At the end of September, the police offered a reward for information leading to the arrest and conviction of Scorpio; in October, the *Sunday Times* offered to double the reward.

Finally, the police arrested two men. The first, Desmond Welthagen, had already appeared in local newspapers, complaining of being terrorised by 'some left wing troublemakers'. He was the secretary and founder of the National Anti-Terrorism Organisation (NATO) – an organisation that does not seem to have commanded any significant membership – and had publicly supported the police in their use of violence against protesting students.[30] He was charged with six counts of criminal libel and one of illegally possessing explosives. However, the judge in the trial disregarded most of the prosecution's evidence, characterising it as inconsistent, and dismissed the charges against Welthagen. His co-accused, David Beelders, was only convicted of one

---

26 *Cape Times*, 11 September 1972.
27 *Cape Times*, 4 October and 29 September 1972.
28 *Cape Times*, 13 September 1972.
29 *Cape Times*, 11 September 1972.
30 *Cape Times*, 25 September 1972.

charge: writing the words 'Communist Den' on a wall belonging to the University of Cape Town. He was required to pay a fine of R150.00 (the wage of about one week for an urban professional). Most importantly, though neither of the men was convicted on the most serious charge – that of illegally possessing explosives.[31]

Although seemingly minor, these incidents suggest something of the heated context within which white students were operating. Threats of violence were most acute in the course of protests and public actions – but could exceed them, and spill over into everyday life. Embarking upon confrontational forms of politics was not in any sense a safe endeavour: it brought students not only to the attention of the state, but also to the attention of other opponents. It also brought them into the criminal justice system, and branded them as opponents of the state. In the context of violent reaction, NUSAS's experiments in protest worked to place their participants outside of white society – and thus outside of the field of racial privilege that would otherwise have protected them from the depredations of radicalised reactionaries.

Experiments in response and reaction

Direct violence was not the only form that official reaction took. In the immediate aftermath of the May and June protests, the state sought to consolidate its control over university campuses and student life – and, in doing so, starve student movements of their support. The effects of these efforts differed dramatically between white and black campuses – with white universities resisting the state, and black universities aiding its work.

In the wake of the violence deployed against white student protests in Cape Town and Johannesburg, the administrations of UCT and Wits both attempted to develop legal strategies to prevent a repeat of the police assault – and, hopefully, to prevent the state from proceeding to prosecute their students. The first test of this strategy occurred in Cape Town on Wednesday 7 June 1972. Students at UCT had announced that they planned to mount a picket on the steps of Jameson Hall – a venue on the university grounds, one that was visible from the main road that bisects the Cape Town campus. Early on the same morning, the Minister of Justice issued a notice prohibiting the gathering. The students chose to ignore it. The police then came onto the campus and forcibly dispersed the protest, once again assaulting students.

Almost immediately, the university administration swung into action. It filed an injunction in the Cape Supreme Court arguing that the university campus was private property – and thus not a public space.

[31] *Cape Times*, 16 and, 15 December 1972.

The police should not have entered the campus without the explicit permission of the administration, and thus their actions were extra-legal. Furthermore – and perhaps more importantly – the university argued that the Riotous Assemblies Act did not apply to any demonstrations or meetings held on private property. It could not therefore be used to prosecute students arrested on the 'private' campus.[32]

This two-pronged argument – both prongs of which rested on the assertion that the university campus was not a public space – came before the court two days later. Justice Watermeyer noted that the Riotous Assemblies Act stipulated that a public place was: 'any street, road, passage, square, park or recreation grounds or any open space to which all members of the public habitually or by right have access. It includes any place described in the definition notwithstanding that it is private property.' He then asked the university administration whether this did not in fact describe their campus. In response, the administration argued that the campus was a strictly private space to which no members of the public had the automatic right to access; the campus grounds, buildings, etc., were not habitually used by the public in the sense of the Act. The police did not accept this, and insisted that members of the public did access the campus grounds. Watermeyer postponed the case, but granted a temporary injunction in favour of the university, preventing the police from enforcing the Act on the campus until the court next sat.

On the same day, police in Johannesburg moved onto the Wits campus to break up an already-dispersing picket and, in so doing, assaulted several students, and arrested seventy-one of them. Immediately following these arrests, the principal of the university, Professor G.R. Bozzoli, filed an application in the Witwatersrand Supreme Court, calling for the charges to be dismissed and the arrested students to be released. The same argument was made: the campus was not a public space and, therefore, the students' picket was not in contravention of the Act. The police were not entitled to enter the campus, the arrests were invalid and the students' detention was illegal.[33]

However, unlike in Cape Town, the presiding judge, Justice Snyman, was notably unsympathetic to the university's claims. He immediately dismissed the suggestion that the public was not permitted to access the campus; he also dismissed the idea that members of the public did not habitually make use of it, either as a thoroughfare or to attend cultural and sporting events. He did not necessarily base his interpretation of the case solely on that supposition, however, but also

[32] This and the following paragraphs are based on the records of this and other trials preserved in WHP AK3166/3 (Raymond Tucker, Attorney) WITS Students vs Minister of Justice – and Minister of Police. See: 'Supreme Court, Cape of Good Hope Provincial Division. Case no. M777/72'.
[33] WHP AK3166/3, 'Supreme Court, Witwatersrand Local Division. Case no. M1351/72'.

argued that even if the campus grounds could plausibly be described as private, the particular space on which the picket had taken place was inarguably public. This stretch of land faced directly onto a major public road; Snyman noted that the picket was clearly presented towards this road, and not towards the campus itself. He found a precedent in a case of indecent exposure, dating from 1909, in which the defendant – although on his own property – had been seen from a public place. The defendant had thus been successfully prosecuted for contravening statutes against public nudity. Justice Snyman added a second analogy, suggesting that if a person chose to stand 'on a private verandah' and shout 'obscene language to a person passing on a public road' this would still count as public obscenity, even though the words had been uttered on private property. These comparisons suggested that 'the demonstration [was] intended that others might see, and [that] it would be nonsense to pretend that they were not demonstrating to the people on the street and passersby'. The picket was therefore public and fell under the provisions of the Act.

Snyman dismissed the university's application and permitted the police to continue to hold the students, and to charge them with contravening the Riotous Assemblies Act. Only days later, however – on 13 June – a second judge in the Cape Supreme Court – Justice J.F. Beyers – upheld Watermeyer's original injunction and extended it indefinitely, thus challenging the interpretation made by Snyman. The police were not entitled to enter the UCT campus, so long as the university undertook to discourage members of the public from it and so long as any gathering of students – 'to which members of the public are not invited' – took place within a delineated area on the campus. This area was set between the steps leading from University Avenue to the entrance of the Jameson Hall, 'including the sidewalk on the mountain side of University Avenue'. As this street could function as a public thoroughfare, Beyers' judgment permitted these students to do what students at Wits had been forbidden to do: demonstrate in the sight of a potential audience.[34]

The two judgments set differing precedents – neither of which were developed in the years following. However, the shared approach of the universities to the defence of their students is notable, and established a model for the protection of the rights of students to act politically.

This was not the model followed by the administrators of black universities, however. At these universities, administrators assumed responsibility for suppressing protests. Protesting students were either expelled or suspended for an indefinite period of time and, consequently, were forced to leave the university grounds – and possibly to abandon their studies entirely. When students did not obey the university's expulsion

[34] WHP AK3166/3, 'Supreme Court, Cape of Good Hope Provincial Division. Case no. M775/72'.

order and chose to remain, administrators rarely hesitated before inviting the police to enforce their shaky authority. The most dramatic example was the end of the protests at the University of the North, in May 1972, but a similar sequence of events marked the conclusion of protests at UDW, UWC, the Springfield College of Education, the Transvaal College of Education and the M.L. Sultan Technical College. Students at these universities were suspended until they submitted letters of apology to the university administration. Only then were they to be readmitted under newly stringent conditions.[35]

The role of the police in the protests on these campuses was significant. At the University of the North they starved the students out of the sit-in; at UWC they detained and interrogated members of the local SASO committee; at Fort Hare, they arrested the head of the SASO committee, while conducting a series of night raids for the purpose of disrupting the student boycott of campus food services and lectures. In each of these cases, their presence on campuses was enabled by the weak institutional authority of the administrators at these universities, and their effectiveness was enhanced by the spatial confines of the student protests.

In regard to the first of these two factors, the Rectors and governing councils of black universities and colleges were appointed directly by the country's President, on the advice of the government and the Minister of Bantu Education. They were not, therefore, answerable to their respective academic communities and struggled to command the loyalties of either staff or students. Turfloop provides an example. It had only recently, in 1970, been reorganised under the formal designation of a university. It was administered by a Rector, assisted by a governing Council consisting of seventeen people. This Council – until 1974 – consisted only of white appointees. A second body – the 'Advisory Council' – consisted of eight black appointees who were expected to be available to the Rector whenever he decided that he ought to consult them. They had no formal decision-making authority within the university's structures. In addition, the President and the Minister of Bantu Education retained the power to appoint not only the Rector himself, but also fifteen out of the seventeen members of the governing Council, and all eight black members of the Advisory Council. (The final two members of the governing Council were elected by the faculty; they were the only academic appointees in the administration.)[36]

Following the university's reorganisation, a new Rector had been appointed – the second in the institution's history. Professor J.L. Boshoff was taken from an administrative position in the Depart-

[35] Horrell et al., *Survey 1972*, pp. 387–92.
[36] J.G.E. Wolfson (ed.), *Turmoil at Turfloop: A Summary of the Reports of the Snyman and Jackson Commissions of Inquiry into the University of the North* (Johannesburg, SAIRR: 1976), pp. 3–8.

ment of Bantu Education; he had never worked as an academic and had never occupied any position, administrative or otherwise, in any tertiary education institution. His appointment was criticised by the university's academic staff, as well as by the student body. In a set of 'reminiscences' printed for the university's Jubilee, Boshoff observed that he had been perceived as an 'ogre' by both the faculty and the students of the university.[37] (He also maintained that he had been able to overcome this characterisation in the course of his years at the university.) Attempts were made to ease tensions by holding a series of official inquiries into the problems faced by the university in 1972 and in 1974 – both years in which major student protests occurred. Both inquiries reached similar findings, including noting 'the desirability of appointing a black chancellor and a racially-mixed Council' and 'the need for administrative staff to conduct themselves in a polite, tactful manner towards the students' – findings which echoed SASO's call for the Africanisation of the university in the latter half of 1971. Both inquiries also emphasised that these problems – of the administration's perceived illegitimacy and its heavy-handed approach to student relations – had contributed significantly to the rise of student protests on campus.[38]

The institutional weaknesses of the university's administrators left them without the ability to discipline students. They suspended and expelled in part because they were incapable of using less punitive means of discipline. Likewise, their practical inability to enforce even these stringent measures led them to invite the local police forces onto the campuses.

The enforcement of these methods of repression by the police was often dependent on the recognition of the spatial constraints of these campuses. Unlike the protests undertaken by students at UCT and Wits, those at the Universities of the North and Fort Hare took place almost entirely within the confines of their campuses. They took the form of boycotts of lectures and of food services; these boycotts were rendered more effective by the relatively large numbers of students resident on campus. The relative smallness of the towns surrounding Fort Hare and the University of the North, too, may have contributed to containing these student protests to the campuses. Although students at some black universities – most notably at UDW and Zululand – adopted more publicly confrontational forms of protest, including picket lines, these forms of protest were notable largely for their absence from the

[37] See: C.H. Muller (ed.), *University of the North Jubilee Publication 1980* (Pietersburg, University of the North: 1980), 17–18, 'Reminiscences of the second Rector of the University of the North'.
[38] Wolfson, *Turmoil at Turfloop*, p. 97. For a very detailed account of the frustrations of the black academic staff, see: G.M. Nkondo (ed.), *Turfloop Testimony: The Dilemma of a Black University in South Africa* (Johannesburg, Ravan: 1976).

majority of black campuses. Most protests were therefore contained, and directed internally at the administrators, not at an external public.

Expulsions can therefore be seen as attempts to end the protests by displacing students. They were expelled from the campus, and then kept away from the university – through period of mass suspension – until the moment of crisis seemed to have passed. The actions of the police at the University of the North – expelling students, and then preventing them from returning – fit into this pattern of response. Later actions, such as the harassment of SASO leaders at the University of Fort Hare or the University of the Western Cape's promulgation of new regulations banning SASO from organising on its campus, can also be seen fitting this general pattern.

The result of these actions was a radical curtailment of the already limited opportunities for black students to express any form of political protest. The new regulations at UWC, for example, prohibited students from either joining or belonging to any organisation that had not been formally vetted by the administration. They also prohibited the production or distribution of any written statements that had not been examined by the administration. The university did not hesitate to enforce these regulations. In July 1972, the newly elected president of SASO, Jerry Modisane – a student at Fort Hare – attempted to visit UWC; on his arrival, the university administration summoned the police. Modisane was arrested and fined for trespassing; other students involved in his visit were detained and interrogated by the security police. Several black lecturers criticised the university's decision to involve the police, and were themselves to be detained and interrogated before long.

Under these circumstances, black students were encouraged to abandon their formal studies. Karis and Gerhart record that more than half of the student body of the University of North – over 500 students – refused to accept the conditions placed by the administration on their readmission and vowed not to return. Of these, at least 100 chose to abandon their studies; at the University of Zululand another thirty students followed suit. Karis and Gerhart note that the figures offered in the records varied widely, and that these figures are conservative. Horrell's annual survey suggests that up to 160 students may have also left the Fort Hare in the same month. For purposes of comparison, it is worth noting that 1,146 students were enrolled at the University of the North, 837 at Zululand and 2,004 at Fort Hare.[39] The proportion of students affected by suspension was high – and although in this first year of protests only a small number dropped out, this number would only increase in the coming years.

[39] Karis and Gerhart, *From Protest to Challenge, Volume 5*, p. 126; Horrell et al., *Survey, 1972*, p. 383.

Ambiguities of engagement

Not all of this story was readily available to commentators on political developments at the time. Karis and Gerhart suggest that, in this period, protests by white students overshadowed the protests organised and conducted by black students – both in the general public view, and in the view of the state – and, in doing so, acted to obscure SASO's political radicalisation.[40]

This is confirmed by an exchange in the course of the parliamentary debate on 5 June 1972, following the protests both at the University of the North and at other campuses. In his speech, the Minister of Police, S.L. Muller, linked NUSAS to black student protest. He described the events on the various black campuses, and acknowledged the influence of SASO in attempting to coordinate the separate protests. Immediately, however, he suggested that: 'NUSAS did everything in its power in an attempt to retain the favour of the non-White students.' He added that NUSAS had 'promised its unqualified support to SASO' and was thus attempting – through these protests –'to enhance its prestige amongst Black students'. It appears that the Minister believed that protests at black universities could only be explained by invoking the baleful – and largely imaginary – influence of NUSAS's members on black students.[41]

It is important to avoid falling both into this trap and into another. The state's fantasies of NUSAS's influence on SASO's action were clearly untrue – paranoid exaggerations that presumed the intellectual and political subservience of black students. This is the first trap. We should not replicate these fever dreams. Yet, nor should we assume that in rejecting the feverish assertions of the government we must necessarily reject all connections between NUSAS and SASO, between white and black students. To assume this is to fall into a second trap – one that inverts the fantasies of the state to refute them, but does not engage with actual political practice.

In the years after the formation of SASO, both student organisations were engaged in an implicit dialogue. The leaders of NUSAS sought to reclaim some of the moral authority they had lost when SASO broke away – and some thought that they had found this in a practice of confrontational protest. The comparative radicalism of their public actions – and the visibility of their successes in the press – led them to attempt to suggest practices of protest to SASO. Unsurprisingly, these attempts to regain the leadership of the student movement were not appreciated by SASO's leaders, who rejected NUSAS's attempts to direct them. They sought instead to develop an alternative mode of action. The members of SASO, however, were less concerned about

[40] Karis and Gerhart, *From Protest to Challenge, Volume 5*, p. 127.
[41] RSA Hansard, 5 June 1972, cols. 8710–11.

NUSAS's pretensions than they were concerned about the conditions on their own university campuses. Despite the strong rhetorical divide between SASO and NUSAS, the practices of protest were commonly available to both – and once black university students began to embark upon protests, it was highly likely that their efforts would strongly resemble those of white students.

The two movements influenced each other: NUSAS changed its focus, while SASO ended up adopting similar methods of protest. Their actions, too, were shaped by the shared ambiguities of students' position in a social order: neither children, and thus innocent of responsibility, nor working adults, and thus incorporated into a class system, students occupied a liminal place. In the liberal arts model of a university, these institutions provide a space within which young people can experiment with their own identities, allegiances and beliefs while, at the same time, being exposed to and learning about the long tradition of scholarly thought. In South Africa, it was perhaps only the universities attended by white, Anglophone students that sought to live up to this ideal, but even those institutions which provided a restricted education to black students were not able to fully divorce themselves from it. Despite the attempts of the state, and appointed university administrators, black students were still exposed to a range of ideas that allowed them to share experiences and develop new models of private and public thinking. Given this, they were soon led to challenge the limitations placed on their education by the paternalistic attitudes of administrators – and, before long, they were forced to confront and challenge the repressive actions of the police on and off campus.

4 The Durban Strikes
'SOULS OF THEIR OWN'

Students were not the only group beginning to protest in South Africa.

Early in the morning of 9 January 1973, before the sun rose, workers at the Coronation Brick and Tile works in Durban moved through the company's hostel.[1] They knocked on the dormitory walls, and told their colleagues that they were about to embark upon a spontaneous strike. That morning, instead of going to their workplace, between 1,500 and 2,000 black workers marched from their hostels to a nearby football field. They demanded that their weekly wage of R8.97 be increased to R20.00. When faced by the demands of the company's management, they refused to elect representatives to negotiate on their behalf, and insisted instead that all communication between management and workers take place on the field, in the sight and presence of all.[2]

The provincial Department of Labour sent a spokesman to the field in an attempt to mediate between the company and its workers. He was, however, notably unsuccessful in engaging the workers. The day ended in a stalemate, with neither the workers nor the company's managers any closer to reaching an agreement. The next morning, the Paramount Chief of the Zulu nation, Goodwill Zwelithini, arrived at the field promising to negotiate on behalf of the workers. After a representative had announced his imminent arrival, he then kept the workers waiting for several hours while he consulted with the company's management; after this wait, the workers were at first reluctant to allow the monarch to take on their cause. Indeed, their scepticism was highly visible: one worker was heard to call out, during Zwelithini's speech, 'We've heard this all before!'[3]

---

[1] This chapter draws upon work previously published as Julian Brown, 'The Durban Strikes of 1973: Political Identities and the Management of Protest,' in William Beinart and Marcelle C. Dawson (eds), *Popular Politics and Resistance Movements in South Africa* (Johannesburg, Wits University Press: 2010). This chapter makes a different argument, and presents the material in the light of this book's overall schema.

[2] *Daily News*, 9 January 1973; *Natal Mercury*, 10 January 1973. See also: Institute for Industrial Education, *The Durban Strikes 1973: 'Human Beings with Souls'* (Johannesburg, Ravan: 1974).

[3] *Daily News*, 10 January 1973.

It was only after they were told – by one of his representatives – that in refusing to accept Zwelithini's authority they were impugning the honour of the Royal House that the workers finally agreed to cede responsibility for the negotiations. A farcical sequence of events then followed, as Zwelithini was taken to task by Chief Mangosuthu Buthelezi, the KwaZulu Authority's Prime Minister. He insisted that the Paramount Chief had no authority to embark upon negotiations; he also suggested that such an endeavour might negatively impact upon the prestige of the monarch.[4] Zwelithini then chose to withdraw from the negotiations, leaving the workers to finally choose to appoint their own representatives – ordinary workers, although they were in fact at first misidentified by the local press as being themselves members of the Zulu Royal House.[5]

Meanwhile, as this situation unfolded, the strikes began to spread across Durban. On 10 January – the day that Zwelithini spoke at Coronation Brick – a group of workers at A.J. Keeler, a transport firm based on Durban's Point Road, downed their tools.[6] Over the next week, several hundred workers at six different companies – primarily in the transport and marine sectors – initiated their own small strikes and pickets. Although the workers at Coronation Brick were able to resolve their dispute by Thursday 18 January, strike fever had spread. In the last week of January, the textile industry became the focus of new strikes. At first, hundreds of workers at the Frametex factory – located in the New Germany industrial area, south of Durban – downed tools; they gathered in an open area within the factory compound, where they were addressed – from a distance, through a loudhailer – by a company representative. He asked them to elect a negotiating committee, and to return to their work. The striking workers refused, and simply remained where they were.

This strike then spread to the other four textile mills owned by the Frame Group in New Germany. At first 1,000 workers were said to be taking part in the strike; then, as the strike stretched on over the weekend and into the first days of the following week, the number of participating workers rose to between 6,000 and 7,000.[7] The strike then spread to other textile factories outside the area. On Monday, 29 January, a group of 650 workers at the Natal Canvas Rubber Manufacturers embarked on a strike. A day later, workers at the Consolidated Textile Mills in the Jacobs-Mobeni industrial area began their own strike. This strike moved – apparently with the encouragement of the workers themselves – to the 2,600 employees of the neighbouring

4   *Natal Mercury*, 11 January 1973.
5   *Natal Mercury*, 15 January 1973; *Daily News*, 15 January 1973.
6   *Natal Mercury*, 11 January 1973.
7   *Natal Mercury*, 30 January 1973.

Consolidated Fine Spinners and Weavers and the Consolidated Wool-
washing & Processing Mills.[8]

At this point – almost three weeks into the strikes – at least
twenty-nine Durban companies had been affected by the strike wave,
and well over 10,000 black workers had embarked on labour action.

But these strikes were only the tip of the iceberg. Between 9 January
and 31 March 1973 about 61,410 black workers in Durban embarked
on strikes across a wide range of different sites.[9] This was the largest
single strike wave since the election of the National Party in 1948,
and the institution of apartheid. More black workers were on strike in
Durban in these months than in the entirety of the preceding decade:
in any given year of the 1960s, no more than about 2,000 black workers
had embarked on strikes.[10] It is also notable that these earlier strikes
were isolated within individual industries and did not threaten either
to combine into a general strike or to spill out into the central spaces
of the affected cities themselves. By contrast, the 1973 Durban Strikes
not only involved tens of thousands of workers across all of the city's
industries, but also, early in February, they left the workplaces and
compounds to occupy the city streets of the Durban central business
district itself.

In this moment, the strikes intensified: in the first days of February,
workers at over thirty-five more companies launched their own strikes
– several of which involved well over a thousand workers apiece.
According to one estimate, only four factories in the Jacobs-Mobeni
region remained open during this week.[11] Then, on Monday 5 February,
Durban's municipal workers downed tools. Over the course of several
days, 16,000 municipal workers embarked upon public protest action,
marching down the city's streets in uncoordinated groups over the
course of the week.[12]

Unlike the earlier student protests, these events attracted widespread attention within South Africa. In initial responses to the
strikes, scholars and activists sought to identify the seeds of a potential labour movement in the events of January to March 1973.[13] For the
government's opponents, the strikes seemed to promise a new set of
possibilities: the organisation of African labour suddenly emerged as
a viable political strategy. In the years since, these strikes were often

[8] *Natal Mercury*, 30 January 1973.
[9] This figure was quoted by the Minister of Labour in Parliament: RSA, *Debates of the
     House of Assembly* (Hansard), 24 April 1973.
[10] Muriel Horrell, *South Africa's Workers* (Johannesburg, SAIRR: 1969).
[11] WHP AH1999/C3.15.2 (FOSATU).
[12] *Daily News*, 6 and 7 February 1973.
[13] In particular, the Institute for Industrial Education (IIE)'s publication, *The Durban
     Strikes 1973*, which provided a detailed account of the strikes in terms of labour
     politics and practice. All subsequent efforts to write about the strike wave have been
     significantly shaped by the IIE's initial account, including this chapter.

interpreted through the lens of the later successes of African trade unions in mobilising a mass base for political opposition to the apartheid state.[14] Both the immediate account and its later developments tended to position the strikes as an originating moment – the ground zero, as it were, of a new labour politics. As such, they also tended to displace the strikes from another potential context – the context of public protest and political dissent of the decade before 1976.

In doing so, these accounts implicitly – and sometimes explicitly – separated the protests of workers from the protests of students. The workers' protests were positioned as the source of later developments, and the influence of students was nudged into the background – or out of the story. These accounts divided the different elements that made up the specific historic conjuncture of the period, and ran the risk of denying the possibility – which may not have always been achieved – of connection and solidarity between different social groups. Any analysis of the period that presents workers without students was, of course, the mirror image of the widespread analyses of the French events of 1968 in which students displaced workers, and the possibility of cross-class alliances were hidden.[15] The effect of such a separation has been to obscure the specific historical conjuncture as it emerged in a particular moment, in favour of an abstracted model of political organisation and progress.

If it is a mistake to separate the actions of students and workers in this way, it is also a mistake to separate out the development of protest from the context created by the state's responses to it. In the previous chapters we have seen the state's response to the public protests of students: intense moments of brutality, followed by the separation of activists from their fellow students through banning orders, and – lastly at Turfloop – the mass expulsion of dissenting students. In each case, the state acted to constrain the space available for student protest, and to shrink the possibilities of insurrection. These actions shaped student politics. They encouraged white students to engage with their

---

[14] These include the accounts of the strikes found in D. du Toit, *Capital and Labour in South Africa: Class Struggles in the 1970s* (London, Kegan Paul International: 1981); Steven Friedman, *Building Tomorrow Today: African Workers in Trade Unions* (Johannesburg, Ravan: 1987); and Jeremy Baskin, *Striking Back: A History of COSATU* (Johannesburg, Ravan: 1991). The Durban Strikes have also been the subject of a number of shorter pieces that adopt a similar perspective. The most notable of these are R. Toli, 'The Origins of the Durban Strikes 1973' (University of Durban-Westville, MA Thesis: 1991); and Ari Sitas, 'Thirty Years since the Durban Strikes: Black Working-Class Leadership and the South African Transition,' *Current Sociology* 52.5 (2004), 830–49. More recently, Grace Davie's *Poverty Knowledge in South Africa: A Social History of Human Science, 1855–2005* (Cambridge, Cambridge University Press: 2015) has situated the strikes in the development of a discourse around labour and income in the social and human sciences.

[15] See the analysis in Kristin Ross, *May 68 and its Afterlives* (Chicago, University of Chicago Press: 2002).

university administrations, and thus to remain in some sense part of a public system. At the same time, they refused that possibility to black students – driving them outside the university, and refusing to recognise their actions as even potentially legitimate. The particular tactics of protests, too, were shaped by the likelihood of the state's violence, as students sought to get around legal restrictions on gatherings and activism.

In Durban, though, the responses of the state and businesses to the strikes were notably different. Instead of suppressing the individual protests, they sought to limit the impact of the strike wave by containing each strike within a particular space and context, and thus limiting the possibilities of connection. Instead of brutality, the local authorities tried a tactic of containment.

In this chapter, the emphasis of the argument turns away from the internal considerations of oppositional groups and organisations towards a focus how the state sought to shape the development of protest in Durban through its responses to the challenge posed by the strike wave. In part, this is due to a shift in the nature of the protest: the Durban Strikes had neither leaders nor spokespeople, and no archives of meetings and discussions. It was a series of independent and spontaneous strikes – each one of which was organised by workers within their own workplaces. There are therefore few sources that are able to give us a sense of how this process worked on the shop floor. Instead, the existing records of the strike wave focus on the actions of the state and business, and how these responses shaped the context of the strikes.

In the context of this book's argument, these records provide an opportunity to consider the ways in which state action shaped the possibilities of politics in Durban – and to consider the ways in which the state sought to resolve the disruptions to the social and economic order caused by protests. These processes involved building a consensus explanation for the strikes that reduced the disruptive potential of their political claims; they also involved developing methods of response – both by businesses and by the police – that emphasised the rapid restoration of social order within Durban. Together, these efforts moulded the events of the strike wave.

'Other influences in this strike'

Such a consensus did not come immediately.

In the course of a parliamentary debate on the strikes, held on 5 February 1973, a member of the ruling party, P.R. de Jager, presented an explanation for the outbreak of strikes in Durban:

I know them [the workers] and I am convinced, as regards labour done by the Bantu in Natal and the level at which they move, they do not have it in them to come together and agree that a thousand of them should strike. There are other influences in this strike.[16]

The conspiratorial account of the sudden development of strikes in Durban offered by de Jager in this speech represents one of the two most common modes of talking about the strike wave. For example, on the second day, the managing director of the A.J. Keeler transport company – the second company to be affected – suggested that the majority of workers did not entirely understand the implications of their own actions. Instead, a small minority of 'agitators' had provoked the majority into striking. As his remarks were reported, he said that 'it was always the same, the ringleaders had intimidated the others into taking the action they had.'[17] His remarks were echoed, at the end of January, by the financial director of the Frame Group of textile companies. He emphasised that 'a small group of agitators' at the Natal Canvas and Rubber Manufacturers – where the strikes across the Group had first started – were driving the process. They had even, he suggested, 'threatened to kill' workers who did not participate in the strike.[18]

In the same period, the figure of hidden agitators was given prominence in a press statement released by the national Minister for Labour, Marais Viljoen, who suggested that agitators from outside the workforce were attempting to manipulate workers into taking part in public protests. He announced that, 'the strikes in Natal follow a pattern from which it is clear that it is not merely a question of higher wages'. This was proven by the fact that while 'there were cases where existing works committees in factories hit by strikes regarded the workers' wage demands as unreasonable and urged them to return to work', in these cases, 'this advice was ignored by workers'. To Viljoen, this demonstrated that there was every indication of 'planned action' and that, therefore: 'The action and willingness of the workers concerned shows undoubtedly that the agitation for trade unions is not the solution, and is merely a smoke screen behind which other motives are hidden.'[19]

The Minister did not elaborate on what these 'other motives' might be – other than suggesting that the strikes might be intended 'to bring about disorderliness prejudicial to the order of the state'. The absence of any specificity in his statement was seized upon by his political opponents. An editorial in the *Daily News* – one of two newspapers published out of Durban – pointed to the emptiness of

[16] Hansard, 5 February 1973, 90–91.
[17] *Natal Mercury*, 11 January 1973.
[18] *Natal Mercury*, 30 January 1973.
[19] WHP AH1999/C3.15.2 (FOSATU), Departement van Inligting. Persverklaring 9/73(K). The English translation is in part taken from: *Daily News*, 2 February 1973.

Viljoen's 'clod-hopping' rhetoric, and suggested that 'not even the Minister himself believes the tired old clichés about agitators and hidden forces' and that his statements were nothing more than 'obligatory political noises' of the government.[20]

Stung by these comments, the Minister responded by giving specifics: a series of political organisations within South Africa were, he argued, behind the strike wave. These organisations included NUSAS, the Black Workers' Project (which was an offshoot of SASO, although the Minister clearly assumed that it was driven by NUSAS members) and the 'pro-Leftist Trade Union Council of South Africa'. He explicitly linked the student protests of the recent past with the labour unrest: the same small group of political agitators was currently manipulating Durban's black workers in the same ways that they had already manipulated white students. Both sets of protests, he argued, were intended to achieve the same end – the destabilisation of the apartheid order and the National Party government. In the face of the state's successful efforts to repress student protest, agitators now saw 'Black unrest as the only remaining way to bring the Government to a fall'.[21]

It was in the context of this same parliamentary debate that de Jager made his comments about the inability of black workers to organise themselves, and drew the conclusion that this demonstrated the likelihood of 'other influences' lurking behind the 'smoke screen' evoked by the Minister himself.

Of course, these accusations had very little substance. Despite the Minister's statement – and the willingness of other politicians to repeat his allegations – the police on the ground could not substantiate his claims. The senior police spokesman in Durban at the time of the Minister's speech, Brigadier H.J. Schroeder, the Divisional Commander of the Port Natal Police, was reported by the *Sunday Times* as saying that 'there was still no definite proof that agitators were behind the stoppages'. He added that, if such proof existed, 'we would have taken action'.[22]

This proof never arrived – even though several politicians would no doubt have desired it to. During February, for example, the Mayor of Durban was quoted suggesting that '95% of ... workers had not wanted to strike but had been stirred by agitators'. When reminded of this statement a month later, he was forced into the embarrassing position of saying that while he still 'believed that agitators were responsible' he had to admit 'obviously nobody can prove this'.[23]

But the absence of proof did not mean that the state refrained from acting on these ideas.

[20] *Daily News*, 3 February 1973.
[21] Hansard, 5 Feb 1973, cols. 50–51; *Daily News*, 6 February 1973.
[22] *Sunday Times*, 4 February 1973.
[23] *Daily News*, 15 March 1973.

In February, as the strikes continued and the minister's accusations festered, parliament debated the Schlebusch Commission's first interim report on the actions of certain opposition organisations, including NUSAS. The Commission had been established to investigate student protest, and to draw up recommendations for controlling its spread.[24] In this first report, the Commission suggested that the political policies adopted by NUSAS were being determined by 'a small group of activists' within the organisation, and did not represent the wishes of its general membership. It suggested that NUSAS's 'leadership consequently from time to time took extraordinary steps to create provocative situations aimed at emotionally activating the greater student body'. On the basis of these premises, the Commission concluded that 'the continued participation of these persons [that is, NUSAS's leaders] in student politics is extremely undesirable' and recommended that eight of these leaders be restricted under the provisions of the Suppression of Communism Act.[25]

In practice, this meant that these student leaders – Paul Pretorius, Paula Ensor, Philippe Le Roux, Neville Curtis, Chris Wood, Clive Keegan, Sheila Lapinsky and Rick Turner – were removed from public life, and banned from participating in any form of political organisation. This had immediate consequences, not just for the men and women themselves, but for NUSAS. Pretorius was the current president of NUSAS. Ensor and le Roux were the sitting vice-presidents, and Lapinsky the secretary-general. These four activists were at the heart of NUSAS's organisation. The remaining four – Curtis, Keegan, Turner and Wood – held no office in NUSAS at the time, but undoubtedly had significant influence in the organisation and on student politics in general.[26]

In the contexts of this chapter and the timing of these banning orders the inclusion of Turner on this list was especially significant. He was a lecturer sympathetic to radical student politics, based in Durban. He had been instrumental in suggesting that students turn their attentions to supporting the activism of workers in 1972, before the wave of the Durban Strikes erupted in January. By placing his name on this short list of agitators and activists, the recommendations of the Schlebusch Commission were explicitly linked to the strikes taking place in Durban at the same time. Even without the direct link, the timing of the decision to restrict NUSAS's leaders – even if it were in fact coincidental – drew a connection between the events.

---

[24] The Schlebusch Commission will be discussed in further detail in the following chapter.

[25] Hansard, 27 February 1973, cols 1485–91.

[26] See: Muriel Horrell and Dudley Horner, *A Survey of Race Relations in South Africa 1973* (Johannesburg, SAIRR: 1974), pp. 24–38.

The state's actions against students did not end with the banning of these eight NUSAS members. A month later, in March – while the strikes were still continuing in Durban – the state turned its attention to SASO and its affiliated organisations, the Black Peoples' Convention (BPC) and the Black Community Programme (BCP). A further eight activists were banned: Steve Biko, Barney Pityana, Bokwe Mafuna, Drake Koka, Strini Moodley, Harry Nengwekhulu, Jerry Modisane and Saths Cooper. In parliament, the Minister of Justice defended the banning orders against these men, saying that they were necessary to prevent the students from using the 'platform' provided by formal courtroom procedures for political ends.[27] Gerhart, meanwhile, linked these banning to the Durban Strikes, writing that, in launching its 'first major offensive against SASO' the state had acted 'as if to acknowledge that blacks had won a round with the Durban strikes'.[28]

The effect of these banning orders – both on NUSAS's leaders, and the leaders of SASO, the BPC and the BCP – was to throw all these organisations into institutional disarray. NUSAS replaced its banned officials with interim leaders, with relatively limited experience and authority. SASO and the BPC attempted to replace their banned leaders – only to see these replacements themselves served with banning orders after a few months in office. From February onwards, student organisations were forced by the state's action to concentrate their efforts on survival – on ensuring that their organisations continued to operate in any possible effective way and to remain active.

This, of course, had a knock-on effect: any desire that these organisations might have had to support the striking workers in Durban – whether through aboveground solidarity protests, or through the underground subversions that the Minister of Labour so feared – was made impossible to realise. Students were being neutralised as a political force in this period, primarily because of their protesting activities in preceding years, but also with the encouragement of those sections of the ruling party that saw them as representing the 'other influences' that were shaping the strikes.

In other words, the discourse of 'agitators' and 'outside influences' in the Durban Strikes helped move the actions of the state away from the local arena, and towards the national political sphere. In this sphere, it provided additional justification for the state's desire to take urgent action against student politics, and student activists. It also permitted the state to focus its attention on its existing opponents, and to overlook the possibility that a new challenge was emerging in Durban.

---

[27] Mafika Pascal Gwala (ed.), *Black Review 1973* (Durban, Black Community Programmes: 1974), pp. 92–103; Horrell and Horner, *Survey 1973*, p. 344.

[28] Gail M. Gerhart, *Black Power in South Africa: The Evolution of an Ideology* (Berkeley and Los Angeles, University of California Press: 1978), p. 297.

'Human beings with souls of their own'

In Durban, though, this luxury was not possible. As the Minister for Labour emphasised the need to expose the agitators behind the strikes, and as the state acted to remove student activists from the public realm, the Durban Chamber of Commerce sought to advise its members on how to respond to the strikes. At the core of its advice was an emphasis on the apparently apolitical nature of the majority of the city's workers. In doing so, the Chamber set out an argument that resonated with part, but not all, of the Minister of Labour's argument.

In a confidential memo circulated to its members, the Chamber outlined its explanation. The first pages of this memo laid out a detailed account of 'the causes of the present work stoppage'. Three causes were identified. First, workers had been receiving generally low wages – 'in many cases without review or appreciable revision for a number of years'. Second, there had been a substantial rise in the cost of living in Durban over the past year – significantly outstripping inflation. Third, a recent rise in the cost of local rail fares and transport may have galvanised workers to demand wages that were more in line with their real everyday expenses.

The Chamber tied these three factors to recent reports of an updated national 'Poverty Datum Line' – that is, the minimum income that a family needed to earn if it were to avoid falling into poverty. The Chamber went into some detail on this figure, ensuring that the readers of its memo were aware both of the logic underpinning it and the methods by which it had been reached.[29] Having established this, the Chamber then emphasised that a typical 'Bantu family of 5' would need 'in terms of the absolute minimum categories of expenditure' an income of R85.15 a month. Assuming that the main male earner in the family contributed two-thirds of its overall income, then his weekly wage would have to be at least R14.74 for his family to avoid falling into poverty.[30] By contrast, many of the striking workers at Coronation Brick were earning a weekly wage of R8.97 – about 60 per cent of the minimum wage they needed to ensure that their families avoided poverty.[31]

In this context, the explanation for the strikes was self-evident: economic constraints had placed the workers in a condition of severe material deprivation. They could not live on their wages. Driven by desperation – and perhaps the blindness of some employers – they had begun to strike.

---

[29] The Poverty Datum Line is discussed in fascinating detail by Davie in *Poverty Knowledge in South Africa*.

[30] WHP AH1999/C3.15.2 (FOSATU), 'The Current Bantu Labour Stoppage' (9 February 1973).

[31] *Daily News*, 5 February 1973.

For the Chamber of Commerce, this was all the explanation that the strikes required. Alternative explanations were considered and shelved in a single paragraph of its long memo: the Chamber noted that 'there was a possibility that the existing unrest has in certain cases been used to further political or ulterior aims'. But it said no more, and allowed this possibility to fade.

Much the same approach was adopted by the editorial pages of Durban's two daily newspapers. As already mentioned, the *Daily News* was particularly scathing in its dismissal of the idea that politicised agitators lurked behind the strike, suggesting that if the Minister of Labour were to remove his 'white-tinted spectacles' he would be 'less disposed to regard an eight-rand a week striker as a political agitator'.[32] Indeed, from the first days of the strike wave these newspapers emphasised the economic motivations behind the workers' actions: on 12 January, the *Daily News* drew attention to these same figures, suggesting that 'to exist on R40 a month undoubtedly accelerates frustration. These workers get R8.97 a week. For those who support a family on this wage it means they are doing so with R43 a month less than the poverty datum line.'[33]

In February, the newspaper was still emphasising the material deprivation suffered by the striking workers: their wages were 'a pittance for survival' and bore 'a relationship to the increases in the cost of living' that was clearly 'remote, to say the least'.[34] There was no question, in the eyes of the *Daily News*'s editorial team, about the causes of the strike: they were economic, not political.

These ideas were shared by many of the workers themselves. During interviews conducted in Durban in the immediate aftermath of the strikes, workers emphasised the material constraints placed upon them by low wages: 'African workers have decided to strike because of the working conditions and because of a very low wage.' Or, as another worker put it: the strikes had occurred because 'the child that does not cry dies ... we should cry for ourselves for working hungry'.[35]

But although the brute fact of the material deprivation suffered by the workers was the primary reason offered to rebut the presumption that the strikes were being driven by external agitators and other political troublemakers, it was not the only such reason offered at the time.

[32] *Daily News*, 6 February 1973.

[33] *Daily News*, 12 January 1973. The discrepancy in figures in this quote and those offered by the Chamber of Commerce lies in the calculation the Chamber made – that the individual worker contributed two-thirds of the family income. The *Daily News*'s figure presumes that the individual worker contributed the entirety of his family's income. Perhaps obviously, both claims would have had some substance to them.

[34] *Daily News*, 3 February 1973.

[35] Alan Paton Centre UKZN PC126 (Natal Room, Gerhard Maré collection), 'African Workers Interview'.

Commentators also emphasised the presumed ethnic homogeneity of the local workforce.

From the moment of Goodwill Zwelithini's intervention during the first strike at Coronation Brick, the local media repeatedly emphasised apparent ethnic homogeneity of the striking workers. Before Zwelithini's appearance, the workers were referred to in the generic language of race: they were 'African workers', 'chanting Africans' and 'marching Africans'. The day after Zwelithini's speech, the same crowd was described by the same newspaper as consisting of '1500 Zulu men'.[36] The *Natal Mercury* emphasised the performative aspects of this ethnic identification, describing the crowds as forming an *impi* and translating their shouts in Zulu for their English readers: '*Hobe Usuthu* (Zulu Warrior)' and '*Asiyi* (We are not going)'.[37] From this moment onwards, the striking workers across Durban were described in ethnic terms – no longer Africans, but Zulus.

This ascription of an essential Zulu-ness to the workers shaped many public responses to the strikes. Clear examples of this can be found in the two presentations sponsored by the Chamber of Commerce. In these talks, L.D. Thorne, Barrister-at-Law, told his audience that his credentials as an analyst of the strikes rested on his outsider/insider perspective: he was now resident in Durban, and had been for several years, but before that had travelled extensively. These experiences allowed him to recognise that, in Durban, 'we have a homogenous workforce of virtually solid Zulu' and that 'our Zulu comes from a warrior race and like all good soldiers they will put up with a lot before they blow their safety valve'. He suggested that a model of identity founded on militaristic and masculinist self-discipline had prevented workers from expressing their frustrations with a growing material crisis in the past. This was exacerbated by the divisions between workers and employers: 'unlike in other parts of South Africa, there is here in Natal no common language – and therefore no contact – certainly of understanding. The African basically does not speak English or Afrikaans, and the White generally understands no Zulu.'[38]

These homogenous ethnic identities also explained how it was that – once the complaints of workers had been made public – the strikers were able to organise without the influence of outside agitators. For Thorne, this ability was a by-product of the essential nature of Zulu society: 'in my experience in my life in India and in other parts of Africa it just could not have happened, except with the Zulu'.[39] In

[36] *Daily News*, 9 and 10 January 1973.
[37] *Natal Mercury*, 10 January 1973.
[38] WHP AH1999/C3.15.2 (FOSATU), 'An Appropriate Form of Labour Organisation for African Employees' (7 March 1973).
[39] WHP AH1999/C3.15.2 (FOSATU), 'Some Comments on Labour Unrest' (27 February 1973).

the context of his other statements, the implication of this is clear: the ethnicity, language and cultural inheritance shared by the workers had provided them with a model of organisation and the means by which to achieve it. The successes of the strikes were the product of the ability of Zulu workers to recreate their historical identity as disciplined 'warriors'.

In the face of this rhetoric, it is important to recognise that the actual demographic makeup of Durban's workers made this idea very unlikely. Although African workers made up the majority of the workforce, and although workers who identified themselves as Zulu also undoubtedly made up the single largest group in that workforce, they were never the entirety of the workforce. Within the broader category of African workers, significant minorities identified as Shangaan or Pondo. Beyond this, these accounts ignored the presence of Durban's many Indian workers in several of the largest strikes in January and February. Finally, the ways in which all workers were described tended to emphasise a model of masculinity associated with Zulu cultural norms, and thus also obscured the presence of women in the strikes, particularly in the textile industry.

Nonetheless – despite its demographic inaccuracy, and despite the stereotyped notions of culture and identity underpinning this discourse – the idea of the ethnic homogeneity of Durban's workforce held currency at the time, and underpinned many of the discussions about the causes of the strikes. This idea was regularly folded back into the discourse around economic deprivation, and helped complete an explanatory model that took hold amongst Durban's liberal and capitalist elites: that the workers were prompted to strike by their inability to live on the wages being paid by employers at the time, and that their ability to organise and sustain these strikes was a product of their inherent ethnic identity. This model served to explain the undeniable fact of the strikes, while – at the same time – dodging the implication that these strikes represented political dissent.

These two sets of ideas about the strikes – that they were the product of the malign influence of external agitators, on the one hand, and that they were motivated by material deprivation and shaped by ethnic inheritances, on the other – publicly competed during the first month of the strike wave. Both narratives persisted throughout the strikes: the Mayor of Durban's statement crediting agitators for the strikes, for example, was made in the middle of March. However, the weight of public opinion soon swung behind the second set of ideas, about material deprivation.

A week after the Minister for Labour's intervention, the Prime Minister, B.J. Vorster, made a lengthy speech distancing himself from the more outré aspects of his government's initial statements. Vorster did not use the word 'agitator' in his speech. Instead he adopted the economic model of explaining the strikes, placing primary responsibility on the employers who had not recognised the growing discrepancy between wages and the cost of living. In this speech, Vorster coupled the absence of agitators and the agency of the employers with an absolution of his government, and a displacement of the strike from the political realm to the economic:

> in the past there have unfortunately been too many employers who saw only the mote in the Government's eye and failed completely to see the beam in their own. Now I am looking past all party affiliations and past all employers, and experience tells me this, that employers, whoever they may be, should not only see in their workers a unit for producing for them so many hours of service a day: they should also see them as human beings with souls.[40]

In other words, it was not political agitation that had caused the strikes. Nor had they been caused by discontent with the government's policies or practices. Rather, the strikes in Durban had been caused by the experience of material deprivation bought about by short-sighted economic decisions on the parts of particular employers. Therefore, it was these employers who were responsible for taking the actions necessary to resolve the strikes, and not the state itself.

Nor was it the responsibility of the workers, because they were not recognised as potential agents, whether political or otherwise. For many contemporary commentators – including the Minister for Labour, the Prime Minister, the members of the Durban Chamber of Commerce, and others – it was impossible to imagine African labourers possessing any kind of political consciousness, let alone agency. Those who believed that agitators were behind the strike clearly believed in the incapacity of African labourers to have organised the strikes on their own. Those who believed that material deprivation had sparked the strikes saw the workers as reactive, driven into action by forces outside of their control. They explained workers' organisations by reference to ethnicity and culture, and not to workers' conscious engagement with each other.

The implication of the arguments put forward by Vorster, and by these other white commentators, was inescapable: African workers were themselves apolitical, or pre-political, merely 'human beings with souls'. This was a conclusion that could resonate with all commentators: even if the strikes were signs of political dissent, this was not the dissent of the workers themselves, but that of mysterious agitators.

---

[40] Hansard, 9 February 1973.

Policing strikes, managing concessions

The triumph of this narrative of pre-political souls shaped the context within which the strikes developed, both before and after Vorster's speech. The belief that the workers were driven by pre-political drives, and the recognition that their economic claims were justified, meant that the striking workers were not treated as political troublemakers by the police. Instead, most local authorities assumed a paternalistic position in relation to the strikers – and acted as if their role was to contain the strikes, rather than suppress them, for long enough for the workers to decide to turn to the negotiations.

The effects of this could be seen in the first week of February, when approximately 30,000 workers were on strike at the same time. About half of these workers were employees of the Durban municipality itself. On Monday 5 February, 3,000 workers in the City Engineer's and Electricity departments downed tools, affecting roads and drains works, street cleaning, and the local distribution of electricity. By Tuesday morning workers in the department of Parks and Gardens had joined the strike, and by Wednesday the local media was reporting that 'all 16,000 of [the city's] non-White employees' had ceased to work.[41] These city streets were these workers' workplaces – and they took their protests into these streets, marching and moving through them.

Their actions shifted the dynamic that had characterised the relationship between striking workers and the local police during the first month of the strikes. This dynamic had been established in the earliest strikes, at Coronation Brick and other industries. These initial protests took place either wholly within the grounds of the affected factories or were located on nearby areas, such as the football field near Coronation Brick. Almost all of the protests that took place in January remained within these informal spatial boundaries and, although there were a few exceptions including the initial march of Coronation workers from their hostels to the football field, these were notable primarily for their rarity. This spatial pattern was reinforced by the actions of the police: officers would generally arrive at the site of strike, and then remain on the periphery of that site. They often set up a loose cordon around the striking workers, shadowing the boundaries of the workplace. Individual workers would be allowed through that cordon, but large groups would more often than not be dispersed. The police rarely entered the workplace or factory, only at the explicit invitation of the company's management. The effect of this was to emphasise existing spatial boundaries, and to prevent workers and police from confronting each other.

The consequences of this can be seen in one of the rare cases in which the boundaries of the workplace were broached by strikers. At

[41] *Daily News*, 5, 6 and 7 February 1973.

the end of January, three weeks into the strike wave, a group of striking workers at the Frame Group's textile mills in New Germany gathered on the sides of the road outside one of these mills. These workers – mainly women – were gathered in the sight of passing commuters. In the words of a newspaper report: 'they clapped hands, sung songs and danced'. Then, after some time, 'sticks and stones were gathered and a large crowd danced in the street in front of the mill's main entrance. They banged against passing vehicles and jeered at police cars.' Despite this, the police took no direct action against the protesting women, even though their protest had exceeded the boundaries of their workplace, and even though their actions could have been seen as posing a threat to public order. Instead, they simply increased the visibility of their presence on the edges of the area, and refrained from acting violently.[42]

This is in clear contrast to the actions of the police in other circumstances – in particular, during student protests in the years immediately preceding the Durban Strikes. In these protests, the police sought to intervene to end the disruptions caused by students and to disperse their crowds. They arrested indiscriminately, and charged dozens and sometimes hundreds of participants. In the process, they used aggressive and violent measures to suppress the protests, beating students with rubber truncheons and, occasionally, setting police dogs on crowds.

Similarly violent confrontations between police and striking workers did occur during the Durban Strikes, but they were exceptional rather than ordinary, and almost always the product of contingent circumstances. They occurred in outlying parts of the city, most notably in Hammarsdale – an industrial area on Durban's inland periphery, half-way to Pietermaritzburg. Here, on one occasion, about 7,000 workers left their factories and – unlike in other strikes – mingled together in a public area, gathering to form a large body of protesting workers. Both the size and the concentration of the group placed the police on edge, and when a relatively small body of 200 workers split off from the main group and advanced towards one of the surrounding factories the police seem to have panicked. They fired tear gas into the crowd, and launched baton charges – both against the small breakaway body and against the main group. For a moment, the scene resembled the confrontations of the past years. But then a degree of control was re-imposed.[43]

One other significant confrontation took place during the period of the strikes, when the Durban municipality's workers took to the streets in early February. On 6 February, a group of just over one hundred men marched down a main thoroughfare near the Electricity Depart-

[42] *Natal Mercury*, 27 January 1973.
[43] *Daily News*, 7 February 1973.

ment's central city depot. According to news reports, the march was 'unruly', and was brought to an end after a policeman saw 'a White man, riding a scooter, being hit over the head'.[44] This one moment of violence provoked several more: the police led a baton charge into the group, beating the workers to the ground and then surrounding them. One hundred and six men were arrested, loaded into six police vehicles, and taken to the local police station. The next morning they were charged and convicted in the Magistrate's Court for the crime of disturbing the peace.[45]

In both these cases, though, the aftermath was also notable. After the baton charge in Hammarsdale, the police refrained from arresting any of the gathered workers. After the baton charge in the city centre, the police did arrest workers – but the charges brought against them were the mildest that could have been levied. They were not charged with illegal gathering, they were not charged with the illegal possession of weapons, they were not charged with assault or public violence. Instead, the charge of 'causing a public disturbance', which carried a potential sentence of either thirty days' imprisonment or a fine of R30.00, was brought against the workers. These sentences were not actually levied, however: the presiding magistrate suspended the majority of the sentences on the condition that the workers did not commit any similar act.[46]

These examples – both of the normal responses to individual the strikes, and of the exceptional moments of confrontation – point to the existence of a pattern in the policing of the strikes. By containing striking workers within the boundaries of their workplaces, the police not only ensured that the protest could be rapidly suppressed, if necessary, but also ensured that communities outside the factories were insulated from any disruption caused by the strike. When these boundaries were breached, the police acted to shadow groups of striking workers in the first instance, disarm them in the second, and remove them from the streets in the third. Instead of allowing confrontations to develop – whether between different groups of protesters, or between protesters and the police – the pattern of police practice emphasised control and constraint, containment rather than engagement, and disarmament rather than confrontation. In the context of the strikes, the pattern of apparent restraint shown by the police was not philanthropic – but nor was it accidental. Instead, this pattern aimed to protect the public order, and to restore it rapidly.

[44] *Daily News*, 7 February 1973.
[45] Gwala, *Black Review 1973*, p. 141. See also: IIE, *Durban Strikes 1973*, p. 20.
[46] To be precise, the magistrate suspended twenty-five of the thirty days of the sentence, or R25.00 of the R30.00 of the fine. The workers did not escape the law – but the law was applied with unusual discretion. See: *Daily News*, 7 February 1973; IIE, *The Durban Strikes 1973*, p.20, Gwala, *Black Review 1973*, p. 141.

A similar emphasis on the preservation of the existing order, or – failing that – its rapid restoration, was at the heart of the Chamber of Commerce's recommendations to employers for how to resolve individual strikes. As the police sought to contain strikes within the workplaces, the Chamber sought to ensure that a strike did not spread from one industry to another and that, were that to fail, the strike would at least be brought to an end before it could fester and swell.

At the centre of the Chamber's approach was the need for the employer to maintain control. The Department of Labour should be 'notified' of a strike, but its services should not be used; the workers' demands should be considered, but only once the striking group had returned to work. Then, 'if you feel an increase in minimum wages is necessary, determine this increase and tell them of your decision. Thereafter stand by your decision.' The Chamber reiterated the need for employers not to bend or show any weakness: 'Do not attempt to bargain as this will only encourage the Bantu to escalate his demands. Action must be positive, definite and final.'[47]

In reality, employers were rarely able to reclaim the initiative from their striking workers. A lone manager standing in front of hundreds – or, occasionally, thousands – of strikers would struggle to project the firm façade of authority suggested by the Chamber: the City Engineer, for example, was jeered at and forced to retreat when he sought to address striking municipal workers. Likewise, employers and managers were unable to insist that workers return to their jobs before engaging with them: faced by large crowds chanting for R10, R20, R30 a week, these employers found themselves entering into negotiations and making concessions without an assertion of authority.

Indeed, in most of the individual strikes, employers entered into some form of negotiation with their striking workers, and in most of these some form of concession was granted by the employer, primarily increases in the weekly wage paid to the workers. During April, the Minister for Labour presented a verbal report to parliament, in which he laid out the pattern of wage concessions. He told his audience that there had been 160 different strikes, spread out of 146 factories and companies located in the metallurgical, textile, transport and clothing industries, the local municipality and others. Of these, wage increases had been granted in 118 cases. In a further twenty-eight, the workers abandoned their strike without an increase. In only seven cases had the workers been fired en masse. In the majority of the cases in which wages increased had been granted, these increases added between R1.00 and R2.00 to the workers' weekly wage packets.[48]

The most notable features of this report are the facts that almost three-quarters of the strikes resulted in wage increases, and that less

[47] WHP AH1999/C3.15.2 (FOSATU), 'The Current Bantu Labour Stoppage'.
[48] Hansard, 24 April 1973, cols. 689–95.

than one-twentieth resulted in the dismissal of workers. In Durban during the first three months of 1973, the decision to embark upon a strike was a good gamble: victories were frequent, punitive losses rare, and the scale of the victories was not insignificant. At Coronation Brick and Tile, for example, where workers were earning R8.97 a week, employers conceded a raise of R2.07 – just under twenty-five per cent of their salary. Workers at Natal United Transport won a fifteen per cent increase, as did Durban's municipal workers. Although no workers were able to achieve the stated demands of R20.00 or more a week, and although few would actually rise above the much-quoted Poverty Datum Line, a wage increase of between 10 and 20 per cent was the normal outcome of the strikes. In at least 107 of the 118 cases, in fact, workers won an increase of over R1.00 a week.[49] This was in itself remarkable.

But it is important to recognise that these increases were granted in particular circumstances: the strikes were all resolved in notably short stretches of time. According to the Minister's figures, thirty-two of the strikes were resolved after less than one day passed, and thirty-eight more at the end of a full day. A further twenty-four strikes lasted between one and two days, thirty-five between two and three days and thirty-eight between three days and a week. The shortest strike lasted a mere ten minutes. The longest continued for a week. In other words: almost half of the strikes were resolved by the end of their first day. A majority were resolved in two days, and only a small number lasted longer than three.

The rapid resolution of the individual strikes and the award of wage increases went hand in hand, each making the other more likely. In the context of the Chamber of Commerce's attempts to ensure that employers acted to control strikes, maintain authority and restore commercial order, the need for these employers to stifle the disruption caused by strikes was paramount. The need to keep wages artificially low – low by reference, at least, to the Poverty Datum Line – was trumped by the need to maintain order and authority. Speedy concessions were necessary to ensure this.

In this light, the victories of the striking workers take on a different complexion: they become signs of the ability of employers to cure the disruption caused by any individual strike. The reduction of the claims of the striking workers to their particular wage demands, and the concomitant erasure of the potential for politics of dissent to emerge in the workers' protests, enabled a managerial response to displace a political one. This had its benefits: overall, workers' wages increased and some of their specific complaints were addressed. But it also had its costs: by taking workers' actions out of the realm of the political,

---

[49] Hansard, 24 April 1973, op cit. See also the documentation in WHP AH1999/C3.15.2 (FOSATU).

the formation of an open alliance between dissenting students and protesting workers was frustrated – not only by the state's desire to prevent such an alliance, but by students, sympathisers and some workers themselves.

After the strikes

In the context of the time, both scholars sympathetic to workers' struggles and activists associated with emerging forms of labour organisation were thus caught between Scylla and Charybdis: on the one hand, they risked disempowering workers by denying their potential political motives; on the other, they risked entrenching the exclusion of African workers from the public sphere by confirming the worst fears of conservative employers. Faced with this dilemma, most sympathetic analyses erred on the side of political caution. They emphasised the unexceptional nature of workers' consciousness, and agitated for the state to recognise the normalcy of labour activism.

An example of this tendency is provided by the work of the Institute of Industrial Education (IIE) in the immediate aftermath of the Durban Strikes. In a comprehensive account of the Strikes, the IIE highlighted the effects of the particular economic crisis faced by workers in the early 1970s on the development of the strike wave. It also sought to emphasise the ease with which the individual strikes were resolved, and the relative sanity of the local response to them. The IIE's interventions seemed aimed at convincing the apartheid state that it was in its interests to expand the spaces available for workers to articulate their own needs and negotiate their own wages. Argument was made that the strike wave had been caused by an economic crisis, and that the likelihood of similar crises continuing or recurring was so great that the state would have to consider means to prevent new strike waves from recurring. The most effective way to ensure that economic pressures did not erupt into crisis, which would then spill onto the streets, was to enable African workers to communicate their needs effectively. From this set of premises, the IIE then argued that the government needed to recognise African trade unions, and to treat the labour activism of Africans as an ordinary part of the capitalist economy rather than a fundamental political threat.[50]

In doing so, the IIE adopted a refined version of the stance adopted by the Prime Minister on the national stage. The title of the IIE's book was taken directly from Vorster's speech – reiterating and emphasising the universal humanity shared by workers and employers, and sidelining the political content of the workers' actions. The book aimed to

[50] IIE, *Durban Strikes 1973.*

dispel the myths that had grown up around the strikes: that they were the product of agitators, that they were driven by ethnic tensions, and that they were somehow the product of a broader political challenge to the state. Instead, the IIE returned again and again to the contingent specifics of the economic crisis faced by African labour in Durban, and yet again to the idea that the recognition of workers' bargaining rights was the best instrument available to the state to prevent further disruption.

This was not uncontroversial. Johann Maree's review of the IIE's account of the Durban Strikes, for example, castigated the Institute for allowing the debate over 'agitators' to determine its approach to the strikes. By spending so much of its energies on countering the Minister of Labour's absurd allegations, the Institute elided the potential political content of the workers' strikes, and allowed the Minister's characterisation of political activism to define political dissent in narrow terms. These terms excluded workers' activism from the realm of the political, and thus risked the IIE replicating the government's devaluing of workers' actions as apolitical and naive.[51]

This critique – premised on the need to recognise the workers' own political agency – was also accompanied on another flank by the assertions of conservative commentators and employers that permitting workers to organise and act would fundamentally disrupt the apartheid order. The fear that the recognition of African trade unions could provide a backdoor through which the recognition of African political parties would inevitably take place drove at least part of the opposition to the recognition of African workers' efforts to organise themselves effectively.[52]

However, it is important to recognise that, despite these critiques, the IIE's argument was visibly successful. In the immediate aftermath of the strikes, several employers in Durban agreed to permit the organisation of 'works committees' within their factories. The continuing pressure from workers and labour activists also drove the government towards establishing a commission of inquiry into the possibilities of recognising labour legislation. This Commission was established in 1977, under the chairmanship of Nicolas Wiehahn, a retired High Court judge, who sat for two years. At the end of the decade, the Commission published its recommendations, which included the need for the state to formally recognise African trade unions. This was linked to an approach that emphasised the ability of individual unions to orga-

---

[51] Johann Maree, 'Seeing Strikes in Perspective', *South African Labour Bulletin*, 2 (9 & 10): 1976.

[52] See the summaries of arguments before the Wiehahn Commission provided by Alide Kooy, Dudley Horner, Philipa Green and Shirley Miller, 'The Wiehahn Commission: A Summary', SALDRU Working Paper 24 (Cape Town, University of Cape Town: 1979)

nise their own membership structures – including the possibility of inter-racial membership structures – but that, nonetheless, precluded unions from participating in the formal political arena by supporting a political party.[53]

These successes opened up a new space for public activism, one in which the ambiguous recognition granted by the state to labour organisation seemed to promise activists a degree of protection from its overtly repressive actions. The opportunities granted by this were then taken up – both in the period preceding the Wiehahn Commission, and after – with real effectiveness.[54]

The usefulness of a dichotomy between students' protests and workers' organisation is thus apparent, both for the state in 1973 and for workers in the years immediately afterwards. Its value at the time, though, is not a sufficiently good reason to continue to accept it forty years later. The workers' protests in Durban were not pre-political: they were not driven by ethnic identity and culture, nor were they driven solely by material deprivation in the absence of political reflection. Instead, workers' protests were founded on their abilities to reflect upon their own experiences – experiences of attempts by employers to divide them along ethnic lines, experiences of material deprivation in the context of a wealthy white economy – and to then translate those reflections into localised calls for action.

Despite various critiques, the effect of the Durban Strikes and the activism that followed the strike wave was to strengthen and entrench the moves towards the creation of a space for African labour organisation. Once established, this space did indeed become the site for the further development of African politics. In the 1980s, African trade unions acted to defend the rights of African workers against state repression, helping found the United Democratic Front in collaboration with other organisations and challenging the apartheid state's ability to govern.[55]

In the early 1970s, though, the rise of the politicised trade union moments was still in the future.

At the time, the adoption of an approach that de-emphasised the political potential of workers' activism – however successful it was in enabling formal labour organisation – also served to sever workers' strikes from the broader politics of protest and dissent in the period. Workers' actions were placed in a separate category to those of students, and their protests were portrayed primarily as part of broader negoti-

---

[53] See: Kooy et al., 'The Wiehahn Commission'.

[54] See: Friedman, *Building Tomorrow Today*.

[55] The literature on the role of unions in the insurgent politics of the 1980s is too large to canvas adequately here. For a sense of the role of the unions in the formation of the UDF see: Jeremy Seekings, *The UDF: A History of the United Democratic Front in South Africa, 1983–1991* (Cape Town, David Philip/Oxford, James Currey: 2000).

ations between workers and managements rather than as signs of a continuing political discontent. This allowed sympathisers to erect a wall between these categories, in part in light of the repressive response of the state to politicised student protest, on the one hand, and, on the other, the restrained actions of the police during the Durban Strikes.

Yet, the Durban Strikes were consistently interpreted at the time through the lens of student protest: whether seen as an attempt by student agitators to spread dissent, or whether seen as an alternate path to the emancipation of the African majority, the implicit reference was to the earlier student protests. In the light of the later success of labour activism, this has been largely forgotten. Nonetheless, it suggests that the particular conjuncture of protest, dissent, and activism in the decade before the Soweto Uprising played a significant role in shaping later labour politics.

The opening up of a space for labour organisation and public activism was thus closely linked to the rejection of the opportunities for dissenting politics that had been created by student protest. This rejection was encouraged by the state's assault on student politics – in which the Schlebusch Commission's recommendations were only one tool in the state's armoury. In the face of this assault, students – both those still in universities, and those now outside – had to reorganise.

5 Reimagining Resistance
'CAST OFF THE STUDENTS-ONLY ATTITUDE'

The reorganisation of oppositional movements did not occur out of the blue. Indeed, as early as 1971, members of SASO's senior leadership had been seriously considering two ways of restructuring the organisation: first, altering its internal structure and, second, establishing a new movement that could provide a home for SASO's members after the completion of their studies.

Their immediate concern was that the institutional structure of SASO might be too unwieldy and, perhaps, too amateurish in conception to respond to the pace of the organisation's development. They recognised that SASO was now a 'going concern' and would 'reach a membership mark of 3,000 by the end of the year' – which meant that it would have to consider increasing the scale of its activities in light of its growing membership. These early proposals focused on developing a core of 'committed leaders' within the university system. SASO did not have the luxury of NUSAS's structures dedicated to identifying potential leaders. In its operations to date, the pattern had been that any activist who demonstrated the potential to lead would have responsibility thrust upon them as soon as he or she began to participate in student politics. This was in part because 'the leadership potential in the black universities is very minimal ... due, mainly, to the conditions prevailing there which effectively stifle the full development of the intellectual being'. The overall effect had been to weaken the organisation. The different ages of the organisation's leaders, the general insecurities of youth, and the uneven distribution of leaders across the country had eroded the effectiveness of SASO: there was 'no intimacy among student leaders and this manifests itself in an obvious lack of cohesion in leadership ranks'. Without reorganisation, the organisation was in danger of coming apart at the seams.[1]

Alongside these discussions about the internal structures of SASO, another group within the national executive was beginning to discuss the possibility of launching an adult wing of the movement – an affiliated organisation that would neither be led by students nor be based on university campuses. In April 1971, this group met with represen-

---

[1] WHP A2675/III/748, 'SASO New Structure: A Proposal' (1971).

tatives of six other organisations, and then again, in August, attended a meeting of twenty-seven aboveground organisations representing different parts of the black community. These meetings were largely successful: although a significant number of the other organisations felt that SASO was too militant in its approach and risked, in Gerhart's words, 'an early clash with white authority', the majority of the represented organisations recognised the importance of this project and continued to engage with SASO on the organisation's plans.[2]

These initiatives – a restructuring of SASO's institutions, and the formation of a new movement that would provide a home for SASO's members after the completion of their studies – were at the forefront of the national executive's agenda when the protests at Turfloop and other black universities exploded late in April 1972.

During that month, Steve Biko met with Themba Sono – the sitting president of SASO – to discuss the possibility of a widespread crackdown on SASO's activities. After the meeting, Biko corresponded with Barney Pityana – the General Secretary – outlining the substance of that discussion, and suggesting further points for discussion within the national executive. He suggested that they consider plans for three alternatives: that the state banned SASO from operating on black campuses, that the state banned individual leaders, and that the state listed SASO as a prohibited organisation – and that, like the ANC and PAC, it be driven underground.[3]

The solutions that Biko suggested echoed and developed upon the proposals already circulating. First, in response to the threat that SASO might be banned from operating on black university campuses, it should embark upon a rapid expansion – establishing local branches in the regions around and outside these universities. The sites suggested for these branches were generally large urban centres – Durban, Cape Town, Port Elizabeth – and not the small towns and villages outside the more isolated black universities. The new branches would admit ordinary members of the public – thus fitting in with SASO's plans to expand – but would also, in the case of an immediate crisis, provide a haven for students: 'the idea is to get immediately as many city branches as possible using the present expelled student population'. In doing this, SASO would develop by taking on 'a youth group approach and gradually cast off the students-only attitude'.

Second, in the event that SASO's leaders were banned, a 'shadow Executive' should be put into place: a set of men and women waiting,

---

[2] See Gail M. Gerhart, *Black Power in South Africa: The Evolution of an Ideology* (Berkeley and Los Angeles, University of California Press: 1978), pp. 292–3.

[3] This letter has been reprinted as Appendix A of Themba Sono's autobiography: *Reflections on the Origins of Black Consciousness in South Africa* (Pretoria, HSRC: 1993). A photocopied version of this publication is filed in WHP A2675/III/749, but I have not been able to locate the original document.

learning by shadowing the existing executive, and ready to replace any banned members with minimal disruption. However, even this might create the appearance of institutional disarray, and so Biko suggested that community leaders be asked to 'quickly react whenever one of us is victimised'. A display of 'backing from the community at large' would help SASO survive the removal of its leaders and strengthen external connections.

However, neither of these responses would work if SASO itself were to be banned – that is, if it were to be listed as a prohibited organisation, and forbidden from organising aboveground. In their discussion, Sono considered that the absence of SASO would create an 'ideological vacuum' that would only ever be partially filled by any alternate body – and no such body existed at the start of 1972. The only practical advice that Biko could offer Pityana and the SASO executive was to consider practicalities: 'who the custodian of your office will be, who will use your machinery, etc., who will inherit your debts or assets, etc., etc.'.

These plans were soon to be put into practice. In the wake of the 1972 student protests, university administrators acted to seriously constrain SASO's presence on black campuses, sometimes by banning SASO from operating, sometimes by withdrawing the right to organise Student Representative Councils altogether. At the start of 1973, during the Durban Strikes, eight leaders associated with SASO and the new organisations set up in the previous year were served with banning orders – and the effective 'shadow executive' that succeeded them were themselves banned a few months later.

In the same moment that student protests reached the zenith of their intensity and frequency, the state began to act to shut down the spaces available to activists on university campuses. The assault on SASO was part of a multi-pronged attack on dissenting organisations. The establishment of Schlebusch Commission (briefly introduced in the previous chapter) provided a structure through which a legal assault on NUSAS and white student politics could take place. Attacks on black student organisations were more direct, driving SASO off university campuses. The state did not restrict itself to frustrating the institutional operation of student movements, however. It also targeted student leaders, banning and harassing members of both organisations. At its most brutal, the state was also involved in the murders of black activists – inaugurating a new and violent phase in the developing conflict between the apartheid state and its challengers.

This assault succeeded in part: SASO branches were closed, NUSAS's institutional abilities were crippled, and student activists were removed from public life. But it did not succeed in its ultimate aim of eliminating dissent: many student activists moved from the universities into other sites of resistance, including – perhaps most notably – labour organisation and the nascent trade union move-ment. These attempts to bridge the apparent divide between students and workers would gain impetus after the Durban Strikes, but were already underway in the run up to 1973. Meanwhile, other activists moved into SASO's sister organisations, the Black Peoples' Conven-tion and the Black Community Programme, which were set up in the face of the state's repressive actions. These sideways moves allowed committed activists to continue to work for a few more years before the state caught up – and kept ideas of dissent and examples of protest alive.

This chapter examines the dynamic of repression and resistance as it played out after the student protests of 1972, as it intensified during the Durban Strikes, and as it culminated in the early months of 1974. These two years were central to the shift away from momentary explo-sions of protest in the first part of the decade, and towards radical experiments in outreach – in the creation of new models of represen-tation, and solidarity – that emerged later. These radical experiments sought to expand the spaces of possibility open to political activists by bridging divides between students and workers, university spaces and public places, youth and the communities within which they had been born and brought up. They were means to erode apparent divisions and dichotomies, and to mutate the Manichaean stasis of the apartheid state.[4]

In these years, a new phase in the struggle against apartheid began: one in which the localised protests of students were transformed, and one in which the actions of the state, too, changed. At the start of this period, the state acted to suppress protest by banning indi-vidual students and prosecuting groups for acts of protest. By the end of the period, student activists faced the routine imposition of banning orders, unjustified arrests and detention, exile, and death.

'Certain organisations'

The roots of the official crackdown on student politics could be traced back to the late 1960s, when the government instituted the first of two Commissions of Inquiry that included the investigation of student politics as part of their remits. The Van Wyk de Vries Commission of

---

[4] I use the language of Frantz Fanon, here, as found in *A Dying Colonialism*, trans. Haakon Chevalier (New York, Monthly Review Press: 1965) and *The Wretched of the Earth*, trans. Richard Philcox (New York, Grove Press: 2004 [1963]). There is much to be said about the relationship between Fanon and the unfulfilled ambitions of Black Consciousness activists – but I'm unable to indulge myself in a discussion of this in the present context. See, however, the work of Nigel Gibson, in particular: *Fanonian Practices in South Africa: From Steve Biko to Abahlali baseMjondolo* (Pietermaritz-burg, University of KwaZulu-Natal Press: 2011).

Inquiry into universities and student affairs was launched in 1968, partly in response to the protests of white students at UCT and elsewhere. In the first months of 1972, a second Commission – the Schlebusch Commission – was instituted into the affairs and operations of 'certain organisations' – these organisation being NUSAS, the South African Institute of Race Relations, the University Christian Movement and the Christian Institute of South Africa.[5]

The Van Wyk de Vries Commission was controversial from its outset. It sat amid accusations of political favours being granted to academics who participated in the Commission. In particular, the awards granted to the Principal of the University of Natal, Owen Horwood – who sat as one of the nine members of the Commission's panel – caused a scandal. After his appointment to the Commission, Horwood was made a Senator by the National Party, and then admitted to cabinet. Once in office, Horwood was quoted in a Senate debate during June 1971 asking what universities were to do with student activists:

> when members of NUSAS who are university students, do the things I have mentioned here and many other things that I have not had time to mention and the many things that they are saying to incite racial unrest in this country, to play into the hands of our enemies outside the country and they do it day by day – what are these authorities doing to stop these nefarious activities?

These comments prompted student activists at UCT to criticise the Commission, suggesting that they demonstrated its pre-existing bias against student activists. The Commissioner himself responded by describing these students as 'impertinent' and 'contemptuous'. He informed the delegation of students from UCT that appeared before the Commission that they would not be heard, and dismissed them. In the same month, NUSAS was called to give evidence. The tone of the Commission's approach to NUSAS can be judged from one question when the Deputy President at the time, Paul Pretorius, was asked 'whether NUSAS would advise its members to fight or not to fight an army attacking South Africa specifically intending to end apartheid'.[6]

In this context, it was expected that the Commission would most likely be highly critical of NUSAS. When the Commission submitted its interim report on student activism to the Minister of Education and the State President at the end of 1972, speculation ran riot about

[5] For a brief survey of these two commissions, see Michael Lobban, *White Man's Justice: South African Political Trials in the Black Consciousness Era* (Oxford, Oxford University Press: 1996), pp. 82–6.

[6] Aluka Online Repository, NUSAS Press Digest: 'Government Commissions of Inquiry', prepared by Paul Pretorius and Nicki Westcott, <http://www.aluka.org/stable/10.5555/al.sff.document.rep19730222.026.022.000>, accessed 7 Dec 2015.

the contents of this report. NUSAS, following reports in the *Sunday Tribune* newspaper, speculated that it would recommend 'blocking overseas funds received by NUSAS and banning its multiracial membership' and establishing powers 'to force universities to withdraw from any "inter-university organisation" like NUSAS, deemed undesirable by the Minister of Education'. The power to enforce these regulations would be linked to the government's funding of universities, which could be suspended or reduced if the administration did not conform to the government's instructions.[7]

At the time, this was merely speculation – but it would turn out to be prescient.

While the Van Wyk de Vries Commission was submitting its interim report, another commission, the Schlebusch Commission of Inquiry into 'certain organisations', began its sittings. Unlike the Van Wyk de Vries Commission, this Commission was not explicitly directed at universities but rather at a loose group of organisations deemed suspicious by the government – apparently in the context of underground communist influence within South Africa. NUSAS, however, was one of the central targets of its investigation. The Schlebusch Commission's remit was broader than its predecessor's: 'to inquire into and report upon the objects, organization, activities, financing and related matters of NUSAS, the SAIRR, the UCM, and the CI, and their subordinate organizations'. Its powers were greater: 'full power and authority to interrogate at its discretion all persons who in its opinion are able to furnish information on the subjects mentioned in its terms of reference or on matters relating hereto … and to conduct investigations in the subject matter of this inquiry in any other authorised manner'. Its operations were also effectively secret: the hearings were closed, and the witnesses forbidden to speak about the proceedings, or to publicise their experiences before the Commission.[8]

At least forty men and women associated with NUSAS, student politics, and the English-speaking universities were subpoenaed to appear before the Schlebusch Commission in 1972. Paul Pretorius was examined on student politics for a full eight days before the Commission. In February 1973, as the Durban Strikes expanded, Schlebusch's first interim report recommended that Pretorius and seven other individuals be placed under restrictive banning orders (as described in the previous chapter). Unlike the Van Wyk de Vries Commission's recommendations, these were made public and were acted upon immediately – throwing NUSAS into disarray.

[7] Aluka Online Repository, NUSAS Analysis: 'Document on the Van Wyk de Vries Commission of Inquiry into Universities', prepared by Charles Nupen, <http://www.aluka.org/stable/10.5555/al.sff.document.rep19740000.026.022.000>, accessed 7 Dec 2015.
[8] Aluka, NUSAS Press Digest.

These banning orders did not represent the end of the Commission's activities, though. It continued to operate through 1973, releasing further 'interim reports' encouraging the state to take action against the investigated organisations. For example the Wilgespruit Fellowship Centre – a site run by the South African Council of Churches, and previously used by NUSAS as a training site – was described as a 'den of iniquity', and its administrator deported from South Africa. The passports of churchmen who refused to testify before the Commission were seized. Further prosecutions under the Suppression of Communism Act, among others, were recommended.[9]

In the fourth (and final) interim report of the Schlebusch Commission, the scope of its comments went beyond the official ambit of its investigation. In this report, the Commission set out its opinion on the connection between SASO, the Black Power movement in the USA and, oddly, international communism. As a Black Consciousness-aligned publication, the *Black Review,* summarised it: 'the Commission noted that [Stokely] Carmichael had an openly expressed admiration for the Chinese version of communism and that the only reason why the two quoted SASO leaders did not continue their philosophy to the logical conclusion was because they lived side by side with laws that would not allow this'. The 'grand conclusion' was that 'Black Consciousness was introduced to South Africa from America; that its basic tenet was a polarization of white and black attitudes towards each other; and that it was an undesirable philosophy bent on conditioning blacks on an overthrow of the existing order.'[10]

Although the Schlebusch Commission did not make explicit recommendations about SASO and its sister organisations, the decision to focus on Black Consciousness in this fashion was significant. At the start of the Commission's enquiries, the standard account of student politics circulating among government ministers emphasised the agency of white students in NUSAS and assumed that Black Consciousness organisations were – when they acted politically – either directed inspired by white students' actions or, more conspiratorially, actually controlled by white students. By the end of its hearings, though, the actions of black students were beginning to appear on their own – without the convenient explanation offered by agitating white students.

The conspiratorial logic underpinning the Schlebusch Commission's analysis of oppositional organisations fed into prosecutions brought by the state against activists – members of NUSAS, members of the Christian organisations under investigation by the Commission, and members of SASO. These prosecutions set out to confirm the

[9] Muriel Horrell and Dudley Horner, *A Survey of Race Relations in South Africa, 1973* (Johannesburg, SAIRR: 1974).
[10] Thoko Mbanjwa, *Black Review 1975/75* (Durban, Black Community Programmes: 1975).

Commission's allegations, and to ensure that these organisations were prevented from acting in South Africa. Several were successful.[11]

These prosecutions took place against the backdrop of an already narrowed public space for protest. At the start of 1974 – a year after the Durban Strikes, and the initial banning of eight NUSAS leaders and eight Black Consciousness activists – the final reports of both the Schlebusch and Van Wyk de Vries Commissions were published, and adopted by the government. These reports recommended everything that commentators and observers had feared: in addition to the banning orders levied in the past year, and in addition to the legal harassment faced by activists and organisers, severe restrictions were to be placed on the funding of NUSAS and other affected organisations. In response to these recommendations, parliament passed an act allowing the State President to declare certain organisations to be 'affected organisations', thus prevent them from receiving any financial support from sources outside of the country.[12]

These restrictions had a crippling effect on NUSAS. In the years immediately prior to their imposition, NUSAS's South African funding streams had begun to shrivel. The Durban campus of the University of Natal and the Johannesburg College of Education elected to disaffiliate themselves from NUSAS, leaving only three university campuses centrally affiliated with student union in 1975: the University of the Witwatersrand, the University of Cape Town and the Pietermaritzburg campus of the University of Natal.[13] Without foreign funding, the union would struggle to continue to operate, and could not continue in its existing national form.

By the end of 1973 and the beginning of 1974, the investigations of both Commissions of Inquiry had ended and their most restrictive recommendations were in the process of being implemented. Oppositional organisations had been under constant pressure for several years, and now were facing state action. The sites and sources of dissenting politics that had flourished, briefly, between 1969 and 1972 were no longer safe: university administrators were encouraged to suppress protest on black campuses, and discouraged from protecting dissent on white campuses. The organisational frameworks that encouraged students to act were being eroded, and the vital financial support that allowed NUSAS and other bodies to operate was being cut off.

In the face of these actions, the affected groups had little option but to either shut down or explore alternative forms of organisation.

[11] Lobban, *White Man's Justice*.
[12] Muriel Horrell, Dudley Horner and Jane Hudson, *A Survey of Race Relations in South Africa 1974* (Johannesburg, SAIRR: 1975).
[13] Muriel Horrell and Tony Hodgson, *A Survey of Race Relations in South Africa 1975* (Johannesburg, SAIRR: 1976).

For students, this meant leaving university spaces and beginning to engage with a broader public – one which included former students among its members, but which was not limited to them: a public that could include workers, youth, urban professionals and possibly even members of rural communities.

Expansion in the face of repression

SASO's plans for alternate forms of organisation were already underway before the state began to detain its leaders, and challenge its right to exist. The discussions begun in 1971 matured in 1972, and were taken up at the annual General Student Council (GSC) in July – just a few weeks after the spread of protests across black university campuses. The council introduced new policies, often based on the discussions between Biko, Pityana and Sono, within SASO's existing organisation.[14] Four new local branches were formally accredited in Durban, Springs, Pretoria and Kimberley. The council also discussed the formation of a range of new organisations, including a Continental Students' Movement and a Black Workers' Council (later re-named the Black Workers' Project). In addition to these proposals, the council also announced the formal launch of the Black Peoples' Convention, a new political movement that would soon run alongside SASO.[15]

These proposals all formed part of SASO's plans to expand their organisational capacities in anticipation of potential repression. Of these, the most significant were the Black Community Programme (BCP), which had been part of SASO's planning for several years, the Black Workers' Project, which would play an important role in the government's statements about the potential role of student activists in the Durban Strikes, and the Black Peoples' Convention (BPC).

The BCP was first discussed in 1971, with its principal aim to 'build up community awareness and liaison between students and the people'. This was imagined as an educative process: SASO sought to use the BCP to 'instil in the black community a sense of self-reliance ... to create an awareness and consciousness of the social, economic and political forces that frustrate their development; [and] to teach them skills and techniques that will help them develop as a community'. In effect, this meant that students should plan to

[14] It is important to note that Sono's position at this GSC was extremely controversial. After a Presidential Address that argued for considering whether to engage with state-directed structures of African representation, the gathered students passed a motion censuring him and removing him from the meeting. The further discussions about the future of Black Consciousness took place without his presence.

[15] WHP A2675/III/750, 'Motions of the General Students Council' (1972).

conduct 'research into the problems of a society', develop a popular literacy scheme, give seminars, set up 'physical work-camps', and embark upon a range of education programmes, including educating 'the community' about 'health', 'home economics', 'family planning' and 'recreation.'[16]

This, at least, was the intention. In practice, the ambitious project of community engagement and education was put into action in dribs and drabs. In 1972, when the BCP was formally launched, its principal activity was the publication of a small number of handbooks and the *Black Review* – a book-length survey of the activities of both Black Consciousness organisations and other community bodies over the past year. In 1973, the BCP expanded into a set of church programmes – linked to a 'Black Theology Agency' – as well as a set of further education programmes aimed at black youth and women. In 1974, these efforts expanded again: a home industries project, a health scheme and public clinic, and leadership training seminars.[17]

By comparison, the Black Workers' Project (BWP) was less successful in achieving its aims. The resolution adopted at the SASO GSC in July 1972 set out a range of objects for a Black Workers' Council: 'to act as a co-ordinating body to serve the needs and aspiration of the black workers; to unite and bring about the solidarity of black workers; [and] to conscientise them about their role and obligation toward black development '.[18] As the formal proposal developed by SASO after this GSC meeting held, this would offer 'something much wider in scope than a trade union'. Its structure would 'of course ... stem from [the] formation of craft unions. However seeing that most Africans are not craftsmen or skilled labourers they can be organised according to the kind of work they do.'[19] This was to be done by a new body: the Black Allied Workers' Union (BAWU).

As these different names – the Black Workers' Council, the Black Workers' Project, and BAWU itself – attest, the need to bring black workers into the politics of Black Consciousness was both obviously important to SASO and its activists, and at the same time a source of confusion and uncertainty. The struggles to relate the need to orga-nise at a shop floor level with the broad ambitions of student activists clearly shaped the tentative practical suggestions in these early docu-ments. They also shaped the uncertain and unsteady response of these workers' organisations to the Durban Strikes in 1973. BAWU released a handful of press releases, but played no role in organising or co-

---

[16] WHP A2675/III/747, 'Community Development Project Proposals' (Sept. 1971).

[17] See the summaries in B.A. Khoapa (ed.), *Black Review 1972* (Durban, Black Commu-nity Programmes: 1973); Mafika Pascal Gwala (ed.), *Black Review 1973* (Durban, Black Community Programmes: 1974); and Mbanjwa (ed.), *Black Review 1974*.

[18] WHP A2675/III/750, Minutes of the 3rd General Student Council (July 1972).

[19] WHP A2675/III/751, The Black Workers' Project: A Proposal (1972).

ordinating the strikes.[20] In the aftermath, however, BAWU did manage to act on some of its aims, boasting a formal membership of 8,000 workers in 1974.[21]

These initiatives sought to move SASO's activities from the universities to communities and workplaces: they placed students in dialogue with non-students, and sought to spread the ideas and tenets of Black Consciousness to a wider public. However, they did not extend existing institutional structures, remaining largely bound to SASO and its initial priorities.

Instead, the most important of these organisations – and the one which was most able to act on its own behalf – was the BPC. Its first public appearance had come in a press statement in January 1972. Signed by an 'ad-hoc committee', this statement called for 'the formation of a Black Peoples political movement whose primary aim is to unite and solidify Black people with a view to liberating and emancipating them from ... psychological oppression'.[22]

The process of organising the BPC was fraught with potential problems. The ad-hoc committee met in February, and then again in May to discuss the practical organisation of the movement, which was facing several minor crises: for example, by May, the draft constitution was ready but had 'not as yet been typed and roneod [sic]'.[23] The meeting in fact began by castigating the chairman, Drake Koka, for 'letting the morale of the Committee run low by not facilitating communication and by not injecting vim into his colleagues'. Despite this – and despite Koka's response that 'individual members should be responsible enough to carry on organisational work without necessarily waiting for directives' – the committee was determined to carry on its work.

A discussion over the best way to launch the movement followed. The committee was split on this: several members argued that the 'grassroots' organisation was too weak to justify launching the BPC in July to coincide with the SASO meeting – the announced date of its formation. Others, however, argued for its immediate launch, suggesting that 'organisational work shall be facilitated when an already structure exists [sic].' This group argued that 'it is difficult to organise people when there is no structure to present to them' and that 'delay could only further dampen the ad hoc committee'. The consensus at this meeting was to hold a larger meeting – but to hold

---

[20] Aluka Online Repository, Black Peoples Convention: Press Release 3rd March 1973, <http://www.aluka.org/stable/10.5555/AL.SFF.DOCUMENT.pre19730303.032. 009.283>, accessed 7 Dec 2015.

[21] Mbanjwa, *Black Review 1974*, p. 136.

[22] Aluka Online Repository, Black Peoples Convention: Press Release 13 January 1972, <http://www.aluka.org/stable/10.5555/al.sff.document.pre19720113.032.009.282>, accessed 7 Dec 2015.

[23] To 'roneo' a document was to duplicate using a precursor of the modern photocopying machine, using a stencil and a rotating ink press.

off on summoning a formal national convention until further organisation had taken place.[24]

It is perhaps significant that one of the members of the committee calling for an immediate launch was Steve Biko, and that this meeting was taking place in the same month as his correspondence with Pityana, setting out the need for Black Consciousness activists to consider possible responses to state repression. In the context of the months of the student rebellion at Turfloop and other black university campuses, the need for Black Consciousness activists to consider immediate – rather than postponed – action was politically important. The consequences of the protests at Turfloop and elsewhere were dire: students were expelled or suspended, universities were closed, and the formal recognition that had been granted to SASO on several of these campuses was now withdrawn. A new organisation would have to be able to accept the membership of activists who had been expelled from their studies and were no longer students. It would have to be able to operate outside of campus spaces – that is, beyond the reach of repressive university administrators.

In this moment, the BPC represented the most plausible version of this new organisation. SASO's other initiatives – the actual launch of a handful of local branches outside of university campuses, and the planned development of a range of other organisations – were either geographically limited, or too far from being implemented.

The BPC held its first national Council in December 1972, six months behind its initial schedule. This meeting saw the election of its first president, Winifred Kgware, and a paid secretary-general, Sipho Buthelezi, as well as the remainder of its national executive. At this meeting, the BPC committed itself to education and outreach programmes, investigating international links, engaging with the press, and otherwise establishing the institutional foundations of the movement.[25] Unlike the other organisations imagined by Black Consciousness activists, the BPC began by setting up new structures at its outset and planned an existence independent of SASO.

But these efforts masked a standing problem, already identified by the BPC ad-hoc committee: without a grassroots network, the movements were at least as vulnerable to the state's assault as SASO itself. All of these plans depended on time – time to educate and conscientise, time to organise, time to institutionalise. Without that time, the efforts of these activists would be a struggle, and most probably fail. That time was not granted to them: in February 1973 the state's assault

---

[24] Aluka Online Repository, Minutes of Meeting: Black Peoples Convention Ad Hoc Committee (28 May 1972). <http://www.aluka.org/stable/10.5555/AL.SFF.DOCU-MENT.min19720528.032.009.282>, accessed 7 Dec 2015.

[25] WHP A2675/III/282, Minutes of First National Congress (17 Dec 1972).

on white student activists began, and in March Black Consciousness leaders joined them in the firing line.

In the absence of mass support and multiple possible organisers, these movements were heavily dependent on a core group of activists. This meant that the BPC, for example, was affected in the same way as SASO was by the imposition of banning orders on Black Conscious-ness activists in March 1973: of the eight banned men, Steve Biko, Bokwe Mafuna, Drake Koka and Saths Cooper were all members of the ad-hoc committee that had been responsible for setting up the BPC, and were all at the time members of its executive. The effects of these bannings was not limited to the BPC. Biko and Mafuna were also local representatives for the BPC, in Johannesburg and Kingwilliamstown respectively. This was not all: Mafuna – possessing a third institu-tional identity – was also a national coordinator of BAWU at the time.

So, although the activists of SASO sought to expand the range of the nascent Black Consciousness movement through the creation of new organisations, intended to cater to different parts of the larger black community and to take up different aspects of social and political struggle, their efforts were frustrated by the state's unexpectedly rapid attack on Black Consciousness activists. The second wave of banning orders, handed down in August 1973, continued this attack. In these moments, the relatively small group of the movement's key personnel became obvious: each banning order affected multiple organisations, and eroded the capacity of Black Consciousness organisations to develop firm roots in communities across the country.

If the efforts made by these activists to expand the range of the Black Consciousness movement had begun earlier – or if the efforts of the state to drive the same activists out of public life had begun later – then these new organisations might have developed a sustained network of resistance. As it was, though, they struggled to maintain their existence in the face of repression.

The Wages Commissions

Meanwhile, as SASO and its activists sought to expand their network of organisations, NUSAS and its activists responded to the changing circumstances of the early 1970s by burrowing deeper into the existing networks of student organisation. As they did so, however, the nature and objects of their activities shifted, moving from campus concerns to broad labour struggles. These processes demonstrated the unwilling-ness of activists to accept the dichotomies that structured the apartheid order – and their need to engage positively across supposed divides.

In 1971, students at the University of Natal in Durban proposed that the SRC on that campus establish a 'Wages Committee' to investigate the wages of African workers employed by the university, and to measure those wages against the Poverty Datum Line. Its proposers argued that the Committee's investigations were necessarily understood as part of campus politics because, although

> students may feel that wages as such are peripheral to student concerns ... in a capitalist society wages are the key to food, shelter, health, education, clothes, transport, and recreation ... The function of students is to redress the imbalance [of society] by using the facilities provided by a university ... to make people aware of the situation of poverty wages.[26]

These aims were elaborated upon in a paper that same year by David Hemson, also based at the University of Natal, in which workers were identified as 'the most important people in South Africa ... those who actually operate the productive processes of the economy'. Because of this, the most significant political action that students could take to disturb the existing society was to support the organisation and actions of these workers. This would not always be easy – 'students cannot be expected to strike up immediate bonds of empathy with workers. There are barriers of class, language and race.'[27] Nonetheless, some communication between classes – between students and workers, in other words – was necessary to permit the development of an effective radical politics. In this light, the question that students faced was crisp: how best to enable workers to act politically, without seeking to dominate or distort their potential consciousness?

The answer, at least as far these activists at this moment were concerned, was to set the instruments of oppression against each other. One of these instruments was the authority of the knowledge produced by the university itself: 'It is important to remember that workers have been created through expropriation of the means of production ... a process which is continuing today to provide the surplus to create universities ... the means to knowledge have not dropped from heaven.' This knowledge could be used by students 'committed to a policy of redirecting the flow of information relevant to the daily industrial activity from the exclusive property of management to the workers as a whole'. In other words, students could act to empower workers by breaking the monopoly of knowledge held by employers – in particular, knowledge about workers' wages.[28]

Instead of attempting to lead protests from the front-lines, white students could now choose to occupy another place in a political

---

[26] University of Cape Town Archives (UCT), BC 586/G3.1 (NUSAS Papers, Wages Commission), 'Proposed Establishment of a Wages Committee Under the Student Representative Council' (1971).

[27] University of KwaZulu-Natal, Alan Paton Centre (APC), PC126/4/5 (Gerhard Maré Collection, Wages Commission Publications), 'Students and Workers' (1971).

[28] APC PC126/45, 'Students and Workers'.

network: making use of their privileged position in a racist and capitalist society to empower black workers to act for themselves. In this
way, these student activists could accept the challenge posed by Black
Consciousness – to cease attempting to shape or guide the politics of
black communities – without surrendering the possibility of contributing to new political developments. In doing so, though, they reimagined the structures of South African politics, by first linking race with
class and then by suggesting how the intersection of class and race
could found a politics that could bring down the structures of apartheid's racial capitalism.[29]

The attraction of this idea was seen by students across the country.
After the University of Natal's initial establishment of a Wage Commission, students at the University of Cape Town rapidly followed – establishing their own Commission before the end of 1971. Within two
years, five such Wages Commissions existed – in Durban, Pietermaritzburg, Cape Town, Johannesburg and Grahamstown. All were structured similarly: simultaneously constituted as a committee under the
university's SRC, and affiliated to NUSAS through its 'social action'
and welfare arm, NUSWEL (National Union of South African Students'
Welfare Secretariat).[30]

These Wages Commissions were immediately active, appearing
in front of official Wages Board hearings in these major centres to
present information on the relation between the Poverty Datum Line
and actual wages for African workers.[31] The Commissions also set
up Workers Advice Bureaus, and – in the aftermath of the Durban
Strikes – disseminated information on the legal situation pertaining
to workers' committees, trade unions and other forms of labour organisation.[32] These activities by the Wages Commissions supported the
emerging black labour movement in its struggle for recognition both
from the state and from employers.

This was not without consequences, of course. After the strikes, the
Wages Commissions attracted the attentions of the government and its

[29] The 'race-class debate' was the subject of intense contestation in the 1970s and
1980s – contestation which continues to erupt in the present. The literature is too
extensive to properly survey here. See, however: Harold Wolpe, 'Capitalism and
Cheap Labour Power in South Africa: From Segregation to Apartheid', *Economy and
Society* 1 (4): 1972 pp. 425–56; John S. Saul and Stephen Gelb, 'The Crisis in South
Africa: Class Defense, Class Revolution', *Monthly Review* 33 (3): 1981, pp. 9–44 and
134–49; and Merle Lipton, *Capitalism and Apartheid: South Africa, 1910–1986* (Cape
Town, David Philip: 1986).

[30] UCT BC586/G3.1, 'The UCT Wages Commission: A Background Paper for New
Members' (1974).

[31] See, for example: UCT BC586/G3.1, Minutes of the Wages Board Hearing on Stone
Crushing in the Transvaal (7 Feb 1972).

[32] See, for example: APC PC126/4/5, 'Why Black Trade Unions' (April 1973) and a
further pamphlet, 'Dirt Cheap' (c.1973), and UCT BC586/G3.1, 'Training Manual'
(c.1973).

various Commissions of Inquiry. In the first months of 1973, the Wages Commissions were seen as a source of potential disruption: employers in Cape Town, for example complained that the publications of the Wages Commission would 'incite their contented and happy workers' – as a confidential report of the UCT Wages Commission quoted them as saying.[33] As a consequence of this challenge, the UCT Wages Commission adopted a range of restrictions, including the appointment of a board of advisors to separate out its 'academic' publications from its other work.[34] This seemed to appease the local critics of the Wages Commission – but highlighted the extent to which the Commissions depended on the authority of their academic positions to defend themselves against assault.

Alongside other oppositional organisations, the Wages Commissions also found themselves criticised by the Schlebusch Commission. Chapter 17 of this Commission's fourth interim report focused on 'The Wages Campaign' of NUSAS – and portrayed it as a revolutionary force. 'The NUSAS leaders concerned and their henchmen are using the wages question, which is charged with emotion, as the fuse, and Bantu workers as the powder to ignite a revolution.' 'Their methods follow the communist guidelines that have been laid down. Communist doctrine also rejects the idea that a revolution could originate spontaneously.'[35] These allegations served to incorporate the actions of the Wages Commissions into the broad critique of NUSAS: that the student activists involved in these organisations were merely the tools of a revolutionary minority, and that the elimination of this minority – and, indeed, these institutions – would restore order.

Ironically, one of the tools that student activists could use to defend themselves in this period had been provided by the state during the Durban Strikes. By placing labour activism outside of the realm of political contest – by emphasising that material deprivation was pre-political, and that wages below the Poverty Datum Line were valid subjects on which workers could express themselves – the state had inadvertently carved out a space of political possibility. In the work of the Wages Commissions, this space enabled some activists to insist that their work was not political – and thus was not subject to the same kinds of restrictions as the activities of, for example, NUSAS.

At the time, the leaders of the Wages Commission of the University of Natal at Pietermaritzburg (UNP) deployed the unique institutional structure of the Commissions to defend themselves against Schlebusch's attacks. The Wages Commission, they argued, was not a part

---

[33] UCT BC586/G3.1, 'Confidential Report of Meetings between Employers and the Wages Commission in Cape Town' (April 1973).

[34] UCT BC586/G3.1, 'Report to the NUSAS Local Committee and the SRC' (May 1973).

[35] As quoted in UCT BC586/G3.1, Open Letter ... from the Wages Commission, University of Natal, Pietermaritzburg (1974).

of NUSAS: it was set up by independent student activists on the UNP campus. Its affiliations with NUSWEL were formal only, and it did not answer to the organisation: 'we reject, further any suggest that NUSAS, NUSAS's leaders, or anyone else is manipulating us ... We function as a completely autonomous body subject only to that accountability. We co-operate ... but only on our own terms.'[36]

This strategy bought the Wages Commissions time. This time was used to continue to develop what Grace Davie calls a 'triple herme- neutic' of political struggle, practical knowledge and official science: 'student activists sought to inhabit workers' frames of meaning and to translate their grievances into the language of social science, but they also attempted to convince their research subjects – whom they also saw as comrades in class struggle – to speak the language of social science themselves'. These efforts, Davie agues, helped to reshape public discourses around labour: the category of 'workers' was solid- ified, and 'notions of universal and comparable basic needs' entered into the ordinary calculus of employers, workers and the observing public. [37]

But it was not enough. As NUSAS was forced to retire from public political action in the face of the Schlebusch Commission's attacks, and the state's imposition of restrictions on external funding, so too were the Wages Commissions forced to retreat from their public efforts. Although the Wages Commissions continued to operate into 1975, they did so under increasing constraints. Some focused on research, and moved away from attempts to organise workers. Others sought to encourage the development of external organisations – advice bureaus, and new labour unions. The successes of these efforts helped justify the retreat of the Wages Commissions (and NUSAS in general) from the public sphere. At the annual NUSAS meeting in July 1975, a 'critical appraisal' of the direction of the organisation suggested that 'NUSAS is withdrawing more and more from the field of direct action, that is, Labour ... bodies like the Wages Commissions can exist independent of NUSAS'. By 1976, the meeting suggested that the Wages Commis- sions 'found it increasingly difficult to define their role' in relation to the new black trade unions they had hoped to encourage.[38] In this context, the Wages Commissions – despite their structural indepen- dence – were unsupported by the national union, and began to drift, unmoored from their original aims.

[36] UCT BC586/G3.1, Open Letter.
[37] Grace Davie, *Poverty Knowledge in South Africa: A Social History of Human Science, 1855–2005* (Cambridge, Cambridge University Press: 2015), pp. 196–7.
[38] Both quoted in Martin Legassick and Christopher Saunders, 'Above-Ground Activ- ities in the 1960s', SADET, *The Road to Democracy in South Africa, Volume 1* (Johannesburg, Zebra: 2004), pp. 869–70.

Taking stock

In the years between 1971 and 1974, student activists could thus feel the slow descent of the hand of the state: first, the Van Wyk de Vries and Schlebusch Commissions were clearly oriented against white student politics and then – later – the black politics of SASO; as they sat, black campuses became increasingly hostile to student organisations in the wake of the university protests that began at Turfloop in 1972; and then, at the height of the strike wave in Durban, the government levied banning orders against sixteen activists associated either with NUSAS or with SASO. From this moment onwards, every act taken by student activists took place under the eyes of the state – and every act took place in anticipation of the government's inevitable reaction.

In these circumstances, students activists sought to broaden the reach of their political ideas. Activists within NUSAS sought to re-orient white student politics away from a focus on public forms of protest towards using the tools of the academy to support the efforts of labour activists to organise themselves into a significant social and political force. For this, the Wages Commissions needed to move off campus and to engage with black workers in the country's metropolises. At the same time, activists within SASO were also beginning to re-orient their politics: as activists left universities, either by graduating or as a consequence of expulsion, organisations needed to be developed in alternate spaces. The Black Community Programme provided a set of ways in which activism could move off campus, the Black Workers' Project provided a way for black students to engage workers, and the Black People's Convention provided a space in which former students could continue to develop their political projects.

All of these efforts shared a goal: to reach out to communities beyond the student body. Their motives, though, were mixed and sometimes inconsistent. For the white students involved in the Wages Commissions, outreach was premised on a mix of political imperatives: an acceptance of SASO's critique of attempts by white students to protest on behalf of the black majority, a belief in the revolutionary potential of the working classes, and perhaps a faith in the potential for applied scholarly knowledge to alter popular perceptions. For the black students of SASO, their efforts at outreach were premised on an ambivalent relationship to broader black communities: how could they as students relate to those who had not been to university, but who had instead been excluded from the ambiguous benefits of a relatively elite education? Should students return to their home communities to learn from these different experiences, or should they return to lead? The Black Community Programme was the product of this tension, as was the Black Workers' Project. The BPC, however, served a different purpose: to provide a home for explicitly political struggle outside of the institutional and ideological framework associated with student politics. ·

These projects were not driven by identical motives, or even structured particularly alike, but they were all products of the particular context of this moment – of the historical conjuncture of the early 1970s. Activists were responding to the same events and pressures: the repression of student politics, and the explosion of labour activism outside the universities. Their different visions of community activism were reshaped by these events and pressures, coming to emphasise community organisation and engagement with workers as the central elements of their actual political praxis. This meant that – whatever their original aims – students in NUSAS and those leaving SASO found themselves moving on parallel paths, towards a new form of politics.

If these movements had been able to take stock of the successes and failures of their efforts at outreach, a year or two after the Durban Strikes, they would have been likely to regard their achievements with ambivalence. SASO had organised new branches and had launched new organisations – but as these were developing, its original core was being stripped. Black students were leaving universities in droves; those that remained were often forced to hide their political interests, as the administrators forbade aboveground organising. The Wages Commissions communicated political knowledge to workers, challenged the official public consensus on wages and set up a series of advisory and support bureaus that assisted workers to organise themselves. But at the same time, the leaders of the Commissions struggled to maintain the interest of NUSAS in these projects, and seemed to be in the process of rendering themselves obsolete as new groups of workers – organised in trade unions – began to form and engage in their own interests.

The new form of politics – of engagement with labour, and with localised community organisations – would later come to constitute the core of the renewed public politics of the coming decade, linking new trade union federations with churches and other movements to form the United Democratic Front against the apartheid state.[39] But its later successes were by no means predictable in the moment of its emergence: both SASO and NUSAS struggled to establish these links, and the early advances promised by the initial connections between students and workers, in particular, were frustrated by the state's attack on activists and organisers in 1973, and after.

[39] See: Jeremy Baskin, *Striking Back: A History of COSATU* (London, Routledge: 1991); and Jeremy Seekings, *The UDF: A History of the United Democratic Front in South Africa, 1983–1991* (Cape Town, David Philip/Oxford, James Currey: 2000).

'Died in the struggle'

These attacks were brutal – and increased in violence throughout this period. The state did not only use legal means – such as imposing banning orders on individuals, or declaring organisations 'affected' – to stifle its opponents. From these years onwards, it also began to use illegal and covert forms of violence to brutalise these opponents – even, by 1974, murdering activists.

One of the first signs of this new wave of brutish violence came with the death of Ahmed Timol in detention in October 1971. Timol had been a student activist, left the country during the height of the post-Sharpeville repression, returned, and was, by the early 1970s, working as a schoolteacher in Johannesburg. He was arrested and detained, interrogated and tortured. On 27 October, Timol fell from a tenth floor window of the national police headquarters, John Vorster Square. He was 29 years old when he died. The police claimed that his death was suicide.[40]

At the time, this explanation was viewed with scepticism. A wide range of South Africans – including student activists, but also members of the Progressive Party and the liberal parliamentary opposition – embarked upon protests, and demanded a judicial commission of inquiry into Timol's death. Perhaps unsurprisingly, the official investigation was run by a compliant magistrate, who held that Timol had died 'from serious brain injuries and loss of blood when he jumped from a window ... The cause of death is suicide and nobody is to blame.'[41]

This death was soon followed by others.

In December 1972, a year later, Mthuli Shezi – an activist associated with SASO for several years, and one of the founders of the BPC and BWP – was killed in the course of a strange altercation at a railway station in Durban. According to his father's testimony to the Truth and Reconciliation Commission, twenty-four years later, Shezi confronted a white man 'pouring water over some women' on the platform. The two men exchanged insults, and then the white man pushed Shezi off the platform and in front of a moving train. Shezi was fatally wounded in the fall; taken to hospital, he spoke to his father, and then died in the course of the night. He was 24 years old.[42]

The authorities took an unusual interest in Shezi's untimely death. His father was harangued by railway officials, who told him that his son was mentally ill; at the mortuary he was told his son had died

[40] See Imtiaz Cajee, *Timol: Quest for Justice* (Johannesburg, STE: 2005).
[41] Quoted in Truth and Reconciliation Commission of South Africa, *TRC Report – Volume 3* (Cape Town, Truth and Reconciliation Commission: 1999), p. 543.
[42] Truth and Reconciliation Commission, Human Rights Violations hearings, Testimony of Ambrose Shezi (Alexandra, 28 October 1996).

because he was a 'politician'; and, after the burial, Shezi's grave was desecrated:

> After the funeral when we got back to the grave we found the police had overturned the tombstone, they have shot it and it was just lying down scattered and when we asked we were told this was done by the police. And we asked why are they killing him for the second time because they have already killed him. I was asking them because I didn't know he was involved in politics and they said to me he is fighting against the government.

For activists in the Black Consciousness movements, Shezi's murder brought home the potential consequences of opposition. Whether intentionally planned by the police, or merely accidental, the mysterious circumstances of his death – and the vicious action by the police in the days afterwards – cast Shezi's murder in the light of his political commitments. He was seen as a martyr: in a flyer prepared during December 1972, Shezi was described as 'a young, black man who was assassinated in defence of black mothers, black children and the black community. He died whilst defending and protecting them against moral, psychological and physical assaults.' The conclusion to be drawn was clear: he was 'a black martyr who died for black people'.[43]

A year after his death, the BPC issued a further 'tribute' to Shezi. It once again described his death as a 'violent assassination … inflicted by an agent of protection of White racism superiority and oppression'. This notice now pointed out, though, that the violence demonstrated in this murder 'should not be regarded as being directed towards him alone, but should be regarded as a concerted assault on the entire Black Community'. The tribute concluded with a call to arms:

> In defence of the inherent dignity and pride of the Black man he will rank as a Black martyr and shall live in our minds as a symbol of Solidarity with the Black struggle for liberation. His violent assassination is a clear call to you and to me of the urgency with which we are faced in the struggle – liberation of the 23,000,000 Blacks in this country.[44]

Shezi's murder shifted the discussions within the BPC and other Black Consciousness organisations. It had an immediate impact on their work: Shezi had been an active organiser in both the BPC and the BWP. His death at the end of 1972 – and thus the absence of a committed and engaged organiser in Durban – may have contributed to the BWP's inability to respond effectively to the strike wave of the first months of 1973.[45] But, more than this, Shezi's death shaped the ways in which

[43] A2675/III/282, Mr Mthuli Shezi, Our Black Martyr (Dec 1972).
[44] WHP A2675/III/284, 'Tribute to the late Mthuli ka Shezi' (Dec 1973).
[45] This is Gail Gerhart's suggestion: *Black Power*, p. 293.

Black Consciousness activists began to perceive themselves in relation to the state, a state which was encouraging universities to expel troublesome students, which was banning student leaders, which was covering up deaths in detention, and which was celebrating the murder of one of SASO's own. Activists now knew themselves to be embattled.

The extent to which this shaped their existence can be seen in the development of Onkgopotse Tiro's life in the eighteen months after his expulsion from Turfloop, following his rousing speech at the university's graduation ceremony.[46] Tiro was expelled from a graduate programme – and so, unlike many or most of the black students leaving their studies, he did possess a university qualification. He also was highly regarded by SASO's leadership, as well as the executive committee of the newly formed BCP. These two things both helped direct his progress after May 1972.

Tiro returned to his mother's house, in Soweto. Shortly thereafter – about a month after his expulsion – he was employed to teach at the Morris Isaacson High School. Morris Isaacson was one of the oldest schools in Soweto, and one of the township's 'islands of learning', sites in which, despite the constraints imposed by the state's African education policies, a reputation for intellectual excellence developed. It had, in Clive Glaser's words, a 'tradition of more open-minded, critical education' than the state's policies would have encouraged. It was also led by a charismatic school principal, who was willing to allow – or even, at times, encourage – the politicisation of his student body, and who was willing to risk employing a troublemaker like Tiro.[47]

This decision was not without consequences: Morris Isaacson's headmaster spent much of the remainder of 1972 and early 1973 in a dispute with the national Bantu Education Department, which refused to countenance Tiro's appointment. After the Department froze Tiro's salary, the school sought to raise private funds to pay him – but this was not sustainable. In February 1973, less than a year after joining the school, Tiro was relieved of his teaching position.[48]

In the months that he was based at the school, though, Tiro used his connections with SASO and the BPC to help entrench a new movement of school-going students – the Southern African Students Movement (SASM) – at Morris Isaacson. According to Nozipho Diseko, SASM had been operating in one form or another since 1968 – and was, in many ways, independent of SASO and other national organisations.

[46] For a more detailed account of Tiro's life see Anne Heffernan, 'Black Consciousness's Lost Leader: Abraham Tiro, the University of the North, and the Seeds of South Africa's Student Movement in the 1970s', *Journal of Southern African Studies*, 41 (1): 2015, pp. 173–86.

[47] See Clive Glaser, 'Soweto's Islands of Learning: Morris Isaacson and Orlando High Schools Under Bantu Education, 1958–1975,' *Journal of Southern African Studies*, 41 (1): 2015, pp. 159–71.

[48] Heffernan, 'BC's Lost Leader', p. 183 and Glaser, 'Soweto's Islands', p. 169.

Instead of acting as a 'junior division' of SASO, or as its 'school-student arm', SASM had its own aims and understandings of the principles of Black Consciousness.[49] During his stint at Morris Isaacson, Tiro liaised between SASO and SASM and taught several of its emerging leaders. He was a charismatic figure for these school-going students, and helped encourage closer links between their activism and SASO's own aims.[50]

In June 1973, SASM held an electoral conference and voted Tiro as its national president.[51] He would work with SASO's Permanent Organiser, as that year's national student council voted to mandate him to work with SASM to build a united front of student organisations.[52] Their first task was to set up an office for SASM across the border, in Botswana – where the formally transnational movement might be secure from the apartheid state. Tiro was central to this task, as one of the few members of SASO with a passport permitting him to enter and leave South Africa legally.

This project would soon take over Tiro's life: soon after this student council reports began to circulate that he was 'being hunted by the South African Security Police, so that he could be served with banning orders'.[53] In the face of these threats, he joined other Black Consciousness activists underground and – in September – crossed the border into Botswana along with Bokwe Mafuna and Harry Nengwekhulu. In the next months, he sought to establish a base for Black Consciousness activists in Botswana, while raising international knowledge about SASO's work.

This phase of his life lasted almost five months. Then, on 1 February 1974, Tiro received a parcel. It was marked to look as though it had been sent by the International University Exchange Fund (IUEF) – a Swiss-based organisation that supported student struggles in South Africa and elsewhere. The parcel contained a bomb – which exploded.

Tiro died in the explosion.

In the words of Tiro's mother, two decades later:

> The next morning someone called from Lobatse, looking for Tiro, and he telephone the next-door neighbours. They sent a child to tell Tiro he has a telephone call from Lobatse. This child found Tiro's corpse there ... Because he was a child he ran away and he said oh there's a man lying on the floor and people started flocking to the house and they discovered it was true.[54]

[49] Nozipho Diseko, 'The Origins and Development of the South African Students' Movement (SASM): 1968–1976,' *Journal of Southern African Studies*, 18 (1): 1992, pp. 40–62. In its first years, SASM was known as the African Students Movement (ASM) and only adopted its later name in 1973.

[50] Heffernan, 'BC's Lost Leader,' pp. 181–3.

[51] Khoapa, *Black Review 1973*, p. 67.

[52] WHP A2675/III/752, Minutes of the 5th GSC (July 1973).

[53] Khoapa, *Black Review* 1973, p. 67.

[54] Truth and Reconciliation Commission, Human Rights Violation Hearings, Testimony of Moleseng Anna Tiro (Gauteng, 19 April 1996).

Tiro's death shocked activists, and revealed the violence of the state to a broad audience. The IUEF immediately disclaimed responsibility for sending the parcel, and pointed out that all its mail to Botswana would have to transit through South Africa. The Botswana government went further, stating that in its opinion, Tiro was killed for 'speaking out against the denial to Black South Africans of their human rights' after having 'incurred the displeasure of certain powerful circles in South Africa'. In response, the South African Minister of Justice and the Police denied that he had been involved in the assassination, and the South African Postal Services disclaimed all responsibility.[55]

Later, the South African Truth and Reconciliation Commission (TRC) found that, 'in all probability, Tiro's death was the result of the work of ... members of the "Z Squad", the operational arm of BOSS, the intelligence-gathering agency of the government at the time'. It also found that 'the former state and the Minister of Law and Order were responsible for the assassination'.[56] In doing so, the TRC confirmed what activists had suspected from the first moments after Tiro's death: that the apartheid state had crossed a significant line. Where before it may have merely celebrated the deaths of its opponents, it now was committed to acting well beyond the bounds of its public commitment to legality. In place of lip-service to a legal order, the police would now act illegally to bring about these deaths, through brutal and covert acts of violence.

In 1974, SASO issued a memorandum listing significant information about the Black Consciousness movement. Among these lists was an account of thirty-one 'Black Leaders who have been silenced by the Minister of Justice'. All thirty-one activists had been banned in the year since March 1973. Above this list was another, headed 'Died in the Struggle'.

On this list were the names of Ahmed Timol, Mthuli Shezi and Onkgopotse Tiro.

Their deaths inaugurated a new phase in the struggle against the apartheid state: one in which the state increasingly used underground and illegal forms of violence to directly attack, assault, and murder its opponents. From the start of 1974, the fear of death became a constant presence. In the context of this brutalisation of the state, political opposition could no longer take the forms that it had – localised protest, community organisation and ideological exploration were no longer sufficient forms of resistance. Instead, new strategies of challenge now had to be adopted.

---

[55] Quoted in Gwala, *Black Review 1974*, p. 110.
[56] TRC Report Volume 3, p. 549. The ministry responsible for policing had shifted in the meantime, and was known as the Ministry of Law and Order at the end of apartheid.

6 The Pro-Frelimo Rallies of 1974
'STAND UP AND BE COUNTED'

In March 1973 – as the Durban Strikes continued, and as the state began to impose banning orders on the leaders of SASO, the Black Peoples' Convention (BPC), and their affiliated organisations – SASO released a twenty-four page pamphlet titled 'SASO on the Attack: An Introduction to the South African Students' Organisation 1973'. It set out the movement's position: that it was a response to 'the oppressive clutches of white ascendency … [the] whole decrepit system of values' that condemned 'young black people' to a 'life almost devoid of sanctimonious socio-political values'.

The year before 'must be regarded as the most productive and historic of [SASO's] existence … community development projects were methodologically brought into operation'; the Black Workers' Projects had been set up; a black-run student newspaper was planned; strikes had radicalised university students. Through all this, 'SASO has come to be accepted as one of the most relevant organisations in this search for the black man's real identity and of his liberation.' The pamphlet's introduction concluded by suggesting that now, in 1973:

> Our problems are defined, our strategies cut and dried, but our commitment still leaves much to be desired. It is about time this commitment is heightened … We cannot afford to stand in the corner with split minds and shudder. We cannot shirk the responsibility to transform this society … Now is the time to stand up and be counted.[1]

In the wake of the assault on student protest detailed in the previous chapter, this call would soon take on added resonance. As activists were harassed by the police, banned from public engagements by the state, and sometimes murdered, young men and women sought to build networks of support and solidarity. The Wages Commissions, the Black Community Programme, and the Black Peoples' Convention were all part of this same work. But building organisational networks was not – and could not be – sufficient. Communities and activists needed to stand together, in private and in public, to resist state repression, and to keep oppositional politics alive.

---

[1] WHP A2675/III/752, 'SASO on the Attack' (1973).

In this period – late 1973 and 1974 – Black Consciousness activists sought to mobilise mass support for their struggles. This reached a head in September 1974, when members of SASO and the BPC attempted to organise nationwide rallies to celebrate the victory of Frelimo, the Mozambican armed resistance movement, in its struggle with the Portuguese colonial state. About a week before the rallies were to take place, a series of ambitious proposals were suggested: that mass meetings be held not only on black university campuses, but also in all of South Africa's major urban centres. These suggestions were taken up by activists, and publicised.

This – in combination with the suggestion that members of Frelimo itself, still a banned organisation in South Africa, might attend one or more of the rallies – stirred a wave of public controversy. The rallies were condemned in parliament, and disputed in newspaper letters columns. The police were placed on alert. The struggles of black activists suddenly became national news – reaching an audience that had previously passed over these struggles without interest.

This heart of this chapter examines these rallies in the context of struggles by student activists to build networks of solidarity, and to galvanise support from other communities. In this light, the rallies represent both a high-water mark in the efforts of Black Consciousness activists to engage black communities in their particular forms of political struggle, and – at the same time – the end of these efforts. The rallies' impact on the public sphere provided the apartheid state with the justification to launch a legal challenge to the right of Black Consciousness organisations to exist. Moving beyond discrete attacks on individual leaders, the state launched a court case against nine SASO and BPC activists – and sought to demonstrate that not only were the accused part of a conspiracy against the social and political order of South Africa, but also that the ideas at the very heart of Black Consciousness thought and political practice constituted a form of treason.

This trial placed Black Consciousness at the heart of political opposition to the apartheid state – and marked the conclusion of a fundamental shift in the state's approach to aboveground opposition. NUSAS and white students were no longer imagined to be at the core of political dissent, agitating or manipulating black student and workers. Instead, the state had now learned to see the politics of black students and the originality of their ideas – and, having seen them, had learned to recognise them as a threat. In the moment of the pro-Frelimo rallies, and in their aftermath, Black Consciousness ascended to national attention, and set the tone for future political action.

These events would also provide the frame through which the explosion of protest in Soweto in 1976 would come to be understood – both by the participants in the protest and by scholars.

This chapter tells the story of this ambiguous ascent to national attention.

A precursor

The rallies in celebration of Frelimo's successes did not, however, represent the first attempts to coordinate student protest and broad community support. In 1973, some months after the end of the Durban Strikes, a protest by students at the University of the Western Cape (UWC) expanded to include local community activists and – significantly – parents in a mass solidarity campaign.

At the centre of this protest was Henry Isaacs, the President of the Students' Representative Council (SRC) at UWC, and the vice-president of SASO. In March, following the banning of Jerry Modisane, he acted as SASO's president. The pamphlet, 'SASO on the Attack', was published under his name and – in the months after the Durban Strikes – he was at the centre of attempts by Black Consciousness organisations to move forward after the strikes and the state's attack on SASO and the BPC. Isaacs was sanguine about this project: in his unpublished memoir, he wrote of the period following Easter 1973 as one marked by 'a mood of optimism and confidence ... Although SASO had lost several key organisers ... the organisation had regained its momentum.'[2]

One of the signs of this momentum would be the coordination of student protests at UWC with a broader public discontent in Cape Town. These protests began in part as a consequence of Isaacs' suspension from the university, along with all other members of the campus SRC, and the institution of the SRC itself. This came after he had organised an event to draw attention to the harassment of student activists on campus by members of the security police.[3] While suspended, Isaacs drew up a list of student grievances, and distributed it amongst students at a meeting on 5 June. By the end of the week, UWC was in turmoil: 'the massive student turnout in the protest and their militancy surprised the SRC. Even students of the natural sciences who normally did not participate in student mass meetings and other activities were present in large numbers.'[4]

The campaign on campus had immediate consequences. Isaacs was arrested by the security police, and interrogated at the local police

[2]   Henry E. Isaacs, 'Full Circle: Reflections on Home and Exile', MA thesis (Johannesburg, University of the Witwatersrand: 2002), p. 62.
[3]   For the history leading up to this event, see: Cornelius C. Thomas, 'Disaffection, Identity, Black Consciousness and a New Rector: An Exploratory Take on Student Activism at the University of the Western Cape, 1966–1976', *South African Historical Journal*, 54 (1): 2005, pp. 72–90.
[4]   Isaacs, 'Full Circle', p. 70.

station. While he was detained, the Minister of Coloured Relations ordered the closure of UWC – and, as had happened the previous year at Turfloop, instructed that all students who wished to return in the second half of the year would have to re-apply for admission. When Isaacs was granted bail, he found an environment ripe for politics. Immediately after his release, a group of student activists worked to develop a plan that would campaign for the reinstatement of all students.

Broad public support was central to the planned strategy: 'the first priority was to obtain the support of the students' parents so that it did not appear to be just another demonstration by irresponsible students'. This would be achieved by the organisation of parent-student committees, set up by the students returning to their home towns after their suspension. These committees would be tasked 'to mobilise community and media support'. Press support was immediately forthcoming: the shuttering of UWC was reported across the media, and the students' demands reprinted in the *Cape Times*. Community support was also surprisingly forthcoming, as local Christian churches and churchmen became involved. They provided students with the spaces to organise – allowing church halls to be used for seminars, training programmes and workshops. They also spoke out in support of the planned campaign.

The visibility of the campaign – in the media, and from the pulpit – undoubtedly helped galvanise public support, and what Isaacs called 'community involvement'. This led people to volunteer 'financial contributions ... services, transportation, and even their homes'. Isaacs also mentions those 'workers who had access to their employers' photocopiers or duplicating machines [and who] reproduced pamphlets and other documents'. All of this activity was vital: it showed how students were embedded in families, in communities, and in black society. It made it impossible to dismiss the campaign as the 'perennial' protests of disgruntled students. Moreover, it made the claim that – as Isaacs says was at SASO's core – 'students were first and foremost part of the oppressed black majority and only secondly a small, relatively privileged stratum of that community'.[5]

The campaign continued from the closure of UWC in early June into July, culminating in a mass meeting at the Athlone Athletic Park in Cape Town on 8 July 1973. The rally was organised by the local Action Committee – set up in the course of the campaign – and not by SASO, in part because the Action Committee could organise a wider range of speakers. These included Fatima Meer, the sociologist and activist, and Mangosuthu Buthelezi – the 'Prime Minister' of the KwaZulu Bantustan. They were joined by representatives of UWC's Black Staff Association, and students themselves. SASO was not formally involved in

---

[5] Isaacs, 'Full Circle', pp. 77–80.

the organisation of the rally, because it publicly challenged the legitimacy of Buthelezi's authority and could not be involved in inviting Bantustan politicians to speak – but, as Isaacs recalls, the Committee 'wanted a panel of speakers who would, in the words of the Action Committee's leaders, "fill the stadium and attract all the media"'. In this context, ideological purity was secondary – and mass participation primary.[6]

The rally was highly successful. Between 13,000 and 20,000 people filled the stadium. The speakers called for unity and solidarity amongst students and parents, and the black community as a whole. Fatima Meer linked the struggle of Black Consciousness with the previous generation's fight against apartheid: 'she pointed in the direction of the Robben Island prison and said: "Power to our brothers beyond Table Mountain," a reference to the black political prisoners.'[7]

Within two days of the rally, the Minister of Coloured Relations modified his earlier position, and announced that all students would be readmitted at the start of the second semester, on 15 July.

This was a significant victory, although it was not the end of the campaign or the students' struggle. The students agitated for a judicial commission of inquiry into their complaints, embarking upon a boycott of lectures. This was also successful, and a Commission under the Judge-President of the Cape Provincial Division was appointed. In addition, a new Rector was appointed to the university, and embarked upon a relatively conciliatory approach to students.[8]

But successes at the university were matched by setbacks and repression elsewhere.

During July, Isaacs was formally elected as the new SASO president – a position he had, in effect, already occupied. A few days later he was arrested while travelling, and served with a banning order, initiating the second phase of banning orders levied against Black Consciousness activists in 1973. For the next eighteen months, he would live in 'internal exile': present in the country, but forbidden from appearing in public, forbidden from completing his studies, forbidden from speaking. In his memoir, he writes of learning of Tiro's death in the midst of an 'existence of isolation, restriction and persecution'. 'I speculated and still believe that Tiro's assassination was aimed at spreading terror among South African exiles ... Certainly, after Tiro's assassination feuding among Black Consciousness Movement exiles in Botswana increased.' Isaacs would still be living in this state of

---

[6] Isaacs, 'Full Circle', p. 81. See also the commentary on the participation of political rivals at the rally in Muriel Horrell and Dudley Horner, *A Survey of Race Relations in South Africa, 1973* (Johannesburg, SAIRR: 1974), pp. 335–9.

[7] The lower figure is Horrell's, the higher Isaacs's. The quote is from Isaacs, 'Full Circle', p. 81.

[8] Horrell, *Survey 1973*, p. 338.

internal exile in 1974, when the next phase of public protests – the pro-Frelimo rallies – erupted.[9]

The campaign and mass rally organised by Isaacs and his fellow students at UWC presents an important precursor to the pro-Frelimo rallies, and speaks to the position of Black Consciousness at the time, as well as to the efforts of activists to build a broad network of solidarity and support outside the spaces of the university. It is notable that although the campaign was planned over a weekend, it was given time to develop – with a month passing between the initial announcement of the public side of the plan and the major rally at Athlone Athletic Park. During these weeks, a distributed network of local organisers – students and their parents, sympathetic teachers and clergymen – worked to drum up organic support. They made use of media attention and press-stories, but did not rely on them. By the time of the mass rally, the Action Committee had mobilised a broad coalition of supporters, not all of whom shared each other's politics. This breadth of political perspective, however, combined with the respectability that accrued to clergymen, helped to legitimise the protest in the eyes of older members of the black community.

It also demonstrates the ways in which the dichotomies of the apartheid order were breaking down, under the pressure of the disruptions of the political protests of the past eight years. Divisions between generations – as well as those between students and workers – were eroding, and student crises were being understood in the context of a broader black experience.

All of these elements contributed to the effectiveness of the efforts to alter UWC's position on student readmissions – and, by extension, the campaign's efforts to expose the continuing discrimination at the core of apartheid. Very few of these elements could be guaranteed, however. A year later, activists in SASO and the BPC attempted to recapture and build upon the successes of this mode of politics in organising rallies to celebrate Frelimo's recent victory. But they did not have the luxuries of time, respectability, or a broad coalition of supporters to develop either friendly media coverage or mass support for their rallies. Instead, they had to use other tactics.

These tactics were dictated not by carefully-laid central plans, but rather by the flood of events.

'Solidarity with the people of Mozambique'

On 7 September 1974, the Portuguese military government – which itself had come to power in a coup only months earlier – announced

9   Isaacs, 'Full Circle', pp. 95–9.

that it had signed a ceasefire agreement with Mozambique's armed rebel movement, Frelimo. It further announced that it would grant Mozambique its independence nine months later, on 25 June 1975. In the meantime, authority would immediately be handed to a provisional government made up of representatives of both the Portuguese and Frelimo. This announcement caused drama and panic within Mozambique: one group opposed to the end of colonial rule attempted to seize the radio station in Lourenço Marques (as the capital, today's Maputo, was then known) and then to incite the Portuguese population to rise up and form a neo-colonial state. This group also called upon the South African government to enter Mozambique, and put down the provisional government of armed rebels.

South Africa did not intervene. Instead, government representatives expressed their sympathy for the reactionaries – but remained reluctant to disrupt the settlement announced by the Portuguese. Instead, the apartheid state sat aside while the reactionary insurgency was crushed and encouraged the fleeing insurgents – and many other Portuguese residents of Mozambique – to find new homes in South Africa. This process continued for weeks after the initial settlement.

Meanwhile – as this drama proceeded – members of SASO and the BPC decided to mount a series of public rallies in celebration of Frelimo's victory, and to hold them nationally on 25 September.[10]

There is some confusion over when this idea first emerged. Some participants have highlighted an early decision of the SRC at the University of the North (Turfloop) to hold a rally in support of Frelimo's struggle. This decision was apparently reached as early as 5 September – two days before the announcement of the ceasefire agreement and Frelimo's victory. The timing suggests that – whatever the intentions behind this particular decision – any plans launched on 5 September would have to have been significantly altered over the course of the coming weeks.[11] A more plausible date is 9 September – two days after the official announcement. On this day, the SASO office in Durban circulated a press statement acclaiming the successes of Frelimo and congratulating the movement on its imminent assumption of power. According to the judgment handed down in the later trial of Black Consciousness activists, this was the start of the process.

One more date, though, is worth noting. On 15 September – a week after the announcement, and four days after the Durban office's statement – the national executive of SASO met during a BPC Sympos-

---

[10] This material in the following sections of this chapter draws upon work previously published as Julian Brown, 'An Experiment in Confrontation: The Pro-Frelimo Rallies of 1974', *Journal of Southern African Studies*, 38 (1): 2012, pp. 55–71. This chapter provides a more detailed version of these events, but does occasionally recast and reuse sentences and phrases from my earlier version.

[11] Michael Lobban, *White Man's Justice: South African Political Trials in the Black Consciousness Era* (Oxford, Oxford University Press: 1996), p. 40.

ium in Durban. Again according to the judgment in the trial, it was here that representatives of the SASO, the BPC, and the Black Allied Workers' Union (BAWU) met to discuss the situation in Mozambique and to coordinate and integrate separate plans for national rallies.[12]

It is worth noticing the abbreviated timelines that each of these initiating dates provide for the planning and organisation of the rallies. The earliest date would have provided a day less than three weeks within which to plan a mass rally; the latest – and, indeed, most plausible – date provided activists with just ten days in which to develop a plan for a mass rally, publicise it, and then put that plan into action. Unsurprisingly, the brevity of the time allotted constrained the possibilities for organisation: it was not easy for the leadership of SASO's Durban office, for example, to set up a distributed network of local activists (as students and parents were able to do during the UWC campaign). Instead, they were forced to rely upon existing connections between SASO and the BPC and BAWU, as well as between these Black Consciousness organisations and other supporters, such as clergymen. They were also forced to use the media – both to announce their plans, and to galvanise disconnected communities to support the rallies.

In using the media, at least, the organisers of the rallies were aided by the rhetorical fervour of SASO's initial public statements – and by the reaction that these statements stirred up in Durban.

The statement issued by SASO's Durban office on 9 September was titled 'Press Statement Concerning the Transition in Mozambique: Riots, Rallies, etc' but focused its attention on the reaction of South Africans to the ceasefire agreement. These reactions were inevitably linked to race: on the one hand, the 'negative reaction by whites' was seen to be characteristic of 'people bent on maintaining an oppressive and exploitative white minority rule system of government' and, indeed, 'perfectly symbolical of the maladjusted schizophrenics' who could not accept any other system of government. On the other hand, 'to us black South Africans' the news of Frelimo's victory and the Portuguese government's concessions, was 'a revelation that every bit of Africa shall yet be free'. In sum, then: 'the dignity of the Black Man has been restored in Mozambique and the white people are turning out to be what they are truly are – violent people'.[13]

The press was not spared in this statement. The statement drew attention to the media's complicity in maintaining public fear: 'until a month ago the word Frelimo appeared [only] accidentally in the paper' and when it did, 'the Frelimo were branded "terrorists"'. Now, however, merely days after the ceasefire, the press was in the process of changing: 'Dr Samora Machel who used to be the "Terrorist President"

[12] WHP AD1719/B, Judgment in State v. Cooper et al (15 December 1976), pp. 118–21.
[13] WHP A2675/III/756, Press Statement Concerning the Transition in Mozambique (9 Sept 1974).

is now the "Frelimo President".' The hypocrisy of the press simply proved SASO's position – at least as articulated here – that the media was not neutral: 'the press is white restricted and whites, particularly South African whites, will always be for whites'.

There is little evidence that this press statement had much impact on the ways in which white South Africans thought about the events across the border, in Mozambique. The same cannot be said, though, for the next public intervention by the Durban office of SASO. On Saturday 21 September, Muntu Myeza – the General Secretary of SASO at the time, and the most senior member of SASO's executive in Durban – spoke to a reporter. He announced that SASO would hold rallies 'to show our solidarity with the people of Mozambique who have been freed by Frelimo'. He also said that a Frelimo leader would be asked to address the rally in Durban.

This suggestion caught the attention of the press. Although Myeza refused to reveal the identity of the speaker, explaining that 'we do not want to risk the possibility of his being stopped at the border', it was this possibility that made SASO's announcement newsworthy. The next day's *Sunday Times* printed Myeza's statement under the headline: 'SASO invites Frelimo to SA'.[14]

The presence of this unnamed Frelimo leader excited the press. Further stories followed, each emphasising the proposed presence of one or more representatives of Frelimo at the planned rallies, and suggesting that SASO was working to smuggle the speakers across the South African border. The organisers of the rally in Durban were willing to encourage this story – at least in part because it was spreading the news about their plans. On 24 September, for example – the day before the rallies were scheduled to be held – two Johannesburg newspapers, *The World* and *The Star*, reported that four Frelimo leaders had already entered South Africa in preparation for the rally. The same day, the police recorded a telephone conversation between Myeza and a reporter for the *Rand Daily Mail*, in which Myeza hinted that there were indeed Frelimo representatives currently incognito in the country – but that he could not officially confirm this.[15] According to the Durban *Daily News*, Myeza continued to confirm the presence of Frelimo on the day of the rally.[16]

The same theme was taken up in SASO's other attempts to publicise the rallies. A flyer, meant for mass distribution, went through two different drafts. The first strongly emphasised symbolic, historical and practical connections between South African opposition movements, including SASO and Frelimo. It announced this connection: 'Viva Frelimo! Support Frelimo! Reactionary or Revolutionary? Afrika is

[14] *Sunday Times*, 22 September 1974.
[15] See the sources quoted in WHP AD1719/B, S v. Cooper, Judgment, p. 129.
[16] *Daily News*, 25 September 1974.

Black. South Afrika??' It added: 'Mozambique has been oppressed for 400 years. South Africa is oppressed for the past 322 years. How long are we prepared to wait? How much longer??' Finally, the flyer stated that speakers from SASO, the BPC and Frelimo itself would be addressing the rally.[17] Some of these statements were edited out of the final version – ostensibly, because they were 'too intellectual' – and the flyer that was actually distributed simply provided the details of the event, asserted that Frelimo would be speaking at the rally, and reminded black South Africans to 'show solidarity with our Brothers in Mozambique'.[18] Nonetheless, the connection with Frelimo – and the possibility of its victory echoing in the context of South Africa's struggle – remained central to the message that Myeza and others were attempting to convey.

Behind the scenes

Not everyone in Durban agreed with this strategy. On 21 September, Aubrey Mokoape – one of the founding members of both SASO and the BPC, and a current member of the BPC's executive – approached the organisers of the rally to complain that he had not been consulted about the plan for 25 September. Mokoape met with Myeza and Saths Cooper, who had been the BPC's first General Secretary, prior to being banned in 1973. They – together with other members of the Durban offices of SASO and the BPC – set out to reassure him of the reliability of their plans.[19]

Apparently, Mokoape was appeased. However, a further problem revealed itself during this meeting: as of 21 September – the day of Myeza's press statement – no one had yet contacted Frelimo to extend a formal invitation to attend the rally, which would be held in four days from then. This group therefore decided to send two activists to cross the border and make an approach to Frelimo.

As it turned out, these activists would not be successful: they left Durban that evening, and crossed into Swaziland. They then contacted the SASO representative in Botswana – at the office Tiro had helped establish, before his death. He referred them to a contact in Lusaka who might know someone in Frelimo. They tried to call this contact from Swaziland, but could not get through. They gave up and returned to Durban in time for the rally on 25 September – never having spoken to a member of Frelimo, or even having crossed the border into Mozambique.[20]

---

[17] WHP A2675/III/276, Viva FRELIMO! Support FRELIMO! (September 1974).
[18] WHP A2675/III/276, Viva Frelimo! Mass Rally (September 1974). See also WHP AD1719/B, S v Cooper, Judgment, p. 122.
[19] WHP AD1719/B, S v Cooper, Judgment, p. 120.
[20] WHP AD1719/B, S v Cooper, Judgment, pp. 122–4.

It is unlikely that anyone in Durban knew the details of the struggle to contact Frelimo from Swaziland. However, it is clear that Myeza and others had announced the planned presence of Frelimo speakers at the rally without having considered from where these speakers would come. Even after activists had been sent out, Myeza continued to announce the imminent arrival of Frelimo speakers, even hinting to the media that these speakers were already in the country.

The single most prominent element of the planed rally in Durban – that is, the presence of representatives of Frelimo – was thus tenuously based in fact. The organisers relied more on the hope that Frelimo would arrive at the rally as proposed, rather than on any concerted effort to arrange their arrival. This speaks to the improvised nature of the rally's organisation: publicity preceded planning, and events rapidly outpaced the skeletal plans drawn up in the Durban office. It was difficult for the organisers to respond to these events: Cooper was banned, the SASO and BPC executives scattered across the country, and Myeza the only public face of the rallies.

There is a stark contrast between the organisation of the pro-Frelimo rally in Durban, and the organisation of the rally in support of UWC students in Cape Town the previous year. Where the earlier rally was conceived of as the culmination of a campaign that lasted several weeks, the Durban rally stood alone – outside of any other organised activism, meetings or connections. The Cape Town rally sought to include other participants, and to build a broad coalition of support; the Durban rally did not. Where the UWC campaign was founded on a set of concrete demands – for the restoration of students to their studies, and the revision of pedagogical practices at the university – the Durban rally was not. It was instead motivated by a desire to register the success of a revolution in a neighbouring country and – if the publicity statements made by Myeza are to be believed – to stir up revolutionary consciousness within South Africa.

This was a vague aim, difficult to particularise, and this difficulty shaped the Durban rally.

However, Durban was not the only site in which a rally was being planned. At the same time that Myeza was releasing press statements, students at the University of the North were developing their own plans. These were already being discussed before the ceasefire was announced, and fed into activism on campus – including the election of a new campus SRC.

This SRC took office on 13 September, and took the lead on the organisation of a rally on the campus. In this, they were assisted by the presence of the national president of SASO at the time, Pascal Nefolovhodwe, who remained in contact with the Durban office throughout this period. The SRC was additionally assisted in its plans by the presence of a Black Academic Staff Association (BASA) on the campus. The protests and mass expulsions after Tiro's graduation speech in 1972 had helped forge strong connections between SASO, the SRC and the BASA at Turfloop. These factors all contributed to the development of an atmosphere of intellectual and political ferment in September 1974.

Over the week between taking office and the beginnings of a public media frenzy around the rallies – centred on the plans for the rally in Durban – the SRC consulted with other bodies on campus. On 22 September, the SRC met to discuss these consultations and agree on a 'tentative programme' of events for the rally on 25 September. Following the opening of the rally at 14h00, the SRC president would speak on 'the historical background of Frelimo'. After this, Nefolovhodwe and the president of the local branch of SASO would each address the crowd. The BASA would be invited to attend the rally, and its chairman invited to give a speech after SASO.[21]

The intellectual content of these planned speeches could be understood in the context of the other event taking place at Turfloop on the weekend of 21 and 22 September – a SASO regional Formation School. The three-page report produced during this meeting reveals that students in SASO and at Turfloop were attempting to understand the political implications of the upheaval around them. The report was titled, 'Freedom struggles of the past – and what we can learn from them to enhance grass-roots involvement'. It opened by noting the 'lack of a thorough insight into the history of the freedom struggle of the past, organisations like ANC, PAC, etc.' Using their 'limited information', they concluded that these organisations had been able to mobilise a mass base because 'the Bantustan system was still in its embryonic stage' during the 1950s, and had not yet diverted black loyalties away from national struggles; because 'they emphasised on basic needs like food ... unlike us, who seem to be more philosophical than practical'; because 'the ANC had a committee in which chiefs were included', thus reassuring rural communities of its respectability; and because 'rallies were also used in an attempt to reach the people'.[22]

The Formation School concluded that SASO needed to develop a mass support base before embarking on further confrontation with the state: 'although resorting to arms (getting to the Bush) is a *practical necessity*, in coming back we might find ourselves fighting an alien war [original emphasis]. Our people regarding us as terrorists. Hence the necessity of preparing the mind of the people.' In this context, rallies were a key tool to help raise the consciousness of the masses – in conjunction with continuing community programmes – and to convince the black public that SASO and the BPC represented them. While it is striking that the participants in the Formation School seem

---

[21] WHP A2675/III/285, SRC Minutes (22 Sept 1974).
[22] WHP A2675/III/756, Freedom Struggles of the Past (Sept. 1974).

to have taken it for granted that they would eventually be forced into an armed struggle with the state, it is important to recognise that they did not see rallies as a means of instigating that confrontation. Rather, they were exercises in enlightenment and persuasion: means of mobilising real support.

This meant that these students had a clearer idea of the purpose behind organising a rally in celebration of Frelimo's victory: the rally would raise public awareness of radical political change in the neighbouring country. It would show that change was possible, and that SASO, the BPC and other organisations associated with Black Consciousness ideas could bring about that change. At the end of the rally, hopefully, more people would be more supportive of the organisers' actions.

'True colours'

The distinction between the improvisational approach adopted in Durban and the intellectual one in Turfloop was, however, lost in the reaction to Myeza's statements and the press reports of Frelimo's planned presence at the Durban rally. Immediately following the *Sunday Times* story, a Durban businessman, Cornelius Koekemoer, sent a telegram to the Minister of Justice, urging him to ban the rally. Koekemoer warned that thousands of whites in Durban were willing to rise up to prevent Frelimo from addressing a mass audience. He noted that this action would lead to further bloodshed, violence and unrest. Jimmy Kruger – at the time, the Minister of Justice – used Koekemoer's telegram to make a public statement about the rallies. He said that this telegram illustrated the depths of the fears provoked by the proposed rallies. This message showed how the rallies had 'evoked a strong emotional response among certain sections of the public'.[23]

Kruger also announced to the press that he would 'take the necessary steps ... to ensure that the meeting will not take place'. He was clear in his intention, if not in the details of his plan: 'I will stop the meeting', he said, 'probably under the Riotous Assemblies Act.'[24] This was widely reported on the morning of Tuesday, 24 September – the day before the rallies were to take place. However, Kruger's statement was not immediately accompanied by any official proclamation: the banning order would only be signed that evening, and published in the *Government Gazette* on Wednesday, the day of the rallies.[25] On Tuesday and much of Wednesday, it was not clear whether or not the

[23] As quoted in Lobban, *White Man's Justice*, p. 41.
[24] *Rand Daily Mail*, 24 September 1974.
[25] *Government Gazette*, 25 September 1974.

rallies had been banned – or if Kruger's threat to do so was no more than empty bluster.

The situation was thus unclear, and at least some activists in the Durban office were afraid that the government and the white press were conspiring to undermine SASO and the BPC by creating the impression that the rallies would not happen. They were concerned that surrendering to these pressures – particularly if they were not backed up in law – would irreparably damage the standing of Black Consciousness organisations with their supporters. They would appear weak, foolish and skittish. On Tuesday, therefore, Cooper and Myeza consulted two experts on the legality of Kruger's notice. Both told them that the statement alone was insufficient; a gazetted notice was needed.

Myeza therefore issued a press statement denying the validity of Kruger's threat and the media frenzy that followed: 'We are not aware of any banning.' He went on, however, to assert that: 'We couldn't care less if it [is] banned. We are going ahead at all costs with the rallies nationally.'[26] Myeza also telephoned reporters to assure them that the rallies would go ahead. These conversations were recorded by the police, and introduced as evidence in the later trial. According to the transcripts, Myeza sought to convince journalists to dismiss the Minister's threat: 'Look, I am telling you everything is going ahead as planned.' 'Right, what we're going to do, we're going to push it until the very last minute. We want to crack them completely.' 'These guys can't stop us with anything.' 'We want to see exactly, we want to call their bluff, you see.'[27]

This was not all, though. Myeza did not stop at asserting that the rallies had not been officially banned, and that the press should be sceptical of the Minister's blustery statements. In conversations with relatively sympathetic journalists, Myeza went much further – and suggested that he, at least, might welcome the state's attempts to suppress the protest. In a conversation with Nat Serache, a reporter for the *Rand Daily Mail*, Myeza said:

> Shit, Nat, we're going to have a ... a very big thing tomorrow. And of course it means I'll ... I'll have to go to gaol for a year or something like that. So we have to take it to the final end ... we want to see exactly, we want to call their bluff ... they must come out clearly, their true colours ... We want to see them shooting us.[28]

Similarly, Cooper told Gerald Phokojoe – the regional secretary for SASO in the Transvaal – that: 'These guys can't stop us with anything

[26] WHP A2675/III/285, Press Statement (24 Sept 1974).
[27] Transcripts, as quoted in WHP AD1719/B, S v Cooper, Judgment, pp. 126–30 and in Lobban, *White Man's Justice*, pp. 41–2.
[28] Quoted in Lobban, *White Man's Justice*, p. 42.

... Mobilise all the resources ... it's an act of warfare, this, and we must retaliate in a like manner.'[29] These conversations were not meant for general consumption, but neither were they entirely private: Serache might have been assumed to be sympathetic, but he was not an insider. These conversations were intended to influence the underlying tone of the articles that would be published – and it seems that Myeza and Cooper hoped that this tone would be rhetorically confrontational, defiant and unapologetically radical.

The rhetoric of confrontation worked to trap the organisers of the rallies: by insisting that the strength of Black Consciousness politics could only be demonstrated by a refusal to back down in the face of the state's threats, the organisers found themselves unable to respond to the actual banning of the rallies on Wednesday morning. At this point, they were forced by their own logic to insist on the right to proceed in the face of a legal prohibition – and to take whatever came.

They did, however, attempt to develop a defence strategy, should they face the attempts of the police to prevent the rally from happening – as seemed likely at the time, and did in fact eventually occur. The organisers sought to identify the possible limits of the banning order, and to discover what type of gathering might be permitted under its provisions. They latched onto a section under which the Minister explicitly prohibited any gathering associated with SASO or the BPC. They suggested that if none of the speakers at the rallies were members of either organisation at the time of their speeches, then the rallies would not fall under the ambit of the order. Although admitting that this sophistry was unlikely to convince the police, Myeza insisted that 'the onus of proof' would rest on the state: it would have to establish 'for instance ... that you have not resigned from SASO'. He thus suggested that speakers should claim to have officially resigned from SASO and the BPC; this might be enough to insulate them from later prosecution.[30]

Myeza also drew up a handwritten document, 'Statement re: Viva Frelimo Rally – Durban'. This document was not released, but was seized during a police raid on the Durban office of SASO.[31] In this document, Myeza mingled misleading statements with defiance. He planned to suggest that the absence of Frelimo's representatives at the rally had been intentional: 'we have decided that our guests of honour [should] excuse themselves from addressing the rallies in the country ... they have since left.' He also planned to announce that the 'rallies are going ahead despite the threat from violent irate whites'. The document suggested that 'white civilians and several white mercenaries'

[29] Quoted in WHP AD1719/B. S v Cooper, Judgment, p. 128.
[30] Quoted in Lobban, *White Man's Justice*, p. 42.
[31] The seizure of this document is recounted in WHP AD1719/B, S v Cooper, Judgment, pp. 139–42.

were conspiring to 'massacre our people and disrupt our meetings'. The Minister's banning order meant that 'the Black Community now realises exactly where they stand with regard to the white racist regime': it knew that it had been 'maimed, massacred, butchered, assassinated and emasculated of our dignity and manhood' by the apartheid order.[32]

This, then, was where things stood on the morning of the rallies: after two days of scandal and reaction in the press, the Minister had finally and officially banned the rallies. Myeza and Cooper, as the primary organisers in the Durban office, were anticipating further reaction – even to the point of imagining violence. Nonetheless, they were certain that the rallies would have to go ahead, even if the state showed its 'true colours': to do otherwise would be admit weakness and failure, and risk losing the support of the black community. These threats shadowed the rallies, as they developed through the day: first at Turfloop, at 14h00, and then in Durban, from 17h00.

The rally at Turfloop

At Turfloop, students began to make placards on Tuesday evening while, in their offices, members of the SRC painted banners. Some slogans drew attention to the potential connection between Mozambique and South Africa: 'The dignity of the Black man has been restored in Mozambique and so shall it be here', 'Mozambique Free. Azania?', 'Frelimo killed and won. SA Blacks?'. Others referred to the situation in South Africa, with little reference to Mozambique: 'Down with Pretoria Regime!', 'Azania my love don't let pigs rape your children', 'Down with Mulder up with terrorism. To hell with Vorster Government', 'Who next if not Vorster?'. Yet another juxtaposed the two:

> Viva Frelimo!!! Azania is bored and from this boredom a revolution shall erupt. Down with Vorster and his dogs (Boers)! Power!!! We shall overcome.[33]

A further banner referenced the role of SASO and the BPC, reading: 'Vacancies. Government of Azania. Majors, Lieutenants, Captains, Duties. To train and lead 50 million Blacks. Apply: SASO, BPC before the reach of the 4th Century of racist oppression.' This banner positioned Black Consciousness at the centre of a coming revolutionary

---

[32] WHP A2675/III/285, Statement re Viva Frelimo Rally – Durban (Sept 1974).
[33] Photographs of these placards can be found in WHP A2675/III/285. Transcriptions of some of these placards can be found in WHP AD1719/B, S v Cooper, Judgment, pp. 180–3, and in J.G.E. Wolfson (ed.), *Turmoil at Turfloop: A Summary of the Reports of the Snyman and Jackson Commissions of Inquiry into the University of the North* (Johannesburg, SAIRR: 1976), pp. 28–9.

change – as the brokers of a future government. This banner – and the other slogans, placards, and posters prepared by students – represented a far more confrontational approach to protest that had previously been seen in public: the obvious willingness of students to invoke threats against the state, and to imagine a post-apartheid order, distinguished the tone and style of these protests from earlier examples.

These banners were distributed across the campus on Tuesday night. The next morning, the official publication of the Minister of Justice's banning order prompted discussions of the advisability of proceeding with the rallies. BASA – despite having participated actively in SASO attempts during the Formation School over the past week – decided to withdraw from the rally. G.M. Nkondo, the chairman of BASA, sent a letter to the SRC president, explaining that the Association believed that, 'the banning order imposed on the rallies which were to be organised by SASO and BPC is in substance applicable to the rally (or celebration) that your SRC envisages'. This posed 'serious legal implications' and, 'in the circumstances', BASA could not participate. Nonetheless, Nkondo concluded his letter with a wish to 'express [BASA's] sympathy with the stand you have taken' – i.e., to hold the rally regardless.[34]

Although BASA was not convinced of the legality of the rally, it appears that the SRC was able to persuade the university's conservative Rector that the role of the SRC in organising it was sufficient to insulate it from legal sanction. According to the Rector's memory of the morning, he met with the SRC and – as he had not yet seen the official banning order – was not overly concerned. He believed them when they told him that the rally was organised by the SRC, and not by SASO. He decided that he did not 'want to start a war over placards' and would overlook the confrontational rhetoric of the slogans that had appeared across the campus overnight. After the meeting, though, he did remember being disturbed by an encounter with a group of students who did not respond to his 'usual friendly greeting' and, instead, snapped 'the Bantu word for "dog"' at him. According to the gloss given to his testimony by a later Commission of Inquiry, 'this unusual behaviour made him realise more keenly that there was something seriously wrong with the attitude of the students'. Nonetheless, he left the campus at lunchtime to play a round of golf with the university's Registrar. Neither was present on the campus when the rally began.[35]

By 14h00, several hundred students had congregated in the campus's main hall. Gilbert Sebide, the SRC president, once again emphasised

---

[34] WHP A2675/III/285, Correspondence: Nkondo to SRC (25 Sept 1974). See also: Wolfson, *Turmoil at Turfloop*, pp. 21–3, and G.M. Nkondo (ed.), *Turfloop Testimony: The Dilemma of a Black University in South Africa* (Johannesburg, SAIRR: 1976), pp. 43–4.

[35] Wolfson, *Turmoil at Turfloop*, pp. 28–9. Lobban, *White Man's Justice*, p. 43.

that this would be a SRC rally, not a SASO rally. He followed this by saying that anyone who wished to address the rally would have to do so in his or her own personal capacity – not as a representative of any organisation. He outlined the programme of speakers, and spoke on the history of Frelimo. Finally, he called upon the crowd to shout, 'Viva Frelimo! Viva Machel!' and raised a clenched fist in the Black Power salute. He then called upon Nefolovhodwe to speak. Despite being the national president of SASO, Nefolovhodwe also insisted that he was speaking on his own behalf. He told the students that they were gathered 'to commemorate those who had suffered for freedom's cause and those who had ultimately gained their humanity'. He 'called upon them to re-dedicate themselves to their won struggle in South Africa'. He then stepped down, and was followed by someone only identified by the police as a 'lady-speaker' – who was interrupted by the police's violent entry.[36]

The leaders of SASO and the BPC in Durban had discussed the possibility of police intervention in the days leading up to the rallies: their appearance in the university's hall now demonstrated the accuracy of these predictions. The police were well prepared: that morning, a force of thirty-two white and fifty black policemen had gathered at the nearby Mankweng police station. Each policeman was armed with a rubber baton. The white policemen also carried service revolvers. Two were equipped with shotguns and four others carried launchers for tear-gas canisters. Police dogs were put on long leashes. According to the report of the Commission of Inquiry: 'Orders had been issued that no fire-arms should be used or action taken ... a minimum of force should be used.'[37]

The police arrived at 14h20. According to their testimony, they found the students 'whipped up to a highly emotional state'. The commanding officer entered the hall and informed the students that the meeting had been banned, and that they were required to disperse within fifteen minutes. According to the police's testimony, this resulted in 'mass pandemonium'. According to Nefolovhodwe, and others, however, the police megaphone was squeaking so loudly that the announcement was inaudible. This led to confusion, and students were merely slow to respond.[38]

Over a thousand students trooped out of the hall – but not all of them dispersed. Instead, about 700 regrouped on the nearby sport field. According to the police, they were singing and marching in formation. Male and female students separated – in part, in response to a sugges-

---

[36] There is no transcript of these speeches. They were paraphrased in police reports, and can be found in WHP AD1719/B, S v Cooper, Judgment, p. 188.

[37] Wolfson, *Turmoil at Turfloop*, p. 29.

[38] Police testimony: Wolfson, *Turmoil at Turfloop*, p. 30. Nefolovhodwe: WHP AD1719/B, S v Cooper, Judgment, p. 188.

tion they return to their sex-segregated hostels. The police continued to count down the time given to students to disperse – and then, at the end of the time, they clashed with the gathered students.

According to students, the police suddenly began to attack the crowd: tear gas was released, dogs were allowed to roam at the end of the long leashes and encouraged to bite students, officers assaulted male students with batons. At least two injured students were hustled into large police vans.[39] According to the police, though, their actions were the consequences of the students' own acts of violence, each one matching like for like. The baton charge was a response to students pelting the police with stones, presumably found on the sports field. During this stoning, a dog handler was struck in the face and – stunned – let slip his dog's leash. The dog then targeted and attacked the student that had thrown the stone. In a rather more plausible alternative, the assault happened when a dog handler had moved to arrest someone, and had allowed his dog to bite the student.[40]

Whatever the exact sequence of events, both the police and students agreed that violence had been used by each other in the course of the confrontation. The police assaulted students, and students had attempted to assault the police – using stones and any other makeshift weapons they could find. The episode remains remarkable, no matter whether one accepts the police's version, in which students attacked first, or the students' version, in which they defended themselves against the police. No similar confrontation had developed during the earlier student protests. No similar confrontation had marked the Durban Strikes. The insurrectionary temper of the students at the University of the North was new, and marked a shift in South African politics.

The rally in Durban

Meanwhile, in Durban, the organisers waited for reports to arrive from Turfloop. At 16h00, Nefolovhodwe telephoned Mokoape to report on the rally. Cooper, Myeza and Mosiuoa 'Terror' Lekota – another senior member of SASO – were all present. They heard Nefolovhodwe describe the rally: 'there were policemen with tear-gas, some 15 students were injured and there was a lot of throwing of batons'. Nefolovhodwe misrepresented the clash between students and police, painting it as an unambiguous victory: the students 'had to order the police to leave them because it was a university, and they then left'. He could not say how many students had been arrested, stammering in response.

[39] WHP AD1719/B, S v Cooper, Judgment, pp. 188–91.
[40] Wolfson, *Turmoil at Turfloop*, pp. 29–31. WHP AD1719/B, S v Cooper, Judgment, pp. 191–7.

Serache, the *Rand Daily Mail* journalist who had been present at the rally, then took the telephone and explained that he considered the rally to have been violent. He 'heard shots being fired'. In response to questions, he said that he did not know whether fifteen students had been injured, but did know that one had been taken to hospital.[41]

The Durban-based audience was excited by this news. Myeza told Nefolovhodwe that he thought 'it was beautiful'. He agreed with Serache that the event 'was truly a victory for the Black people'. He was heartened both by the successful organisation of the rally, and the refusal to bow to the force of the police: it appeared as though the rallies might be capable of sparking further insurrectionary moments. This was not a general belief amongst the organisers, or those participating in ongoing debates over the advisability of continuing with the Durban rally. Nonetheless, the telephone conversation bolstered support for proceeding boldly and publicly.

In truth, though, the question was moot by the time of this telephone call. According to a newspaper report, 'two hours before the rally was scheduled to go ahead the crowds began to gather outside the locked gates at Curries Fountain' – the site planned for the rally.[42] According to the police, between fifty and sixty black men and women were gathered outside the site at 15h15. Two hours later, over 1,000 people were said to have gathered. The crowd was not permitted to enter the site, though: the police had locked the main gates and had stationed themselves at 'strategic points in the sports grounds'. The crowd thus gathered both on an open area between the entrance to Curries Fountain and the road, and then across the road on a ten-foot high sloping embankment. According to the police and others, the crowd was silent until 17h30.[43]

Shortly after this, part of the crowd began to move from the embankment onto the road itself. A few minutes later, they began to sing – apparently under the direction of Vino Cooper, Saths Cooper's wife and an activist in her own right. According to the *Daily News*, the crowd 'began to sing "Inkosi sikele Africa" and other ANC songs'. According to the police testimony, parts of the crowd chanted an eclectic mix of words and slogans, including: 'Viva Frelimo!', '*Amandla Uwetu!*', 'White Man go Home', and '*Uhuru!*' According to Myeza's own description, he arrived at the site to find people 'singing, dancing and making whoopee, it was jolly, some were hugging'.

The police, though, found the crowd threatening. They were primed for this: more than 200 policemen had been seconded to the local police station. Another group had been seconded to a neighbouring station. In addition, half of the city's police dog force – thirty dogs and their handlers – had been deployed to the Curries Fountain site. A

---

[41] As paraphrased in WHP AD1719/B, S v Cooper, Judgment, pp. 148–51.
[42] *Daily News*, 26 September 1974.
[43] WHP AD1719/B, S v Cooper, Judgment, pp. 155–6.

large part of the city's police force were therefore at or around the rally, prompted to prepare themselves for the eruption of violence.

They arrived at Curries Fountain hours before the rally was scheduled to begin. They gathered at different sites, both inside the stadium and on the streets. According to the summary of the events, prepared in the course of the later trial, the dog handlers were 'kept out of sight' until needed. The *Daily News* reported that 'plain clothes and uniformed officers, dogs, cars and vans were strategically placed' throughout the area, and estimated that there were more than 300 officers at the site. The area around Curries Fountain was thus surrounded by police, while the actual site remained off-limits. Protesters were hemmed in, but – in contrast to the model of policing adopted a year earlier, during the Durban Strikes – protesters were not contained, and the spaces of their protest were neither separated nor clearly delimited. Perhaps it was the unease caused by closeness that caused the police to read the crowd as dangerous: making 'rhythmic movements ... They made contemptuous and provocative remarks to the police and moved up to the police and retreated again ... some of the people made finger gestures.' One of the senior officers present believed that 'the shuffling movements of their feet were the kind used in Zulu war dances.' They saw the crowd raise their fists, and heard them call: 'Power!'.

Then, shortly before 18h00, Myeza arrived at the site of the rally – 'a little west of the gates, more or less on the apron between the road and the gates'. He said that as he arrived he learned that the police had just ordered the crowd to disperse. He told his companions: 'Let us get the people away from here. Let us move off.' He began to sing 'Shosholoza' – a Zulu-language workers' song – and began to lead the crowd away from Curries Fountain. They moved twelve paces, according to Myeza. Then the people in front of him began to turn around and rush back. Through the opening they created, Myeza could see a group of policemen and their dogs.

He said: 'You can't stop us from going away' – and then the dogs attacked.

The police interpreted these events differently. They claimed to have seen Myeza giving 'the Power salute ... [and] the crowd again responded to this by giving the Power salute and shouting "Power"'. Myeza pointed to the police and said: 'These guys can't stop us.' The crowd 'formed a mass-formation behind him, one holding the other from behind, and with shuffling movements moved in a semi-circle towards the east gate'. This was once again perceived as part of a Zulu war-dance, and thus as an implicit threat. The police charged, 'to surround and arrest the crowd'.

Regardless, the crowd rapidly dispersed after the police charge.

Lobban suggests that Myeza was at Curries Fountain 'for less than five minutes', and that the crowd did not respond to the police violence. That evening, SASO's Durban offices were raided and documents – including Myeza's planned statement – were seized. The next day, ten people were charged in connection with the organisation of the Durban rally. The day after that, police raided the homes of Black Consciousness leaders, including Biko in Kingwilliamstown, as well as the Johannesburg offices of the BCP and BPC. Activists were arrested as part of a general round-up, while the state considered how to proceed with what became a trial of a political ideology.

The rally in Durban thus melted into its end: a brief flurry of activity, followed by retreat and collapse. The state proved relentless in its efforts to bring the disruptive possibilities of Black Consciousness organisation to an end: by the end of the week, the activities of these organisations had been thrown into disarray, their leaders arrested, and a final repression could be seen coming. Whatever the organisers of the rallies had expected, this was not it – even the year in gaol imagined by Myeza did not measure up to the penalties that the state would request.

Black Consciousness on trial

In their brief description of the rallies, Karis and Gerhart suggest that: 'the abortive rallies might have caused little stir had they been allowed to proceed unobstructed ... to the security police, however, the rallies presented a convenient pretext to step up repression of the black consciousness movement'.[44] The story told in this chapter challenges the first part of that conclusion: the rallies were not unimportant in themselves, nor were they strictly speaking abortive. They represented the conjunction of two tendencies within Black Consciousness organisations – on the one hand, towards moving outwards and engaging with non-student communities and, on the other hand, towards courting the catharsis of confrontation in protest. These were not easily reconciled, and the differences between the campaign and rally in Cape Town in 1973 and those in Durban and Turfloop in 1974 speak to these obvious difficulties. In attempting to bridge these tendencies, the pro-Frelimo rallies served as a watershed for Black Consciousness politics – regardless of whether they succeeded in their explicit aims or not.

But the second part of Karis and Gerhart's conclusion nonetheless retains its force: the preparations of the police in Mankweng and Durban show how the police were prepared to disrupt and disperse the rallies before they began. In addition, the months following saw the state and

[44] Thomas Karis and Gail Gerhart (eds), *From Protest to Challenge: A Documentary History of African Politics in South Africa, 1882–1990: Volume 5: Nadir and Resurgence, 1964–1979* (Bloomington and Indianapolis, University of Indiana Press: 1997), p. 143.

its police forces ramp up their actions against SASO and the BPC. By the end of 1974, at least twenty activists belonging to various Black Consciousness organisations had been placed under banning orders, and at least thirty-five other activists were held incommunicado under similar forms of detention. Many of these were tortured in efforts to amass the evidence to try SASO's leadership.

In January 1975, thirteen members of SASO and the BPC were arrested and charged under the Terrorism Act. After a series of preliminary hearings, nine men remained on the final charge sheet. They included four out of the five members of SASO's national executive – Nefolovhodwe, Myeza, Lekota and Rubin Hare – as well as Cooper, Mokoape, Sebide, Nkwenkwe Vincent Nkomo and Strini Moodley. Nkomo was the national organiser of the BPC; Cooper, Mokoape and Moodley had all been instrumental in its founding, but were already banned – and thus already prohibited from holding positions in the organisation at the time of their arrest.[45] The charges against them were twofold: first, that the nine defendants had 'conspired to commit acts to bring about revolutionary change by (i) unconstitutional and/or (ii) violent means and/or (iii) the threat of unconstitutional and/or (iv) the threat of violent means' while, at the same time, aiming 'to cause, encourage or further feelings of hostility between the Whites and the other race groups in South Africa'. The second charge was more specific, claiming that 'the Accused, in concert and in common purpose with certain others who are listed, with intent to endanger the maintenance of law and order, organised and/or arrange Pro Frelimo Rallies'. These rallies were intended to:

> cause or encourage an insurrection or forceable resistance to the Government; to further or encourage the achievement of any political aim, including the bringing about of any social or economic change, by violent or forceable means; to cause bodily injury or to endanger the safety of any person ... [and] to embarrass the administration of the affairs of the State.[46]

The trial itself was dramatic, and long lasting. For sixteen months it provided the leaders of SASO and the BPC with an unusual platform from which to raise public awareness of their existence, and to present their ideas to a broad audience. The key moment in this process came when the defence subpoenaed Steve Biko to explain the intellectual and political content of Black Consciousness. His testimony was compiled soon after the end of the trial and served – in the trial itself, and in its published incarnation – as a lengthy tutorial in black politics, history and ideology. In responses to questions from the defence as well as from the judge, Biko set out to establish the foundation of Black Consciousness

---

[45] WHP A2176/16, Arrests, Detentions and Trials (1976).
[46] WHP A2021/14.1, S v Cooper, Heads of Argument.

while emphasising the earlier non-confrontational gradualism of SASO. In doing so, he undercut the prosecution's core argument – which was an attempt to link insurrectionary rhetoric and ideas to revolutionary organisation, activity and, ultimately, violence.[47]

Biko's testimony was heard over five days in May 1976 – over a year into the trial. As he was speaking in court, school students across Soweto were beginning to meet to discuss protesting against the decision of the national Department of Bantu Education to impose Afrikaans as the medium of instruction in their schools. They drew their organisational framework from the Southern African Students' Movement (SASM), and their ideas from the knowledge of Black Consciousness and other student protests, as relayed to them by charismatic teachers such as the murdered Onkgopotse Tiro. But they translated these ideas and these models in terms of their own experiences, and – in doing so – catalysed a true insurrection on the streets of the township.

The Uprising came – but not from within the existing structures of resistance created and nurtured during the past decade. Neither the white students of NUSAS or the black students of SASO would lead this Uprising, but their ideas and their examples would be reinterpreted and reinvented by the students of Soweto. The path that they had set out upon would continue without them.

---

[47] Steve Biko, *The Testimony of Steve Biko*, ed. M. Arnold (London: Maurice Temple Smith: 1979).

7 The Soweto Uprising
EVENT AND AFTERMATH

In January 1976, at the start of the school year, the state expanded the curriculum of Afrikaans-language instruction in black schools in the Transvaal. Half the subjects studied in the first year of junior secondary schooling would now no longer be taught in English, but rather in Afrikaans.

This language policy was not the first or the only imposition placed upon this particular group of students: from the start of the year, they were suffering from the consequences of a decision taken in 1975, intended to reduce overcrowding in black schools over time. The Bantu Education Department aimed to even out classroom sizes across the country by abolishing a year of studies between the end of junior school and the start of secondary school. In the short term, this meant that double the normal number of students were taking part in the first year of junior secondary schooling in 1976 – 'creating an unwieldy bulge of numbers that meant yet more crowding and double shifts, more shortages of textbooks and qualified teachers', as Karis and Gerhart put it.[1]

These factors – both national and provincial – angered students, and helped prompt them into action. The first significant protests against these changes in education policy took place in March and April 1976, amongst the 13- and 14-year-old students most affected by them. Pupils at Phefeni Junior Secondary School embarked on a 'go-slow' in March. According to Sifiso Ndlovu, a pupil at the time, this meant that the students refused to go to class after lunch and, instead, 'dedicated the afternoon lessons in our class, from 2 o'clock to about 4 o'clock to discussion about the directive that Afrikaans should be the medium of instruction in our school'.[2]

Ndlovu recalled that discussions were limited to 'issues that affected us directly in the school and classroom' and did not drift into questioning the legitimacy of the apartheid system. Older students,

---

[1] T. Karis and G. Gerhart, *From Protest to Challenge: A Documentary History of African Politics in South Africa, 1882–1990. Volume 5: Nadir and Resurgence* (Bloomington and Indianapolis, Indiana University Press: 1997), p. 166.

[2] S.M. Ndlovu, *The Soweto Uprisings: Counter-Memories of June 1976* (Johannesburg, Ravan: 1998), pp. 5–7.

prefects, teachers, 'and other authorities including the principal' were excluded from these meetings. The meetings provided a space where very young students could engage with each other, and reflect upon and engage with their own experiences, without outside guidance.

It is possible to cast these meetings as the true starting point of the Soweto Uprising: they linked experience to reflection, and reflection to action. This action – the learning go-slow that permitted the meetings – was coordinated locally, and in response to particular conditions and complaints. The students were forming themselves into a politicised group, and were acting for themselves. This emergent form of communal organisation was a local reinvention of the trends of a decade of protest and political experiments, a rooting of these trends in Soweto itself. The Uprising began in Soweto, and began because students sought to act on their own experiences and for themselves.

They did not do so in isolation, however: these students were able to meet in this way in part because Black Consciousness activists had reshaped the structures of teaching within state schools in Soweto. The introduction of a generation of teachers into these institutions after the protest waves of 1972 and 1973, and the integration of their practices into classrooms in Soweto with the complicity of administrators, meant that structures of thought and organisation were already in place by the beginning of 1976. The young students of Soweto were able to take advantage of these structures, and use them to give form to their own frustrations. In this way, these students were the direct inheritors of the contentious struggles of university students over the past decade.

The Soweto Uprising of 16 June 1976 – a mass march that turned into an insurrection when school-going students responded forcefully to the police's use of deadly violence – has been written about more often than any or all of the other strikes, protests and rallies described in this book. It was immediately recognised as a turning point in the history of mass resistance to apartheid, but (as I suggested in the Introduction) scholars nonetheless struggled to place the Uprising in a political history. For some, this was because none of the events of the previous dozen years were recognised as political, and so the roots of the Uprising were found in the organised activism of the ANC and PAC during the 1950s. Others recognised one or another aspect of these events as political: the work of Black Consciousness activists, but not others, or the protests of workers, but not others. They linked the Uprising to Black Consciousness ideas (although, rarely organisations) in the first case, or to the trade union movement, in the second.[3]

---

[3]   E.g. J. Kane-Berman, *Soweto: Black Revolt, White Reaction* (Johannesburg, Ravan: 1978); B. Hirson, *Year of Fire, Year of Ash: The Soweto Revolt – Roots of a Revolution?* (London, Zed: 1979); A. Brooks and J. Brickhill, *Whirlwind Before the Storm: The Origins and Development of the Uprising in Soweto and the Rest of South Africa from June to December 1976* (London, IDAF: 1980).

More recently, scholars have emphasised the role played by the local context of Soweto in shaping the Uprising. The details of the schooling system have been central to several narratives, as has the presence of the South African Students' Movement (SASM) in a number of Soweto schools.[4] Clive Glaser, in particular, has drawn attention to the ways in which the context of gang membership and extra-curricular social-isation amongst Soweto's youth shaped the development of the student protest.[5] And in the past decade, a loose group of researchers have shown how the development of the Uprising was shaped by the ways in which different communities within Soweto were constituted.[6] These approaches have deepened our knowledge of the Uprising.

But these different works – the early interpretations which sought political antecedents, and the most recent ones which locate the Uprising in social histories – run the risk of replicating the dichoto-mies that underpin accounts of this period. These include the splits between political and social history, between the activism of black and white students, between student activists and workers, and between the slow processes of organisation and the disruptive explosions of protest.

This chapter instead argues that the Uprising was the product of a tension between invention and inheritance, integrating local expe-riences into recently developed forms of organisation, consciousness and political activity. In the process, these forms themselves mutated, altering with the ever-shifting struggles of activists against the stric-tures of the apartheid order. Starting inside the schoolroom, student organisation moved between different schools and different year groups; students planned massed activities and protests and then, once the event was underway, these students built networks of soli-darity and support with parents and adults across Soweto.

4   Jonathan Hyslop, *The Classroom Struggle: Policy and Resistance in South Africa, 1940–1990* (Pietermaritzburg, University of Natal Press: 1999); Clive Glaser, 'Sowe-to's Islands of Learning: Morris Isaacson and Orlando High Schools Under Bantu Education, 1958–1975', *Journal of Southern African Studies*, 41 (1): 2015, pp. 159–71; Nozipho Diseko, 'The Origins and Development of the South African Students' Movement (SASM): 1968–1976', *Journal of Southern African Studies*, 18 (1): 1992, pp. 40–62.

5   Clive Glaser, *Bo-Tsotsi: The Youth Gangs of Soweto, 1935–1976* (Oxford, James Currey: 2000); but see also: Motlatsi Thabane and Jeff Guy, 'The Ma-rashea: A Partic-ipant's Perspective', in Belinda Bozzoli (ed.), *Town and Countryside in the Transvaal* (Johannesburg, Ravan: 1983); and Gary Kynoch, *We are Fighting the World: A History of the Marashea Gangs in South Africa, 1947–1999* (Athens, Ohio University Press: 2005).

6   See: Philip Bonner and Lauren Segal, *Soweto: A History* (Cape Town, Maskew Miller Longman: 1998); S.M. Ndlovu, Noor Nieftagodien and Tshepo Moloi, 'The Soweto Uprising,' in SADET (ed.), *The Road to Democracy in South Africa, Volume 2: 1970–1980* (Johannesburg, Zebra Press: 2004); Philip Bonner and Noor Nieftagodien, *Alexandra: A History* (Johannesburg, Wits University Press: 2008); Noor Nieftago-dien, *The Soweto Uprising* (Johannesburg, Jacana: 2014).

This chapter therefore places the event of the Uprising in the context of a series of productive tensions, as laid out in the chapters preceding this. These tensions shape the narrative that follows, as classroom activism gave way to the forging of connections between school-going students in the run up to the planned mass march of 16 June 1976 and then, in the course of that day and those that followed, as the solidarity and sympathy of others in Soweto helped shape the further evolution of the Uprising and the social and political changes it set in motion.

The build-up

The student go-slow at Phefeni Junior did not attract any public attention in March and April, and seems to have been confined to the one school. In May, however, these students decided to escalate their protest and embark on a full strike, refusing to attend any of their classes.

According to the Cillié Commission's report, the principal of the school informed the local inspector of the proposed strike on Sunday 16 May; the strike began on Monday and in its course the students 'pelted the school principal's office with stones and let the air out of the tyres of his motor car'.[7] On Tuesday, students threw out Afrikaans textbooks and threatened the principal again: according to a report in *The World*, they 'seized a tape recorder from the vice-principal, Mr F. Nhlapo, accused him of being a police informer and threatened to beat him up'.[8] Over the next days, the strike spread to three neighbouring schools: Thulasizwe, Belle and Emthonjeni higher primary schools. At Thulasizwe, 300 students held a demonstration protesting against the use of Afrikaans. They left the school premises, then marched up and down the neighbouring streets bearing placards. At Belle, the protesting students locked the school gates and refused to allow either teachers or non-participating students to enter the school property. By Monday morning, *The World* reported that at least a thousand students were participating in these demonstrations.[9]

The strike continued to spread across higher primary and junior secondary schools in Soweto. It reached its peak in the first week of June, when approximately 2,700 students were thought to be participating.[10] Several of the demonstrations were confrontational. According to the Cillié Commission, students at four different schools threw stones at observers during their protests.[11]

[7] RSA, *Report of the Commission of Inquiry into the Riots at Soweto and Elsewhere from the 16th June 1976 to the 28th February 1977* (Cillié Commission) 2 vol. (Pretoria, Government Publisher: 1980), p. 78.
[8] *The World*, 19 May 1976.
[9] *The World*, 24 May 1976. See also: RSA, *Cillié Commission*, pp. 80–81
[10] *The World*, 1 June 1976.
[11] RSA, *Cillié Commission*, p. 85–6.

After this week, however, the number of students on strike began to decline. By Tuesday, 15 June, all but three of the original schools – Phefeni, Belle and Emthonjeni – had resumed classes. *The World* was still reporting the protest, suggesting that 300 students were still refusing to be taught 'Social Studies and Mathematics – the subjects taught in Afrikaans'.[12] But it appears that – despite the strike being discussed by parliament, local authorities and the police – these protests declined through students' exhaustion rather than in response to any effort made to bring them to an end.

These protests were organised by the students most affected by the change in the language policy – that is, the students entering into junior secondary classes. According to Ndlovu's memories of the period, only one of the older students at his school was permitted to take part in the afternoon discussions. This student, Seth Mazibuko, was a school prefect and, apparently, respected by the younger students. Ndlovu's memories – like those of the other students he quotes – place Mazibuko solely in the context of Phefeni, and portray him as a minor influence within their own lives. Mazibuko, however, had a political life outside of the school as one of the leading activists in SASM. His connection to these protests raises the question of the ways through which students outside Phefeni and outside of the age group most affected by the new policy came to be involved.

Although the older school students in Soweto were not directly affected by the change in the language policy – the new curriculum was being phased in, and students above junior secondary classes would continue to be taught in English – they were nonetheless aware of the way in which this policy was being imposed upon their juniors, and were spurred into actions of their own. SASM was one of the key instruments through which these students could express their solidarity.

This should not be mistaken for anything more than support – national organisations of students did not organise these protests, nor did they claim to do so at the time. Late in May, the Black Peoples' Convention rejected a report linking it to the protest, suggesting that such a link was simply an attempt to divert attention from the struggles of the students. Similarly, in a SASM general conference held during the last weekend in May, the organisation resolved 'to fully support the students who took a stand in the rejection of this dialect' without claiming to have played any role in originating or organising the protests.[13]

This point is important, because the proposer of this resolution – Tebello Motapanyane, the secretary-general of SASM – would later claim that he had played a more active role in the organisation of these

---

[12] *The World*, 15 June 1976.
[13] RSA, *Cillié Commission*, pp. 83–5.

protests. In an interview published in *Sechaba*, the official publication of the ANC in exile, he suggested that he and other SASM members from Naledi High School had visited Phefeni in March 1976, and had incited their protest: 'the students there agreed with us and started destroying their books and refused to go to class'.[14] Indeed, among the most active leaders of SASM there may have been some intention to organise, and to link the activities of students to the African National Congress in exile and underground. Diseko argues that, by the early months of 1976, SASM was looking for models of politics beyond the relatively young South African Black Consciousness tradition. They were 'impressed' by Malcolm X's critique of the apparent passivity of the Civil Rights Movement in the USA, as well as by the victories of Frelimo's armed struggle. In addition, despite the very limited presence of the ANC Underground in Soweto at the time, its growing ability to distribute samizdat pamphlets and flyers brought the movement's existence and history to the attention of student activists. Diseko suggests that the ANC's underground network was in touch with a small number of SASM's leaders at the start of 1976, and – although there was little direct influence – these core activists in the student movement in Soweto were increasingly becoming aligned with the ANC's ideas.[15]

Against this, Ndlovu insists that he did 'not remember any liberation movement, such as the Black Consciousness Movement or the Southern African Students' Movement (SASM) contributing to our daily meetings and discussions'.[16] In all, Ndlovu's approach is convincing – Motapanyane's account is the only one that exists of his visit, and the chronology does not fit other events: students at Phefeni only destroyed their textbooks in May, for example, and not in March.

Indeed it is clear that support and solidarity – rather than incitement or organisation – was what most of the students in SASM believed themselves to be offering. The resolution adopted at the SASM conference connected the fight against Afrikaans with a broader condemnation of the Bantu Education system: 'The recent strike by schools against the use of Afrikaans as a medium of instruction is a sign of demonstration against schools' systematised producing of "good industrial boys" for the powers that be.'[17] These older students may even have been considering embarking on their own campaign, alongside and in support of the struggles of their younger colleagues. But this did phase of organisational separation not last.

Before long, SASM was brought to the attention of the state – and, once the police became involved, events worked to bring older students

[14] *Sechaba*, 1977, p. 55.
[15] Diseko, 'Origins and Development of SASM', pp. 60–61.
[16] Ndlovu, *Counter-Memories*, p. 7.
[17] Quotes in RSA, *Cillié Commission*, p. 84.

to the foreground in the first weeks of June 1976. A member of the SASM branch at Naledi High School wrote a letter to SASO's head office in Durban, 'asking for support for the campaign against Afrikaans'. This letter was intercepted by the police, who arrested and then immediately released the student on Friday 4 June.[18] Four days later, two officers of the Security Police returned to Naledi High to question Enoch Ntushana, the secretary of the school's SASM branch. According to the account given to the Cillié Commission, the policemen parked their car on the school property and, while the white officer went to find Ntushana, his colleague, a black policeman, 'was being intimidated by pupils; they called him a sell-out and even threatened to kill him'.[19] The officers telephoned for reinforcements, before the students apparently cut the telephone wire. Then, according to another account of the incident, 'as [the officers] were walking back to the car students started to stone them. They let go of the boy they had arrested and fled to the principal's office, where they locked themselves in.'[20]

According to the police, about 800 students took part in this attack, and had to be forcibly dispersed. The following day, the police returned to the school. Again, according to the account given to the Commission by the police, a police photographer was driven away by stone-throwing students. According to the memories of participants in the protests, the police were present in force – possibly supported by a group of Bantustan soldiers – and were once again prevented from making any arrests. A year later, Motapanyane recalled confronting the police with obvious pleasure: 'Hey, it was unfortunate for them to be seen by the students. They were beaten.'[21]

The clashes between students and police at Naledi suggest how a confrontational mood was developing in Soweto in the autumn of 1976. The defiance of authority figures such as principals and teachers was accompanied by a defiance of the representatives of the state, and was notably confrontational. This marked a shift from earlier student protests – indeed, it is only at the pro-Frelimo rally at the University of the North in 1974 that a comparably aggressive response to state authority can be found. However, as with earlier protests, these were still confined within school grounds, and largely isolated from each other. The events at Naledi had little direct impact on other schools, while the go-slow and then boycotts at Phefeni, Belle, Emthonjeni and other schools, remained restricted to the particular student bodies. In this, at least, the protests of April and May 1976 resembled the workers' strikes of 1973, where workers at factories scattered across Durban

---

[18] Brooks and Brickhill, *Whirlwind*, p. 89.
[19] RSA, *Cillié Commission*, p. 92.
[20] Pat Hopkins and Helen Grange, *The Rocky Rioter Teargas Show: The Inside Story of the 1976 Soweto Uprising* (Cape Town, Zebra: 2001), p. 85.
[21] *Sechaba*, 1977, p. 56. See also, RSA, *Cillié Commission*, pp. 93–4.

downed tools individually, each factory protesting against conditions and wages independently of each other factory. These protests coincided with each other, creating the conditions under which further strikes and further activism became thinkable, instituting a wave of labour activism.

In Durban, of course, the strikes were never coordinated: although the wave lasted for almost three months, each strike continued to be resolved independently. In Soweto, three years later, students recognised the problems that came from disconnection, and sought instead to connect.

On Sunday 13 June 1976, four hundred students from several schools across Soweto gathered at the Donaldson Community Centre in Orlando – a subdivision of Soweto, with a social history of its own.[22] According to Motapanyane, admittedly a problematic source, this was organised by SASM, to discuss 'that there should be a mass demonstration from the Soweto students as a whole'. During the course of the meeting, he recalled: 'We decided to have a committee that would take charge of the whole thing.'[23] It was decided that this committee – namely simply the 'Action Committee' – would consist of an executive elected at the meeting, and two further members from each of the schools in Soweto. The process of integrating these further members into the Committee would have to wait, however, as not all schools were represented at the meeting.

According to other accounts of this meeting, the proposal for a mass demonstration came from the floor. Tsietsi Mashinini, the leader of the SASM branch at Morris Isaacson High School, was elected to the Committee's executive and suggested that a demonstration be held three days later, on Wednesday 16 June. His speech was, in the words of Bonner and Segal, 'greeted with cheers of support'. The discussion then turned to deciding what from the demonstration should take, and how it should be organised. Significantly, the students decided to form a 'pact that parents should not get involved. They should not even be told about what was going to happen on the 16th.' This was confirmed by Murphy Morobe, another student leader, who suggested that 'students had lost so much confidence in the adult population' that they needed to work alone.[24]

It was agreed that the demonstration would take the form of a mass march of school students, and that the Action Committee would establish any further details. On Tuesday, 15 June, the Committee held a brief meeting to ensure that the march had a schedule. The primary concern was that 'if some schools left prematurely, they would get cut

---

[22] For the history of the area, see: Noor Nieftagodien and Sally Gaule, *Orlando West, Soweto: An Illustrated History* (Johannesburg, Wits University Press: 2012).

[23] Sechaba, 1977, p. 56.

[24] Bonner and Segal, *Soweto*, p. 83.

off from the rest'.[25] Each school was therefore to be assigned a schedule and route. According to the Cillié Commission's report – which may overstate the degree of conscious organisation in this period – three streams were identified, moving from Morris Isaacson, Naledi and Sekano-Ntoane schools. Others would join as they passed, and all would congregate outside the Orlando West High School before moving on to the Orlando Stadium. The Commission suggested that 'according to some witnesses, the intention had been to march from there to the offices of the Bantu Education Inspectorate' – but this does not seem to have been a widely held belief.[26] Most members of the Action Committee seem instead to have been uncertain of how they expected the march to end. Morobe, for example, remembered the plan to have been simply to 'pledge our solidarity and sing 'Nkosi Sikelel' iAfrica'. Then we thought we would have made our point and would go back home.'[27]

These plans were rudimentary, but they mark an important shift in the development of protest in Soweto. The confrontational events at junior secondary schools in April and May and the clash between students and police at Naledi High in the previous week were all spontaneous and uncoordinated. The move towards organisation was – at least in the minds of activists – linked to a move away from confrontation. According to one of Brooks and Brickhill's anonymous informants: 'Before we marched on the 16th we decided there should be no placard inciting the police as such. Placards should only be against Afrikaans ... we wanted a very peaceful demonstration – it had to be disciplined.'[28] This avoidance of conflict resonated with the memories of a student at Phefeni, who believed that the march would be carnivalesque – that 'it would be a Guy Fawkes thing'.[29]

This was not to be, however.

16 June 1976

The leaders of the march understood that the peacefulness of students could not guarantee the peacefulness of the police: at most, they could attempt to reduce the opportunities which could be used by the police to justify their own violent actions. Brooks and Brickhill's informants suggest that: 'Yes, we did consider the possibility of police attack but tried to avoid it by being peaceful.' In retrospect, Motapanyane was less

---

[25] An anonymous activist, quoted in Brooks and Brickhill, *Whirlwind*, p. 91.
[26] RSA, *Cillié Commission*, pp. 98–9.
[27] Quotes in Ndlovu, *Counter-Memories*, p. 26.
[28] Brooks and Brickhill, *Whirlwind*, p. 92.
[29] Paul Ndaba, quoted in Ndlovu, *Counter-Memories*, p. 26. See also the first pages of the Introduction in this volume.

sanguine: 'we knew the police would be violent against the students'. He argued that students had sought to avoid initiating violence – but would not refrain from responding in kind should it be needed: 'So we said no, immediately there is violence from the police, we would have to defend ourselves and, if possible, hit back.'[30]

Although this suggestion – like all others made by Motanyane – was made a year after the Uprising, and after the conflict had exploded, it was picked up by the Cillié Commission as a thin piece of evidence to suggest that the students were not completely committed to non-violent forms of protest. The Commission claimed that 'only the organisers knew what dimensions the demonstration would assume and they apparently took no measures to ensure that everything would begin and pass off peacefully'. Instead, 'they gave advice on what should be done if they police should dare to stop the marching crowds; the advice was not that they should disperse peacefully'.[31]

This overstates, though, the extent to which the Action Committee was capable of managing the demonstration. It overstates, too, the willingness of ordinary participants to imagine embarking upon acts of violence – or even to imagine what effective coordination would be like. Instead, in interviews conducted by Elsabé Brink and others, students recalled a swirling, chaotic morning.[32]

For the majority of students, Wednesday began unremarkably: 'we went to school as if it was just a normal day. There was nothing. We even learnt well.' 'We arrived at school and went to assembly ... we entered the classrooms.' 'There was normal schooling.' This was interrupted, though, when students from other schools streamed past and, according to George Baloyi, 'told us that we must knock off because there was Black Power'. Others remembered similar scenes: 'There were these students from the high schools. They entered into our school to tell us that now we will have to stop learning because now is Black Power.' 'These guys just came in and went "Out, out, out, out, out" and "Amandla!" ... it was first just confusion ... I didn't even understand where we were going. I didn't grasp the objective of the march.' Some classes were dismissed by their teachers; others, however, marched out over the objections of the school authorities.[33]

So schools dispersed at different times in the morning: if an orderly schedule had been agreed to by the Action Committee, few of the participating students knew of it or adhered to it. Students met their peers in their own schoolyards, after being roused from classrooms,

[30] *Sechaba*, 1977, p. 56.
[31] RSA, *Cillié Commission*, p. 104.
[32] Elsabé Brink, Gandhi Malungane, Steve Lebelo, Dumisane Ntshangase and Sue Krige, *Soweto, 16 June 1976: It All Started With A Dog ...* (Johannesburg, Kwela: 2001).
[33] All quoted in Brink et al, *Soweto*, p. 40–52.

groups of students discovered each other in the streets, at crossroads and in open spaces. Erick Ngobeni remembered that 'it was so crowded outside ... There was no way that [teachers] could identify us.' Steve Lebelo remembered mingling at a crossroads for 'thirty to forty-five minutes ... We haven't even started marching along.'[34]

Lebelo was still at that crossroads when 'suddenly news filtered that there were problems between the students and police in other parts of Soweto'. This was 'well after nine o'clock, going for ten', and rumours of these confrontations put the students on edge, anticipating violence.

Some of these rumours were repeated over the following days: the *Sunday Express* suggested that there had been confrontation at 08h00, in which a policemen 'drew a gun and fired two shots in the air, then another at a student carrying a placard. He missed.'[35] The Cillié Commission suggested that a number of police officers reported being stoned by students – and that, although they had tried to disperse the crowds with tear gas, their canisters did not go off.[36] None of these incidents, though, developed into a more general confrontation – each fizzled out quickly.

The same cannot be said about the confrontation between police and students outside the Orlando West High School, at about 10h30 in the morning. The police were heavily armed: 'before they left the police station, revolvers, pistols, three automatic rifles, ammunition and tear-gas grenades [were] issued' to these officers. Almost fifty officers moved to intercept students outside the school, accompanied by police dogs.[37] They encountered a large group of students – estimated by journalists at the time to have comprised between 1,000 and 2,000 people, and estimated by the Commission afterwards to have comprised between 5,000 and 6,000 people.

This confrontation rapidly turned violent.

According to the police, in the initial account given to parliament, the students had 'summarily' stoned a police unit 'before they were even given an opportunity to negotiate with the pupils'. The police therefore responded by using tear gas in an attempt disperse the crowd. When this failed, 'it was clear that the lives of the police were seriously endangered as a result of intensified attacks, and they were obliged to make use of their fire arms ... to reach safety'.[38] Translated into clearer language, this means that the police shot at the students with live ammunition until they fled.

According to other observers, though, the police's actions could not be so glibly justified.

[34] Quoted in Brink et al, *Soweto*, pp. 44, 75.
[35] *Sunday Express*, 20 June 1976.
[36] RSA, *Cillié Commission*, pp. 110–11.
[37] RSA, *Cillié Commission*, p. 113.
[38] RSA, *Debates of the House of Assembly* (Hansard), 17 June 1976, cols. 1241–2.

Sophie Tema, a reporter for *The World*, offered an eyewitness account that provided an early alternative to the parliamentary narrative. She had been following a group of students, accompanied by two photographers. The three journalists left their car near Vilakazi Street and approached the students outside the Orlando West High School; she saw at least ten police vehicles arrive at the site and approximately thirty people approach the students. The students were waving placards condemning the use of Afrikaans in school teaching, they sang a Sotho-language version of 'Nkosi Sikelel' iAfrica' and whistled at the police. At this point, 'a white policeman hurled what seemed to be a tear gas shell – which released a cloud of smoke or gas – into the crowd.' The students responded by throwing rocks at the police. Immediately after this, Tema saw 'a White policeman pull out his revolver, point it, and fire it. As soon as the shot was fired other policemen also began firing.' These shots sped into the crowd, killing two students.

Tema saw:

> a young boy whom she estimated to be between six and seven years old ... fall with a bullet wound. 'He had a bloody froth on his lips and he seemed to be seriously hurt so I took him to the Phefeni Clinic in a press car but he was dead when we arrived.'[39]

A second press account confirmed the general thrust of Tema's account, while differing in some of the details. This version emphasised a chain of contingent incidents which had the effect of heightening tensions at the scene, until the police fired – first in panic, then with intent.[40]

Tema's version, however, was the most widely reported, and her testimony to the Commission helped cement it as the best account.[41] The Commission itself concluded that the shooting was the product of a heightening tension:

> on their arrival the police were taunted by the crowd and stones were thrown at them. After the use of tear-gas, the stone-throwing became fiercer, and Col. Kleingeld fired two warning shots ... they were surrounded on all sides by the crowd and stones were thrown at them. Because their lives were in danger, Col. Kleingeld tried to ward off the crowd with rifle fire ... his men also began firing in desperation.[42]

The existence of these alternate accounts highlights the confusing and contradictory nature of a mass event in which violence erupts and catalyses protest. No one memory can encompass all the moments

[39] *The World*, 17 June 1976.
[40] *Sunday Express*, 20 June 1976.
[41] RSA, *Cillié Commission, Testimony* (1976–1977), Vols 9–10, pp. 340–76.
[42] RSA, *Cillié Commission*, p. 120.

leading to the violence, and no account can fully record all the actions that took place.

All these accounts converge, however, on the undeniable presence of a child's corpse.

At this moment, the mass demonstration in Soweto diverged from the patterns set in the recent past. There were precedents for the protests of students within the boundaries of their schools and classrooms, and there were precedents for the reclamation of public space through mass demonstration and marches. But there were no precedents for the death of a child in the midst of protest: police violence had been brutal over the past decade, but rarely deadly. To date, death had come in secret: in prison cells, and in packages through the mail. It did not happen in public, on the streets.

And it did not occur in front of photographers.

Sam Nzima was one of the two photographers accompanying Sophie Tema on Wednesday morning.[43] He caught a photograph of the child's body, carried in the arms of an older youth. This youth is running towards the camera. Beside him is a young girl, her expression twisted into a scream, hands held beside her face. The child's body is slack, seemingly already dead.

The child's name was Hector Pieterson, and this image has come to be inextricably linked to the memory of 16 June 1976.[44] Nzima's photograph was printed in several different newspapers, and shaped a particular response to the police violence.[45] It was used to emphasise the culpability of the police, and the violence of their reaction to the student protest. It was therefore notably absent from those immediate responses that sought to justify police action: in the conservative *Die Transvaler*, there was no visible sign of Pieterson's death. Instead, this newspaper illustrated its coverage with images of a delivery truck in flames, a white man's head seen in profile, with streams of blood from his ear – indicating where he had been hit by a stone, another bloodied white face, and a studio portrait of the sole white casualty of the day. On 17 June, *Die Transvaler* published no images of black students, let alone any images of injured or dead students.[46]

The conservative press had little impact within Soweto, though, and by the time that Nzima's photograph was published it could only serve to crystallise the existing response in the township.

Within minutes of Pieterson's death, events in Soweto began to outpace earlier protests. Solly Mpshe recalled that he was marching

[43] RSA, *Cillié Commission Testimony*, Testimony of Sam Nzima.
[44] See the publication of the Hector Pieterson Museum: A.K. Hlongwane (ed.), *Footprints of the 'Class of 76': Commemoration, Memory, Mapping, and Heritage* (Johannesburg, Hector Pieterson Museum: 2006).
[45] See, for example, *The Star*, 17 June 1976.
[46] *Die Transvaler*, 17 June 1976.

towards Orlando West when he 'heard that several people have been shot already and one was killed'. Ahead of the students, the police had erected barricades. 'And there was tension like we did not expect ... the message was clear that if we try to go beyond certain point, they were going to shoot.'[47]

The students stood in 'a state of uncertainty ... we were just moving around, not knowing where to go. And there was no direction'. Whatever organisation might have existed in the morning had collapsed in the face of the police: 'So basically what happened thereafter was a free for all.'

Instead of wilting under the pressure of the police's threatening posture, though, students began to revolt: 'it started with commercial vehicles who happened to be in the neighbourhood and people started stoning these cars and taking whatever is inside'. Mpshe took part in this assault – although he struggled to explain why. 'We were still disciplined, law-abiding kids. We just wanted to freelance, all right. And even the stoning was done by a handful of silly kids ... some of us were a bit silly, threw stones and looted.' Despite his protestations, though, the assaults that Mpshe took part in were not truly random: 'That afternoon, I learnt the popular word "the system". So, on our way back, anything that was associated with "the system" was stoned.'

Mpshe's political education took place in the midst of the protest – through action and conflict. It crystallised the next day, when he read of Pieterson's death in the morning newspapers. He spent the next several days indoors, avoiding the violence in the streets. 'That is when we really started to talk about politics. That is when we started talking about the ANC, the PAC, Umkhonto we Sizwe. And getting really interested in Black Consciousness ... That is when we really started relating politics and our situation.'[48] Over the coming weeks and months, the unfocused explosion of 16 June would turn – for Mpshe, at least – into a process of self-education and political discovery. It is striking that, in his narrative, the experience of violence, whether suffered or inflicted, is subjugated to a narrative of political awakening. For Mpshe, the violence of the Uprising opened a site of possibilities, and it was those possibilities that remained with him.

For others, of course, the shock of violence loomed larger.

Vusi Zwane, one of the youngest students participating in the march, was initially excited by the chaotic atmosphere on the streets. When the organised march dissolved, he rushed home to change out of his school uniform, sneak out again, and then join the Uprising. He met a group of students near the Esso Garage in Chiawelo, in the south-eastern section of Soweto. By this time, the students' march had collapsed, and localised groups were resisting the police's efforts to

[47] Brink et al, *Soweto*, p. 62–3.
[48] Brink et al, *Soweto*, pp. 134–5.

restore their particular brand of order. The Garage occupied a site on the main road in and out of Soweto; the gathered students threw stones at passing cars, attempted to prevent commercial and government vehicles entering the township, raised ramshackle barricades, and raided delivery trucks. For Zwane, these were all bound together in the politics of what Mpshe would learn to call 'the system' – the network of institutions and ideas that justified and held together apartheid.

But it was not the political aspects of this violence that remained with Zwane. He could not remember how long he spent at the Garage, participating in the stone-throwing. Nor did he recount particular stories of attacking cars or raiding vans. Instead, he remembered participating passionately at the Garage 'until a certain lady died. She was behind me. This happened just at the back of Esso Garage. That is where I got frightened and realised that this can cost one's life.'

Asked whether the dead woman was a student, he replied:

> No, this lady was not a student. She was just an elderly lady who was just passing. She did not know what was happening ... It was just a passing bullet. Maybe it could have got me simply because she was just behind me ... it is where I started to realise that this was a serious issue now, that it can cause the death of a person.

Zwane continued to protest, even after witnessing this death. After that moment, though, his understanding of the day's events changed. Although 'at first' he believed that 'we throw stones at cars and ended there', he now came to realise that these violent events would have unavoidable consequences: 'It was my first time to see a person die ... especially losing her life in front of me.'[49]

These accounts of the events of 16 June 1976 highlight how the planned demonstration was transformed, through the rush of contingent events, into an insurrection. They show how the potential for such an uprising was always present – the same tensions between students and police, the same repressive and brutal practices of policing, and the same heightened sense of possibility occurred in earlier protests. Yet, at the same time, they demonstrate the uniqueness of the event – the unpredictability and open-endedness that Lefebvre identified in the context of the insurrection of May 1968. The students' explosion of consciousness flowed from their experiences during the Uprising, and found the forms established for them over the past decade: dissent from the 'system', Black Consciousness, and the new radicalism of student protests.

The starkest difference between this protest and those that preceded it was the brute fact of death: there was no possibility of avoiding the proof of the state's disregard for the lives of its black subjects. The

---

[49] Brink et al, *Soweto*, pp. 85–8.

stories told by participants return again and again to the shock of witnessing death, while the popular memory of the event revolves around Hector Pieterson's corpse.

There is good reason for this: on 16 June alone, the police killed eleven people. Over the next several days this number would increase dramatically. It was, in part, the undeniable force of the dead – the physical and symbolic presence of mute bodies – that would make the Uprising what it was.

But, of course, the Uprising was not simply the events of one day. It continued, and expanded.

Expansion and aftermath

Shortly after midnight on 17 June, protesters began to burn the regional Bantu Affairs Administration offices, located behind the Meadowlands police station; the police dispersed the crowd, but could not rescue the building. Between 03h00 and 06h00, railway stations and beer halls were attacked by crowds; an hour later, a dozen shops in the Klipspruit area were set alight, further Bantu Affairs buildings were torched, and someone was stabbed to death in a dispute on a football field near Jabavu. Shortly after 08h00, 3,000 people attacked the Naledi Railway Station: 'bottles with unknown contents were distributed to the bystanders. Warning shots by the police had no effect. Someone in the crowd fired at the police with a small-calibre firearm. Three of the inciters were singled out by the police and shot. The crowd retreated but later regrouped.'[50]

Crowds targeted railway stations, Bantu Affairs offices, post offices, beer halls, and shops. Their size ranged from several thousand to several dozen, and there is little to suggest that these groups consisted solely of young students – although the majority of the deaths recorded in this period were of youths between the ages of 15 and 30 years. Instead, it appears that insurrectionary fervour had spread across Soweto's society; the attacks against property were loosely tied to a notion of 'the system' as involving not just openly discriminatory politics, but also all commercial and economic activity that could be said to support the apartheid state.

But most importantly, the police struggled to impose any form of control on these crowds. The Cillié Commission concluded that fifty-four people were shot dead by the police in the course of Thursday 17 June. A further thirty died in ways that the Commission was unwilling or unable to link to the police. Friday 18 June, saw the police kill thirty-one people. Twelve more were killed in other ways. In addition to the

---

[50] RSA, *Cillié Commission, Volume 2*, Annexure D, p. 16.

eleven killed by the police on 16 June, this brought the total death toll for these three days of violence to 138 – a staggering sum, and one that was almost unprecedented.

From Saturday, the violence in Soweto began to subside. On that day, only five people were killed by the police. On Monday 21 June, only one man was killed by the police. Over the following weeks and months, deaths would continue intermittently – without daily figures being needed.

However, acts of protest and dissent, accompanied by violence, had now erupted far beyond Soweto. On 17 June, for example, white students from the University of the Witwatersrand marched in sympathy with the embattled school students in Soweto. This march was assaulted by members of the white public, and forcibly dispersed by the police. At the University of the North, black students disrupted classes, before attempting to burn the office of the head of the Afrikaans department. Meanwhile, school students in Alexandra and Thembisa attempted to organise in support of the students in Soweto: young students in Alexandra attempted to build barricades near a primary school and, in Thembisa, high school students now refused to attend their classes.

On 18 June, Alexandra erupted into violence. Shops, bottle stores, and official buildings were attacked, burned and looted by large crowds. According to the Cillié Commission, many of the targeted shops were owned by Indian or Coloured traders. Nieftagodien, however, argues against the implication of a racial rivalry, suggesting that these 'demonstrations were remarkable for the unity displayed between African and Coloured students, even though they attend segregated schools'.[51] The police used force in an attempt to curtail the violence in the township, and were judged by the Commission to have been responsible for the deaths of twenty-nine people. Similar acts of violence took place across the Witwatersrand. In Tembisa, students from two schools began a march: approximately 2,000 people may have joined in. This march ended at a bottle store, which was attacked and looted; the police fired tear gas at the crowd, but the wind changed and the gas failed to disperse them. The railway station was threatened, and transport into and out of the township was affected. The police killed six people, while shop owners and others were responsible for the deaths of a further eleven.[52]

Over the next week, beer halls and bottle stores were torched in Vereeniging, Mamelodi, Atteridgeville and Pretoria. A post office was destroyed in Benoni, while buses, Bantu Affairs offices, and commercial vehicles were stoned and burned in Bophuthatswana and Lebowa. By the end of June, these incidents had settled into a steady pattern – the Cillié Commission recorded one or more acts of violence occurring

[51] Ndlovu et al., 'The Soweto Uprising', p. 355.
[52] RSA, *Cillié Commission, Vol. 2,* Annexure D.

each day in black townships across the country and in the Bantustans. Only on rare days could it note, as on 14 July, that 'no incidents were reported'.

Meanwhile, in the immediate aftermath of the violence, a number of Soweto's older generation – including Winnie Mandela, Manas Buthelezi and Aubrey Mokoena – formed the Black Parents' Association (BPA) to support the embattled youth. At first the BPA provided transport and refuge for the leaders of the protest; later, it turned its attention to organising funerals. It sought to raise burial fees, organise free coffins and provide religious counselling to the relatives of the dead. Its members did not seek to lead protest, and remained in support roles.[53] For Motapanyane, the task of the BPA was to 'get figures of how many people died' and to speak to the authorities on behalf of the students.[54] The funerals organised by the BPA, however, did provide an opportunity for the further coordination of protest. For example, the BPA planned a mass funeral for the victims of the police shooting but, late in June, this was banned by the Minister of Police, Jimmy Kruger. This order was received with great resentment: it failed to acknowledge the common experience of the residents, and was seen to mock their shared grief. Instead of a mass funeral, therefore, a funeral for Hector Pieterson was held as a symbol for all the other funerals that could not take place. The police erected barricades around the township and patrolled the skies.

Cemeteries became sites of political conscientisation, and attendance at funerals became a means of expressing solidarity. Hirson noted that the funerals were marked by 'the reversal of social custom … adults mourned children, the youth mourned lost comrades'. Many of the adults were unrelated, but were there to express 'political, and not only social, solidarity'. 'Funerals were no longer seen only as rites of passage in which the departed were entering the other world, but also as gatherings at which there could be an affirmation of the demand for a new South Africa.'[55]

Entrenching the Uprising

As the anarchic violence of late June subsided, the student activists of the Action Committee were increasingly able to exert their influence on other emergent groups within the township. By mid-July, its members 'were able to demonstrate that they could effectively speak for the students and structure their political action. Greater co-ordination now began to appear.' A sign of this was the movement of

[53] Hirson, *Year of Fire*, pp. 196–8.
[54] *Sechaba*, 1977, p. 52.
[55] Hirson, *Year of Fire*, p. 207.

172

students away from 'stoning, burning, and more primitive forms of political response' and towards 'the identification and exploration of alternative action-techniques for intensifying pressure upon the white authorities.'[56] On 22 July, schools re-opened – and Afrikaans-language instruction was gone. The Action Committee called on students to return to class.[57]

On Sunday 1 August, the BPA held a public meeting in the Regina Mundi Catholic Church in Soweto, at which Tsietsi Mashinini of the Action Committee called for a mass meeting of students to be held the next day. At this meeting, the Action Committee formally transformed itself into the Soweto Students' Representative Council (SSRC). Mashinini was elected its first president; it adopted the same organisational structure as the Action Committee, aiming to consist of two representatives from each of Soweto's forty schools. It was decided at this meeting that the SSRC would both organise a protest march on Wednesday 4 August, and call for workers to strike on that day. The march would start from Soweto and end at the police headquarters at John Vorster Square; the marchers would hand over a memo calling for the release of all students.

On Wednesday morning, students refused to attend classes. The SSRC march began at Morris Isaacson school at approximately 07h30. Two hundred students soon met up with sympathetic adults, and students from other schools. Large crowds gathered in other areas of Soweto, most probably intending to join together. It was a massive crowd: Hirson suggested that it swelled to number 20,000 people; the Cillié Commission, more conservatively, estimated that it was 15,000 strong. The crowd was prevented from marching from Soweto into Johannesburg. According to Hirson, the 'leadership, in the front ranks of the marchers, had firm control over the students'. They refused to retreat, and eventually the police resorted to using tear gas and live ammunition in an attempt to disperse them. This violence succeeded in disrupting the march and in forcing the protesters – both students and non-students – to flee from the aggressive confrontation.

The success of the SSRC's strike-call was equally significant. Between 50 and 60 per cent of workers in Soweto stayed at home, or joined the protest march.[58] This high rate of participation was associated with a degree of intimidation – students gathered around Soweto's railway stations and public transport hubs to prevent workers from leaving the township. Stones were thrown at buses and vehicles; some workers were assaulted in the evening, on their return to the town-

---

[56] P.H. Frankel, 'The Dynamics of a Political Renaissance: The Soweto Students' Representative Council', *Journal of African Studies*, 7 (3): 1980, p. 170.

[57] Hirson, *Year of Fire*, p. 209.

[58] Karis and Gerhart, *From Protest to Challenge, Vol. 5*, p. 172.

ship.[59] Hirson, however, emphasised that the scale of the strike could not be accounted for simply by the students' action. The students were not able to convince workers into further strike days – whether by force or otherwise – which suggests, at least, that the first strike and the march were indeed supported by workers.[60]

Buoyed by these successes, the SSRC called a second stay-away for 23–25 August. This was marked by 'lower levels of intimidation and a stronger public response', but was still successful. This display of unified opposition was, however, threatened on the following day when a group of largely Zulu workers from the Mzimhlope hostel in Meadowlands rampaged through the township. Although the Cillié Commission claimed that this rampage was encouraged by a group of 'firebrands' within the community, Karis and Gerhart conclude that it was most likely inspired by police provocation. They suggest that the police exploited tensions between the hostel dwellers and the students; students had not attempted to communicate with migrants, nor had 'any apologies been made to them for the destruction of the municipal beerhalls which were a centre of their social life'.[61]

Although these clashes marred the otherwise successful strike, they also drove the SSRC to talk to hostel dwellers and attempt to build networks of support and solidarity in Soweto. Kane-Berman suggests that in a meeting with hostel dwellers, 'the students explained their protest ... emphasising how they as migrant workers were also victims of oppression. Thus was peace restored.'[62]

The flyers distributed by the SSRC after this point appealed for unity between workers, hostel dwellers and students. By September – when the SSRC called for a third stay-away – many hostel dwellers had been convinced, and most took part. This stay-away was held from 13–15 September. Over 80 per cent of Soweto's workforce remained at home. In the next days they were joined by Coloured and African workers in Cape Town, sustaining the protest nationally into 16 September. This was the high-water mark of the Uprising, the largest single demonstration to have been staged by black workers: up to 500,000 workers took part in this protest.[63]

Of course, the SSRC was not the only organisation seeking to organise the insurrectionary fervour of this period. Nonetheless, it was both the most visible and the most effective such organisation. The labour stoppages in August and September demonstrated its ability to reach beyond its core constituency of students and to involve adult workers and non-students. As it grew in confidence, the SSRC began

[59] RSA, *Cillié Commission*, Vol. 2, Annexure D.
[60] Hirson, *Year of Fire*, pp. 210–11.
[61] Karis and Gerhart, *From Protest to Challenge, Vol. 5*, p. 172.
[62] Kane-Berman, *Soweto*, p. 114
[63] Brooks and Brickhill, *Whirlwind*, p. 32; Hirson, *Year of Fire*, p. 254

to expand its activities. In October, for example, the SSRC ordered the closing of shebeens – that is, unlicensed and informal township bars. 'Hundreds of students visited shebeens towards the end of October, asking their owners to observe the period of mourning for people killed since 16 June. "They were most courteous," said one shebeen-owner, "and we feel we must show our solidarity."'[64] There were an estimated 1,000 shebeens in Soweto, and this response was probably not representative. Still – after gaining a week's grace to dispose of their existing stocks of liquor – Soweto's shebeens shut on 31 October and remained closed for a fortnight.

In the same period, the SSRC also embarked on other social campaigns, including one to clean up the litter on Soweto's streets. Refuse removal had been suspended after 16 June, and the township was 'full of ash, papers, tins, bottles, stinking dead animals, rotting garbage, and leaves'. The township was 'reduced to a stinking slum'. The SSRC also pressured the National Professional Soccer League into cancelling its remaining fixtures; despite a lack of cooperation from its leaders, the league was suspended on 3 November – with only two games left to play. (Later, after 15 November, the SSRC gave permission for these games to be played.)[65]

Not all the SSRC's efforts were successful. A further stay-away was planned for the same period in early November, but failed to attract mass support. Students in Soweto boycotted their end-of-year exams under the SSRC's influence – but although this boycott succeeded, the SSRC was then faced with the decision whether to allow students to sit the exams again, early in 1977. A shopping boycott timed to coincide with the Christmas season also achieved mixed success, with some stores registering unusually low sales, while others seem to have negotiated with the SSRC to be allowed to remain trading. These campaigns all achieved relatively limited support from the general population – at least in contrast to the SSRC's other successes.

Nonetheless, it is clear that the actions of the SSRC in the months following the Uprising sought to direct the revolutionary fervour of Soweto's young population. It sought to transform disconnected violent events into a coordinated and developing programme of political opposition: it sought to include all parts of Soweto's society in its efforts, and sought to expand its repertoire of public protests from marches and demonstrations to strikes, stay-at-homes and public displays of mourning. Although incidents of violence remained endemic to Soweto in the period of the SSRC's significance, and although not all of its actions succeeded in achieving their stated goals, nonetheless it is clear that the SSRC was attempting to transform itself from an

[64] Kane-Berman, *Soweto*, pp. 118–19.
[65] Kane-Berman, *Soweto*, pp. 119–20.

organisation concerned with expressing protest to one which sought to organise campaigns.

This move towards sustained political campaigning can be seen in the statements circulated by the SSRC. At the end of October, its chairman, Khotso Seatlholo – who had assumed the role after Mash-inini had fled into exile at the end of August – issued a press release in which he argued:

> We have the full right to stand up erect and reject the whole system of apart-heid … We are neither carbon nor duplicate copies of our fathers. Where they failed, we shall succeed … They carried the struggle up to where they could. We are very grateful to them. But now, the struggle is ours … The ball of liberation is in our hands … We shall rise up and destroy a political ideology that is designed to keep us in a perpetual state of oppression and subserviency.[66]

After the Uprising

The SSRC's greatest success came a year after the June Uprising.

In April 1977, the West Rand Administration Board (WRAB) announced that rents in Soweto would rise from 1 May 1977. This rise would be significantly larger than usual, as a consequence of the loss of income suffered from the destruction of the municipal beer halls over the previous year. The Urban Bantu Council (UBC) – an ineffectual body, intended to represent the residents of Soweto – proved unwilling to oppose the measures; the SSRC saw this as an opportunity to both protest the rent increases and to condemn the apparent collaboration of the Council. On 23 April, the SSRC convened a public meeting at which it was decided that the rent increase should not be paid and that, in addition, the UBC should be suspended. Four days later, the SSRC led a march through Soweto to protest against the rent increases: this march turned violent when it reached the offices of the UBC. The offices were stoned. The police attempted to disperse the crowd using tear gas; the crowd once again reacted violently, stoning vehicles and torching beer halls.[67]

The police shot at the protesters with live ammunition.

But this violence proved insufficient to quell the protests. Before long, the WRAB had suspended the planned rent increase. By the beginning of June 1977, all members of the UBC had been forced to resign – leading the government to formally halt the body's activities. In the course of this campaign, the SSRC appeared to have succeeded

---

[66] 'Press release by Khotso Seatlholo, chairman of the SSSRC, 29 October 1976', published in Karis and Gerhart, *From Protest to Challenge, Vol. 5*, pp. 587–8.

[67] Hirson, *Year of Fire*, pp. 270–2.

in dismantling the instruments of apartheid governance in Soweto. The township was no longer simply governable from outside, or above.

The possibilities of organising further campaigns were increasingly constrained, though. The leadership of the SSRC was under constant pressure: its first leader, Mashinini, fled into exile in August 1976. Its second leader, Seatlholo, was shot by the police in January 1977, and followed Mashinini into exile. Its third leader, Daniel Montisi, was arrested after the success of the campaign against the rent increases and the UBC. A fourth leader, Trofomo Sono, assumed control of the SSRC in June 1977 and attempted to organise a commemoration of the previous year's Uprising; on 23 June he led a march of approximately 500 protesters into Johannesburg, where they were baton-charged outside the police headquarters in John Vorster Square. On the same day, the government approved the creation of a new administrative body to replace the UBCs (across the country), thus undermining the SSRC's recent success in overthrowing the Soweto Council. By August Sono, too, was forced to flee into exile; the SSRC announced that it would be led by a secret committee of six – but the absence of a public leader in effect signified its decline as a public organisation.

It is vital to recognise that the collapse of the SSRC's efforts to organise Soweto's youth into an ongoing campaign of political opposition did not bring about the collapse of the insurrection.

In part this was undoubtedly due to the ultimate inability of the SSRC to ever fully incorporate or otherwise divert the violence of the period into its own campaigns. Acts of violence continued throughout the year-long period of its operations, and although these acts never coalesced into a second uprising they nonetheless demonstrated the continuing willingness of the youth in Soweto and across the country to protest against the apartheid order using whatever means might be at hand – including notably violent means. Over the coming years, the tension between this radicalism and the organising impulses of the ANC underground and the trade union movement would shape the next stage in the development of public protest in South Africa. In the period between 16 June 1976 and the late 1970s, the ANC sought to increase its presence in the country and its influence upon the radical youth; the liberation of Mozambique enabled the underground to resuscitate itself, while the arrests of many of the young protesters brought them into contact with the older generation of imprisoned leaders. The ANC sought to contain the violence of the youth, concerned that it would rupture the political order prematurely; its leaders did not believe it was yet ready to return to the country to present a plausible alternative to the government.

But the terrain of politics had changed. The redevelopment of public forms of protest after the collapse of the underground armed struggle in the 1960s had altered the relationship between organised opposition movements and the mass public. Student protests and workers struggles had developed in the absence of national organisations, and new movements had developed and mutated. A broad public had experienced the empowerment of participating in public demonstrations of dissent, and had also experienced at first hand the violence of the state. They had learned, too – in universities and in the streets and in Soweto – that the state did not have a monopoly on the use of violence; and that resistance – even though overmatched – was possible.

The Soweto Uprising is not therefore best understood as marking the end of a period of quiescence, but rather is better understood as representing a culminating moment in a chain of protests that had occurred throughout this period. Without the student protests of the 1960s and 1970s, the youth would not have found the model of public politics and dissent that they used. Without the attempts of students and workers to build networks of solidarity, the connections that were forged between the youth and the elders in Soweto, and elsewhere, would have been harder to find. And without the precedents of the pro-Frelimo rallies, the Durban Strikes and student protests, the meaning of the insurrection might have vanished: it might have simply been one more localised rebellion, a disconnected act of dissent. Instead, it was the spark that lit the flame of resistance: a flame that would raze the political order.

Conclusion
CONSEQUENCES

Where previous protests had opened up imaginative spaces in which to oppose the apartheid state, the Uprising in Soweto carved out a material space that was beyond the state's ability to control.

In the months following the events of 16 June 1976, Soweto ceased to be governed as an ordinary part of the apartheid system: the state was forced to reveal the violence lurking beneath its everyday operations. The township was isolated from the rest of the country, policed from the outside by the armed forces of the state. Inside, the SSRC and other groups sought to coordinate the masses of protesting students and other community members; in significant ways, these organisations replaced the state – organising the collection of garbage, coordinating public events, and acting as the legitimate alternative to the bankrupt Urban Bantu Council.

The attempts in Soweto to sustain insurgent actions over time suggested how a single protest could develop into more. This had significant consequences for the protests that were to come in the following years. In the years after the march it was impossible for the state, commentators within South Africa, and international observers to repeat the idea that the apartheid order was simply an alternate means of ordering a society – a local variation on the ordinary distribution of power.

The Uprising in Soweto exposed the apartheid order as a structure imposed on the world, designed to divide, and designed to render those divisions permanent. It operated through violence, brutality, and exclusion. By revealing the roots of this order, and its contingency, the Uprising exposed fissures in the existing political system, fissures between those who claimed to govern and those who were supposed to be governed. It showed that the black population of South Africa – treated for so long as subjects rather than as citizens – could no longer be forced to accept their disempowerment and dispossession. And it revealed the fact of that disempowerment and that dispossession to those who had previously chosen not to see it.

After the Uprising, South Africa was a changed place – the dissent of the majority from the apartheid social order was rendered visible, both to the members of that majority themselves as well as to the governing minority. Public protest became the principal means of conducting politics. Over the next decade and half, swathes of the country would become 'ungovernable', the government would declare local and national States of Emergency, and the army would be deployed to suppress or contain the immediate disruptions caused by popular insurgency. Nothing, though, could contain the imaginative disruption that these protests had caused: the established order no longer seemed unassailable, and its end could now be predicted to come within the lifetimes of those protesting against it. The state was vulnerable, and opposition imaginable.

Of course, the struggle against the apartheid order did not end in 1976.

At the end of the year of the Uprising, judgment was handed down in the trial of nine SASO and BPC activists, emerging from charges brought after the pro-Frelimo rallies of 1974. In the main judgment, Justice Boshoff held that the state had been unable to prove that the defendants had been involved in a conspiracy to overthrow the government by violence. Nonetheless, he decided, they represented a protest organisation involved in verbal and intellectual agitation. They were undoubtedly guilty of 'encouraging and furthering feelings of hostility between the Black and White inhabitants of the country'.[1] As such, they were liable to serve lengthy sentences: six of the defendants received sentences of six years of imprisonment each, and the others three to five years each. These activists were to be removed from the possibility of public life.

Meanwhile, other activists were placed in the condition described by Henry Isaacs as 'internal exile'. They were either restricted to small towns or to their homes, often prevented from seeing more than one person at time, and completely excluded from the public sphere. Activists found themselves living half-lives, hiding from the police while haunting their colleagues and friends.

For many of these activists, 'internal exile' was only a step on the path to true exile. Isaacs himself had already left the country by the time of the Uprising. At the end of 1974, he snuck across the border between South Africa and Swaziland, walking down a dry riverbed at night, clambering through a barbed wire fence, and then hitching a lift to the city where he hoped to meet an underground contact. Once there, he applied for asylum and – after some weeks – was allowed to travel to New Zealand to take up a scholarship. For the fifteen years after January 1975, Isaacs lived a peripatetic life in exile – travelling from country to country, under the auspices of the PAC.

Isaacs was not alone in exile. One of his early experiences after leaving South Africa came on a stopover in Melbourne, on his way

---

[1] WHP AD1719/B, Judgment in State v. Cooper et al (15 December 1976), p. 256.

to New Zealand. There he met a fellow traveller and fellow exile, Neville Curtis – the recently-banned former president of NUSAS. Isaacs recalled that he was 'overjoyed' to see Curtis, and to gain his insights both into South African politics of the time and the experience of exile.[2] Student leaders from both SASO and NUSAS found themselves expelled from the country, travelling into estrangement.

Meanwhile, inside the country, the state stepped up its assault against student activists and oppositional organisations. In September 1977, Steve Biko was arrested by the apartheid police, detained, beaten and tortured. Severely injured, he was placed in a police vehicle and driven the long road from the Eastern Cape to Pretoria. The drive almost certainly exacerbated his injuries and, once detained in Pretoria, he died of the wounds he had sustained under interrogation. Biko's death was an immediate scandal. For the Minister of Justice, though, it was business as usual. Kruger dismissed Biko's death as an irrelevance, saying 'I am not glad and I am not sorry about Mr Biko. His death leaves me cold.'

On 19 October 1977, the Minister announced that banning orders had been levied against the South African Students' Organisation, the Black Peoples' Convention, the Black Community Programme, the Southern African Students' Movement, the Soweto Students' Representative Council, and several other organisations associated with the broad Black Consciousness movement. At the same time, *The World* – the most visible black-focused newspaper in the country – was closed down by the order of the Minister of Justice, in part for its role in reporting Biko's death.

The Minister's intention was obvious. He sought to undermine the widening insurgency and re-impose state control over South Africa's black population. He may have been thinking of the state's earlier assault against the aboveground liberation movements after the Sharpeville Massacre in 1960. This assault – arresting and detaining leaders, banning organisations – had proved strikingly successful in driving dissent underground. The public activities of these movements were brought to an end, and public forms of politics had to be reinvented by students and workers over the course of the next dozen years. If such a result could be achieved by assaulting black student activists and banning their organisations, then the state would be safe.

But neither the murder of activists nor the banning of organisations could stem the tide.

The politics that had been forged through protest and dissent between Sharpeville and Soweto were not inextricably linked to personalities or to organisations. Students in NUSAS and SASO had both learned to regard the organisations that they belonged to – student unions and

---

[2] Henry E. Isaacs, 'Full Circle: Reflections on Home and Exile', MA thesis (Johannesburg, University of the Witwatersrand: 2002), pp. 100–13.

Wages Commissions, Community Programmes and trade unions – as expressions of political possibility rather than as the producers of these possibilities. In other words: Black Consciousness, to take one example, existed regardless of the existence of SASO. SASO was merely one tool through which Black Consciousness could be expressed. Likewise, once exploitation had been recognised, workers' consciousness existed regardless of the Wages Commissions, or even of trade unions.

This meant that dissent was not easily suppressed. It meant, too, that it could take many different organisational forms. Activists associated with Black Consciousness would find themselves in the underground movements of the ANC and PAC, in the aboveground Civics that were set up in townships as popular alternatives to the Urban Bantu Councils, in church groups and in new student moments, in trade unions and in professional bodies. A superfluity of organisational forms flourished in the wake of Soweto, and were used as means of expressing political identities that nonetheless could not be contained within them. Trade Unions, for example, were always about more than simply workplace activism – throughout the 1980s, they were a site of oppositional black politics.

The force of this organisational malleability was felt in the 1980s, with the formation of the United Democratic Front (UDF). This brought together representatives of dozens of different kinds of organisations, and provided a loose umbrella beneath which they could co-exist. In their co-existence, these organisations avoided amalgamation while, at the same time, building a broad front of opposition to the apartheid state. A decade after the Uprising, the country was gripped by a wave of public protest – of a mass insurgency in which the example held out by the ungovernability of Soweto in the months after June 1976 was extended across the country.

For obvious reasons, the Uprising itself has come to stand as the moment in which this wave of public protest began: if nothing else, the death toll over the first week of the protest viscerally demonstrated the cruelty of the state. For the first time since the Sharpeville Massacre, photographers had captured the fact of death and disseminated it across the world's media. Images became icons, and the experience of Soweto came to stand for all forms of resistance.

But Soweto did not stand alone.

Not in the moment. Even in the week of the Uprising, it was not alone. Similar protests were erupting across the country, and sites of insurgency multiplied. Even within the sprawl of Johannesburg, other townships participated in the Uprising and fought their own battles.

And Soweto did not stand alone in the past. The Uprising did not explode out of a period of quiescence, resurrecting a buried tradition of struggle. It arose out of the incremental, imperfect and ambiguous struggles of the previous dozen years – the struggles of white and black students, of workers, and of communities. These struggles shaped the terrain on which the school-going students of Soweto acted, providing examples of successful public protest, models of local organisation, and a set of ideas that could provide an ideological framework for action. Without these artefacts of the earlier struggles, the Uprising may not have happened at all – or, at least, would have been very different.

This book has sought to highlight the ways in which the Soweto Uprising was a product of its time, emerging out of a specific historical conjuncture created by the development of new and reinvented modes of politics and protest in the absence of the old organised liberation movements. These modes were the organic product of the experiences of students and workers, as well as other members of excluded communities. They developed in response to shifting circumstances, and to the ways in which each event reshaped the field of political possibility. Most protests were either spontaneous or organised locally, but each can be seen as a response to the same pressures – and each can be placed in an ongoing dialogue with other protests at the time.

This dialogue could be said to have begun at many different points.

After Sharpeville, and after the suppression of the aboveground liberation movements, students in NUSAS found themselves debating amongst themselves what the possibilities of politics were: facing a choice 'between silence and protest', which would they choose? In a stuttering process, the students who remained in NUSAS chose to protest. They risked, though, assuming that they were the only ones capable of speaking. The emergence of SASO disrupted this assumption, though, and forced students to begin speaking to each other, as well as to the state and white society. The dialogue between students was often interrupted, and often contentious. But over a relatively short length of time, both NUSAS and SASO were developing modes of action that reflected each organisation's own priorities – and the substance of the dialogue between them.

Although it is possible to describe these two student movements as existing in parallel to each other, the truth is that their politics of protest and the modes of organisation developed in relationship to each other. This was rarely a relationship of explicit collaboration or cooperation, although it sometimes amounted to that. More often, it was a relationship built on public rejection and private recalculation, on the adoption and mutation of models of protest and organisation. Nonetheless, these tensions produced a constant development of new forms of action, and spurred students to continually remake and expand the spaces of political possibility at the time.

These spaces were suddenly expanded again when workers in Durban embarked upon a series of wildcat strikes, sparking a wave of protest that would reinvigorate labour activism and return it to the national stage. These strikes were rapidly placed in dialogue with the protests of students: the workers were first interpreted through the lens of student activism, and then differentiated from the protests of students in the state's response. As it happened, students were already attempting to enter into constructive dialogues with workers at the time of the strikes – although, despite the government's flirtation with conspiracy theories at the time, these efforts did not directly lead to the wave of activism in Durban in 1973.

Nonetheless, these conversations flourished in the immediate wake of the Durban Strikes. The establishment of the Wages Commissions, as well as the establishment of the Black Workers' Project, both provided spaces within which workers and students could speak to each other, share knowledge and experiences, and build forms of solidarity. These spaces provided activist students with a brief respite from the assaults of the state against student organisations, and allowed for new forms of politics to emerge in the course of the engagements between students and workers.

These new forms of politics were also being developed through other forms of dialogue and engagement. As students left universities – predominantly, black students – they either returned to their home communities, or moved into new ones. In these new environments, activists had to build networks of support – joining family members and colleagues, workers and friends, clergymen and teachers into a web of social and political relationships. These were the networks that activists drew upon in 1973 and 1974, when large rallies were organised to protest the exclusion of students from the University of the Western Cape and to celebrate the victory of Frelimo's armed struggle in Mozambique. These rallies opened up the spaces of activism to a wider range of participants, and once again reshaped the nature of oppositional struggles.

All of these events opened up the space within which the Soweto Uprising was made possible. Student protests re-opened a space for public politics after Sharpeville. The debates between students led to the development of new political ideas, based on the recognition of experience. The protests of workers carved out the possibilities of different forms of organisation, and the networks that followed demonstrated the power of solidarity and sympathy. In Soweto, these networks were able to support the protests of students as they became an ongoing insurgency.

These precedents opened up the possibility of new protests, new politics and new hopes.

There is no privileged site of politics: not the state and its political society, not student groups or trade unions, not community organisations, and not social movements. Politics, as Rancière reminds us can emerge in any of these sites – or can simply remain latent, and unexplored:

the same thing – an election, a strike, a demonstration – can give rise to politics or not give rise to politics. A strike is not political when it calls for reforms rather than a better deal or when it attacks the relationships of authority ... It is political when it reconfigures the relationships that determine the workplace in relation to the community.[3]

Politics occurs whenever a social group refuses to act in a manner expected – when its members claim identities that go beyond the roles assigned to them in the social order. By doing so, they reconfigure the relationships that structure relations between groups in that social order. Politics can occur anywhere that those relationships are rendered visible, and challenged.

Rancière's definition of politics best captures what took place during the years between the massacre at Sharpeville and the eruption of a widespread insurgency in Soweto. In these years, a system that claimed to be founded on natural divisions was repeatedly shown to be contingent on historical events and based on power, privilege and ideology. In these years, a system that sought to present itself as unassailable was repeatedly challenged, and the limits of its ability to enforce obedience on South Africans were repeatedly revealed. These challenges took place on the terrain of public protest: student marches and sit-ins, workers' strikes and large mass rallies.

The effect of this was to remake the relationships between the state and those that it sought to govern: both white and black students ceased to accept their assigned roles within the hegemonic racial order, insisting on acting out of character. They acted not as representatives of their races (as assigned through law and ideology by the apartheid order) but rather as students – and even this was not where their protests ended. As they acted, they came to act not only as students but as active members of society, as men and women who had a stake in the order. When white students acted this way, they posed an initial challenge to the distribution of roles. When black students acted in this way, they shattered the presumptions of the apartheid order.

The protests of the years between Sharpeville and Soweto thus reconfigured the relationships within the apartheid system: the state could not assume that young white men and women were its natural constituency, and nor could it assume that young black men and women were capable of being pacified – whether by co-option or by force. Likewise, the relationships between the protesting groups were also altered: as black students reimagined society and their roles in it, they forced white students to recognise that their relative privilege was not dissolved by their opposition to the system that granted it to them. The struggles of workers – and the relationships that they

---

[3] Jacques Rancière, *Disagreement: Politics and Philosophy*, trans. Julie Rose (Minneapolis, University of Minnesota Press: 1999), p. 32.

developed with students – also changed the ways in which African labourers, in particular, were able to relate to society, as actors within South African politics.

This book has argued that these interconnected reconfigurations created the space within which the Soweto Uprising could take place and, following on from that, the next wave of protests. Without these precedents, the Uprising was only understandable as an explosion of a previously suppressed tension, or perhaps as the product of underground and exile organisation. But once the consequences of the earlier protests are recognised, Soweto is explicable as the product of shared struggles against the apartheid order of the time – and as part of that ongoing struggle.

Instead of representing a break from a period of quiescence, the Uprising can been seen as a catalyst, a moment in which the dissolution of the apartheid order became inevitable. If we see the past in this light, it changes how we can interpret the present.

As I am writing the final pages of this conclusion, in the dog days of 2015, the university where I teach is the site of massive student protests. Young activists are finding themselves in their identity as students, and then developing a critique of their positions in society on the basis both of race and of economic exclusion. In other words: they are students acting not only as students, but also as the excluded. This seems to me to resonate with the protests of the late 1960s, and with the efforts of the students at the time to place their experiences at the heart of a critique of the social order.

One of the most striking aspects of these recent protests has been the solidarity shared by workers and students: over the past several months, students have been agitating on behalf of outsourced workers on campus, and now the workers have been joining the students' protests. Although these connections may or may not amount to anything in particular, it is important to recognise that these protests are seeing a reappraisal of the relationships between students, cleaning staff and the university administration. These relationships are being disturbed and disrupted, and new sources of political struggle – new identities, new dreams – are being forged in the heat of protest.

This is happening in the context of a widespread insurgency in South Africa's urban communities, led by groups of citizens characterising themselves as 'the poor' – asserting a positive identity in the face of economic exclusion, in a way comparable to the efforts of black communities to assert their own identities in the period before the Soweto Uprising. For many commentators, the protests of the poor are simply ways of demanding better service from the state. They are ephemeral and disposable, single-issue struggles – 'popcorn protests' in the words of prominent commentators. Likewise, for many of the same commentators the protests of students are no more than the effusions of youth, a fashionable and brief outburst of discontent.

There are striking similarities between these contemporary dismissals of protest and those that characterised the principal responses to similar protests in the 1960s and early 1970s. These responses do not recognise the actions of students and workers, or of local protesters, as politics: they are pre-political, or naive. The ways in which localised struggles and challenges disrupt the imaginative hegemony of the social order, and expose the contingency of that order – whether the order be that of the apartheid state, or of post-apartheid liberal democracy – are, however, central to the vision of politics set out in this book.

The disruptions of the past made the Uprising in Soweto possible. The disruptions of the present are making a different politics possible today.

The road to Soweto wound its way through student protests, ideological challenges, workers' strikes, mass rallies, and the development of a new form of politics. The road from Soweto continues to wind its way into the future – a future that is enabled by the possibilities opened up in the past. It winds through popular protests and student activism, new identities and ideologies.

The road that leads through Soweto has not reached its end.

Bibliography

1 Archival sources

Aluka Online Repository
  Karis-Gerhart Collection
  NUSAS Collection
Alan Paton Centre, University of KwaZulu-Natal
  PC126 Natal Room, Gerhard Maré collection
Truth and Reconciliation Commission of South Africa
  Human Rights Violation Hearings
University of Cape Town Manuscripts and Archives (UCTMA)
  BC 586 NUSAS
  BC 1072 Sir Richard Luyt
University of the Witwatersrand Historical Papers (WHP)
  A2675 Karis-Gerhart Collection
  AD1719 State v Cooper and Others
  AH1999 FOSATU
  AK3166 Raymond Tucker, Attorney.

2 Government publications

Republic of South Africa, *Debates of the House of Assembly* (Hansard)
Republic of South Africa. 1980. *Report of the Commission of Inquiry into the Riots at Soweto and Elsewhere from the 16th of June 1976 to the 28th February 1977* (Cillié Commission), 2 volumes. Pretoria, Government Publisher.
Truth and Reconciliation Commission of South Africa. 1999. *Truth and Reconciliation Commission Report*. 5 volumes. Cape Town, Truth and Reconciliation Commission.

3 Newspapers and periodicals

Daily News
The Cape Times

Harvard Crimson
Natal Mercury
NUSAS Newsletter
Rand Daily Mail
Sechaba
The Star
Sunday Express
Sunday Times
Die Transvaler
The World

4 Articles, books, research reports, theses, etc.

Badat, Saleem. 1999. *Black Student Politics, Higher Education & Apartheid: From SASO to SANSCO, 1968–1990.* Pretoria, HSRC.

Badat, Saleem. 2009. *Black Man You Are On Your Own.* Johannesburg, Steve Biko Foundation.

Badiou, Alain. 2005 *Metapolitics*, trans. J. Barker. London, Verso.

Baskin, Jeremy. 1991. *Striking Back: A History of COSATU.* London, Routledge.

Beard, T.V.R. 1972. 'Background to Student Activities at the University College of Fort Hare: Conflict, Consensus and Political Mobilisation on a University Campus', in H.W. van der Merwe and D. Welsh (eds), *Student Perspectives on South Africa.* Cape Town, David Philip.

Biko, Steve. 1978. *I Write What I Like: Selected Writings*, ed. Aelred Stubbs. London, Bowerdean.

Biko, Steve. 1979. *The Testimony of Steve Biko*, ed. M. Arnold. London: Maurice Temple Smith.

Birchall, Ian. 2002. 'France 1968', in Colin Barker (ed.), *Revolutionary Rehearsals.* Chicago, Haymarket.

Bonner, Philip and Lauren Segal. 1998. *Soweto: A History.* Cape Town, Maskew Miller Longman.

Bonner, Philip and Noor Nieftagodien. 2008. *Alexandra: A History.* Johannesburg, Wits University Press.

Bourg, Julian. 2007. *From Revolution to Ethics: May 1968 and Contemporary French Thought.* Montreal and Kingston, McGill-Queens University Press.

Brink, Elsabé, Gandhi Malungane, Steve Lebelo, Dumisane Ntshangase and Sue Krige. 2001. *Soweto, 16 June 1976: It All Started with a Dog …* Johannesburg, Kwela.

Brooks, Alan and Jeremy Brickhill. 1980. *Whirlwind Before the Storm: The Origins and Development of the Uprising in Soweto and the Rest of South Africa from June to December 1976.* London, IDAF.

Brown, Julian. 2009. 'Public Protest and Violence in South Africa, 1948–1976'. DPhil Thesis, University of Oxford.

Brown, Julian. 2010. 'SASO's Reluctant Embrace of Public Forms of Protest, 1968–1972', *South African Historical Journal*, 62.4.

Brown, Julian. 2010. 'The Durban Strikes of 1973: Political Identities and the Management of Protest', in William Beinart and Marcelle C. Dawson (eds), *Popular Politics and Resistance Movements in South Africa*. Johannesburg, Wits University Press.

Brown, Julian. 2012. 'An Experiment in Confrontation: The Pro-Frelimo Rallies of 1974', *Journal of Southern African Studies*, 38:1.

Brown, Julian. 2015. *South Africa's Insurgent Citizens: On Dissent and the Possibilities of Politics*. London, Zed.

Buthelezi, S. 1991. 'The Emergence of Black Consciousness: An Historical Appraisal', in Pityana et al. *Bounds of Possibility*.

Cajee, Imtiaz. 2005. *Timol: Quest for Justice*. Johannesburg, STE.

Curtis, Neville and Clive Keegan. 1972. 'The Aspiration to a Just Society', in H.W. van der Merwe and D. Welsh (eds), *Student Perspectives on South Africa*. Cape Town, David Philip.

Davie, Grace. 2015. *Poverty Knowledge in South Africa: A Social History of Human Science, 1855–2005*. Cambridge, Cambridge University Press.

Diseko, Nozipho. 1992. 'The Origins and Development of the South African Students' Movement (SASM): 1968–1976', *Journal of Southern African Studies*, 18:1.

Dubow, Saul. 2014. *Apartheid, 1948–1994*. Oxford, Oxford University Press.

du Toit, D. 1981. *Capital and Labour in South Africa: Class Struggles in the 1970s*. London, Kegan Paul International.

du Toit, A. 1990. 'The National Committee for Liberation (ARM) 1960–1964: Sabotage and the Question of the Ideological Subject'. MA Thesis, University of Cape Town.

Erbmann, Robert. 2005. '"Conservative Revolutionaries": Anti-Apartheid Activism at the University of Cape Town, 1963–1973', BA Thesis. Oxford, University of Oxford.

Fanon, Frantz. 1965. *A Dying Colonialism*, trans. Haakon Chevalier. New York, Monthly Review Press.

Fanon, Frantz. 2004 [1963]. *The Wretched of the Earth*, trans. Richard Philcox. New York, Grove Press.

Fatton, Robert. 1986. *Black Consciousness in South Africa: The Dialectics of Ideological Resistance in White Supremacy*. Albany, SUNY Press.

Feit, Edward. 1971. *Urban Revolt in South Africa, 1960–1964*. Chicago, Northwestern University Press.

Foucault, Michel. 1977. *Discipline and Punish: The Birth of the Prison*, trans. Alan Sheridan. London, Allen Lane.

Frankel, Philip. 1980. 'The Dynamics of a Political Renaissance: The Soweto Students' Representative Council', *Journal of African Studies*, 7.3.

Frankel, Philip H. 2001. *An Ordinary Atrocity: Sharpeville and its Massacre*. Johannesburg, Wits University Press.

Fridjon, Michael. 1976. 'The Torch Commando & the Politics of White Opposition: South Africa 1951–1953', Paper Presented at the University of the Witwatersrand African Studies Institute.

Friedman, Steven. 1987. *Building Tomorrow Today: African Workers in Trade Unions, 1970–1984*. Johannesburg, Ravan.

Gerhart, Gail M. 1978. *Black Power in South Africa: The Evolution of an Ideology*. Berkeley and Los Angeles, University of California Press.

Gibson, Nigel. 2011. *Fanonian Practices in South Africa: From Steve Biko to Abahlali baseMjondolo*. Pietermaritzburg, University of KwaZulu-Natal Press.

Glaser, Clive. 2000. *Bo-Tsotsi: The Youth Gangs of Soweto 1935–1976*. Oxford, James Currey.

Glaser, Clive. 2015. 'Soweto's Islands of Learning: Morris Isaacson and Orlando High Schools under Bantu Education, 1958–1975', *Journal of Southern African Studies*, 41:1.

Gunther, M. 2004. 'The National Committee of Liberation (NCL)/ African Resistance Movement (ARM)', in South African Democracy Education Trust (ed.), *The Road to Democracy in South Africa, Volume 1, 1960–1970*. Johannesburg, Zebra.

Gwala, Mafika Pascal (ed.). 1974. *Black Review 1973*. Durban, Black Community Programmes.

Hallward, Peter. 2009. 'Staging Equality: Rancière's Theatrocracy and the Limits of Anarchic Equality', in Gabriel Rockhill and Philip Watts (eds), *Jacques Rancière: History, Politics, Aesthetics*. Durham, Duke University Press.

Hardt, Michael and Antonio Negri. 2000. *Empire*. Cambridge, MA, Harvard University Press.

Hardt, Michael and Antonio Negri. 2005. *Multitude: War and Democracy in the Age of Empire*. Harmondsworth, Penguin.

Heffernan, Anne. 2014. 'A History of Youth Politics in Limpopo, 1967–2003', DPhil Thesis, University of Oxford.

Heffernan, Anne. 2015. 'Black Consciousness's Lost Leader: Abraham Tiro, the University of the North, and the Seeds of South Africa's Student Movement in the 1970s', *Journal of Southern African Studies*, 41:1.

Hendricks, F. 2008. 'The Mafeje Affair: The University of Cape Town and Apartheid', *African Studies*, 67.3.

Hirson, Baruch. 1979. *Year of Fire, Year of Ash: The Soweto Revolt – Roots of a Revolution?* London, Zed.

Hlongwane, A.K. (ed.). 2008. *Footprints of the 'Class of 76': Commem-*

oration, Memory, Mapping and Heritage. Johannesburg, Hector Pieterson Museum.

Hopkins, Pat and Helen Grange. 2001. *The Rocky Rioter Teargas Show: The Inside Story of the 1976 Uprising*. Cape Town, Zebra.

Horrell, Muriel. 1961. *A Survey of Race Relations, 1959–1960*. Johannesburg, South African Institute of Race Relations (SAIRR).

Horrell, Muriel. 1963. *A Survey of Race Relations in South Africa, 1962*. Johannesburg, SAIRR.

Horrell, Muriel. 1964. *A Survey of Race Relations in South Africa, 1963*. Johannesburg, SAIRR.

Horrell, Muriel. 1965. *A Survey of Race Relations in South Africa, 1964*. Johannesburg, SAIRR.

Horrell, Muriel. 1967. *A Survey of Race Relations in South Africa, 1966*. Johannesburg, SAIRR.

Horrell, Muriel. 1969. *A Survey of Race Relations in South Africa, 1968*. Johannesburg, SAIRR.

Horrell, Muriel. 1969. *South Africa's Workers: Their Organizations and the Patterns of Employment*. Johannesburg, SAIRR.

Horrell, Muriel. 1971. *A Survey of Race Relations in South Africa, 1970*. Johannesburg, SAIRR.

Horrell, Muriel and Dudley Horner. 1974. *A Survey of Race Relations in South Africa 1973*. Johannesburg, SAIRR.

Horrell, Muriel and Tony Hodgson. 1976. *A Survey of Race Relations in South Africa 1975*. Johannesburg, SAIRR.

Horrell, Muriel, Dudley Horner and John Kane-Berman. 1973. *A Survey of Race Relations in South Africa, 1972*. Johannesburg, SAIRR.

Horrell, Muriel, Dudley Horner and Jane Hudson. 1975. *A Survey of Race Relations in South Africa 1974*. Johannesburg, SAIRR.

Hyslop, Jonathan. 1999. *The Classroom Struggle: Policy and Resistance in South Africa, 1940–1990*. Pietermaritzburg, University of Natal Press.

Institute for Industrial Education. 1974. *The Durban Strikes 1973: 'Human Beings with Souls'*. Johannesburg, Ravan.

Isaacs, Henry E. 2002. 'Full Circle: Reflections on Home and Exile'. MA thesis, University of the Witwatersrand.

Kane-Berman, John. 1978. *Soweto: Black Revolt, White Reaction*. Johannesburg, Ravan.

Karis, Thomas G. and Gail M. Gerhart (eds). 1997. *From Protest to Challenge: A Documentary History of African Politics in South Africa, 1882–1990: Volume 5: Nadir and Resurgence, 1964–1979*. Bloomington and Indianapolis, University of Indiana Press.

Keniston, Billy. 2014. *Choosing to be Free: The Life Story of Rick Turner*. Johannesburg, Jacana.

Keucheyan, Razmig. 2013. *The Left Hemisphere: Mapping Critical Theory Today*, trans. Gregory Elliot. London, Verso.

Khoapa, B.A. (ed.). 1973. *Black Review 1972*. Durban, Black Community Programmes.

Kooy, Alide, Dudley Horner, Philipa Green and Shirley Miller. 1979. 'The Wiehahn Commission: A Summary', SALDRU Working Paper 24. Cape Town, University of Cape Town.

Kynoch, Gary. 2005. *We are Fighting the World: A History of the Marashea Gangs in South Africa, 1947–1999*. Athens, Ohio University Press.

Laclau, Ernesto and Chantal Mouffe. 2001. *Hegemony and Socialist Strategy: Towards a Radical Democratic Politics*. 2nd edition. London, Verso.

Lefebvre, Henri. 1969. *The Explosion: Marxism and the French Revolutions*, trans. Alfred Ehrenfeld. New York, Monthly Review Press.

Legassick, Martin. 1967. *The National Union of South African Students: Ethnic Cleavage and Ethnic Integration in the Universities*. Occasional Paper no. 4, African Studies Center. Los Angeles, University of California.

Legassick, Martin and Christopher Saunders. 2004. 'Above-Ground Activity in the 1960s', in South African Democracy Education Trust (SADET) (ed.), *The Road to Democracy in South Africa, Volume 1, 1960–1970*. Johannesburg, Zebra.

Lipton, Merle. 1986. *Capitalism and Apartheid: South Africa, 1910–1986*. Cape Town, David Philip.

Lobban, Michael. 1996. *White Man's Justice: South African Political Trials in the Black Consciousness Era*. Oxford, Oxford University Press.

Lodge, Tom. 1983. *Black Politics in South Africa since 1945*. London, Longman.

Lodge, Tom. 2011. *Sharpeville: An Apartheid Massacre and its Consequences*. Oxford, Oxford University Press.

Lunn, Helen. 2009. '"Hippies, Radicals and the Sounds of Silence": Cultural Dialectics at Two South African Universities, 1966–1976'. PhD Thesis, University of KwaZulu-Natal.

Maaba, B.B. 2004. 'The PAC's War Against the State, 1960–1963', in South African Democracy Education Trust (SADET) (ed.), *The Road to Democracy in South Africa, Volume 1, 1960–1970*. Johannesburg, Zebra.

Macqueen, Ian. 2011. 'Re-Imagining South Africa: Black Consciousness, Radical Christianity and the New Left, 1967–1977'. PhD Thesis, University of Sussex.

Magaziner, Daniel. 2010. *The Law and the Prophets: Black Consciousness in South Africa, 1968–1977*. Athens, Ohio University Press.

Mandela, Nelson. 1994. *Long Walk to Freedom*. London, Macdonald Purnell.

Manganyi, N. Chabani. 1973. *Being-Black-In-The-World*. Johannesburg, Spro-Cas and Ravan.

Mangcu, Xolela. 2012. *Biko: A Biography*. Cape Town, Tafelberg.

Marée, Johann. 1976. 'Seeing Strikes in Perspective', *South African Labour Bulletin*, 2: 9 & 10.

Mathabata, S. 2004. 'The PAC and Poqo in Pretoria, 1958-1964', in South African Democracy Education Trust (SADET) (ed.), *The Road to Democracy in South Africa, Volume 1, 1960–1970*. Johannesburg, Zebra.

Mbanjwa, Thoko (ed.). 1975. *Black Review 1974/75*. Durban, Black Community Programmes.

Michelman, Cherry 1975. *The Black Sash of South Africa: A Case Study in Liberalism*. Oxford, Oxford University Press.

Moss, Glenn. 2014. *The New Radicals: A Generational Memoir of the 1970s*. Johannesburg, Jacana.

Muller, C.H. (ed.) 1980. *University of the North Jubilee Publication 1980*. Pietersburg, University of the North.

Naidoo, Beverley. 2012. *Death of an Idealist: In Search of Neil Aggett*. Johannesburg, Jonathan Ball.

Ndlovu, Sifiso M. 1998. *The Soweto Uprisings: Counter-Memories of June 1976*. Johannesburg: Ravan.

Ndlovu, Sifiso M, Noor Nieftagodien and Tshepo Moloi. 2004. 'The Soweto Uprising', in South African Democracy Education Trust (SADET, ed.), *The Road to Democracy in South Africa, Volume 2: 1970–1980*. Johannesburg, Zebra.

Nieftagodien, Noor. 2014. *The Soweto Uprising*. Johannesburg, Jacana.

Nieftagodien, Noor and Sally Gaule. 2012. *Orlando West, Soweto: An Illustrated History*. Johannesburg, Wits University Press.

Nkondo, G.M. (ed.). 1976. *Turfloop Testimony: The Dilemma of a Black University in South Africa*. Johannesburg: Ravan.

Nolutshungu, Sam C. 1982. *Changing South Africa: Political Considerations*. Cape Town, David Philip.

Ntsebeza, Lungisile. 2014. 'The Mafeje and the UCT Saga: Unfinished Business?', *Social Dynamics* 40:2.

Pityana, Barney, Mamphela Ramphele, Malusi Mpumlwana and Lindy Wilson (eds). 1991. *Bounds of Possibility: The Legacy of Steve Biko and Black Consciousness*. Cape Town, David Philip.

Quattrochi, Angelo and Tom Nairn. 1998. *The Beginning of the End: France, May 1968*. London, Verso.

Ramphele, Mamphela. 1995. *Mamphela Ramphele: A Life*. Cape Town, David Philip.

Rancière, Jacques. 1991. *The Ignorant Schoolmaster: Five Lessons in Intellectual Emancipation,* trans. Kristin Ross. Stanford, Stanford University Press.

Rancière, Jacques. 1999. *Disagreement: Politics and Philosophy,* trans. Julie Rose. Minneapolis, University of Minnesota Press.

Rancière, Jacques. 2012. *Proletarian Nights: The Workers' Dream in Nineteenth Century France*, trans. John Drury. London, Verso.

Reddy, E.S. (ed.). 1992. *The Struggle for Liberation in South Africa and International Solidarity: A Selection of Papers Published by the United Nations Centre against Apartheid*. Sterling Publishers, New Delhi.

Reeve, Ambrose. 1960. *Shooting at Sharpeville: The Agony of South Africa*. London, Gollancz.

Rodgers, Mirabel. 1956. *The Black Sash: The Story of the South African Women's Defence of the Constitution League*. Johannesburg, Rotonews.

Roos, Neil. 2005. *Ordinary Springboks: White Servicemen and Social Justice in South Africa, 1939–1961*. Aldershot, Ashgate.

Ross, Kristin. 2002. *May '68 and Its Afterlives*. Chicago, University of Chicago Press.

Ross, Kristin. 2015. *Communal Luxury: The Political Imaginary of the Paris Commune*. London, Verso.

Ross, Kristin and Henri Lefebvre. 1997. 'Lefebvre on the Situationists: An Interview', *October*, 79 (Winter).

Saul, John S. and Stephen Gelb. 1981. 'The Crisis in South Africa: Class Defense, Class Revolution', *Monthly Review*, 33.3

Schuster, L. 2004. *A Burning Hunger: One Family's Struggle Against Apartheid*. London, Jonathan Cape.

Seekings, Jeremy. 2000. *The UDF: A History of the United Democratic Front in South Africa, 1983–1991*. Cape Town, David Philip/Oxford, James Currey.

Singer, Daniel. 2013. *Prelude to Revolution: France in May 1968*. 2nd edition, Chicago, Haymarket.

Sisulu, Elinor. 2002. *Walter and Albertina Sisulu: In Our Lifetime*. Cape Town, David Philip.

Sitas, Ari. 2004. 'Thirty Years since the Durban Strikes: Black Working-Class Leadership and the South African Transition', *Current Sociology* 52.5.

Sono, Themba. 1993. *Reflections on the Origins of Black Consciousness in South Africa*. Pretoria, HSRC.

Spink, Kathryn. 1991. *Black Sash: The Beginning of a Bridge in South Africa*. London, Methuen.

Suttner, Raymond. 2008. *The ANC Underground in South Africa to 1976: A Social and Historical Study*. Johannesburg, Jacana.

Thabane, Motlatsi and Jeff Guy. 1983. 'The Ma-rashea: A Participant's Perspective', in Belinda Bozzoli (ed.), *Town and Countryside in the Transvaal*. Johannesburg, Ravan.

Thomas, Cornelius C. 2005. 'Disaffection, Identity, Black Consciousness and a New Rector: An Exploratory Take on Student Activism at the University of the Western Cape, 1966–1976', *South African Historical Journal*, 54.1.

Toli, T. 1991. 'The Origins of the Durban Strikes 1973'. University of Durban-Westville, MA Thesis.

Webster, Edward. 2005. 'Rebels with a Cause of Their Own: A Personal Reflection on my Student Years at Rhodes University, 1961–1965', *Transformation: Critical Perspectives on Southern Africa*, 59.

Williams, Donovan. 2001. *A History of the University College of Fort Hare, South Africa – 1950s: The Waiting Years*. Lampeter, Edwin Mellen.

Wilson, Lindy. 1991. 'Bantu Stephen Biko: A Life', in Pityana et al. *Bounds of Possibility*.

Wilson, Lindy. 2011. *Steve Biko*. Johannesburg, Jacana.

Wolfson, J.G.E. (ed.). 1976. *Turmoil at Turfloop: A Summary of the Reports of the Snyman and Jackson Commissions of Inquiry into the University of the North*. Johannesburg, SAIRR.

Wolpe, Harold. 1972. 'Capitalism and Cheap Labour-Power in South Africa: From Segregation to Apartheid', *Economy and Society* 1.4.

Žižek's, Slavoj. 2000. *The Ticklish Subject: The Absent Centre of Political Ontology*. London, Verso.

Index

academic freedom 28, 52, 56, 70
activism 2–10, 38, 64, 93, 113–15,
   157
  black 9–11, 18–19, 42, 52,
    60–64, 67–70, 87–8, 92,
    107–9, 123, 133, 141, 156
  classroom/school 157–60
  community-based 47, 49, 59,
    61–2, 124–5, 133
  white 7, 9–12, 20–22, 26, 29–31,
    38–9, 60, 73, 91, 111, 120–21
  see also labour activism; Black
    Consciousness movement:
    activism
African National Congress (ANC)
    5–6, 21, 43, 45, 142, 156, 168
  alliances 43
  banning of 23, 42, 108
  leadership 23
  Rivonia Trial 5–6
  exiled/underground movement
    6, 21
  Youth League 42, 44
  see also apartheid, resistance/
    struggle
African Resistance Movement
    (ARM) 26–8
African Students Association
    (ASA) 43, 45
apartheid
  bantustan system 49, 135, 142,
    151, 172
  hegemony/status quo 3, 9, 16,
    23, 38, 57, 185
  racial policies 32, 45, 47, 51, 86,
    121, 185

  see also Bantu Education
apartheid resistance/struggle
    2–8, 16, 38, 90, 125, 134,
    179
  and destabilisation of political
    dichotomies 9–12, 19, 41, 110,
    119, 136
  experiments in 3–4, 16–18, 21,
    30, 37–8, 60, 64, 70, 76, 156
  narratives of quiescence 3–6, 9,
    178, 182, 186
  role of trade unions in 3–4, 10,
    12, 87, 125
  underground armed 5–6, 21,
    26, 38, 160, 177
  see also liberation movements;
    public student protest
apartheid repression, post-
    Sharpeville 1, 4–5, 16, 18, 23,
    37, 46, 110, 126, 181–5
  arrests 5, 23–4, 26–7, 38, 81,
    133, 153, 181
  mass arrests 41, 52, 54–5, 63,
    71–3
  role of Minister of Justice in 20,
    27–30, 54, 76, 92, 130, 143,
    147, 181
  States of Emergency 5, 23–4,
    180
  trials of activists 5–6, 18, 38,
    52, 55, 73, 132, 137–8, 144,
    151–4, 180
  see also bannings; detention
apartheid state violence/brutality
    1–2, 14, 52, 64, 73, 76, 87–8,
    109, 126, 179